Diversification and Accumulation in Rural Tanzania

Anthropological Perspectives on Village Economics

Pekka Seppälä

Nordiska Afrikainstitutet 1998

Indexing terms

Tanzania
rural development
informal sector
micro-enterprise
agriculture
labour
diversification

CABICODES:
Labour-and-employment,
income-and-poverty,
distribution-and-marketing-of-products

Language checking: Elaine Almén

ISBN 91-7106-427-3

Printed in Sweden by Elanders Gotab, Stockholm 1998

Contents

Tables

Figures

Money equivalents:
Shs. 450 = USD 1

The field-work was carried out, if not mentioned otherwise, in 1994.

Acknowledgements

This book is a culmination of explorations with economic anthropology as they are applied in a contemporary Sub-Saharan Africa. My explorations have directed me to borrow ideas and seek inspiration through a wide variety of contacts. I have presented conference papers based on this material in ASA and EASA conferences and in the workshops organised by the Nordic Africa Institute in Finland and Tanzania. On these occasions, I have had the benefit of receiving criticism from Deborah Bryceson, Stephen Gudeman, Bertha Koda and Marja-Liisa Swantz. Kjell Havnevik has generously read through an earlier version of the manuscript and given a number of detailed comments. Peter Gibbon was, during his years at the Nordic Africa Institute, a constant source of influence because of his sharp and straightforward way of carrying out research.

This research would not have been possible without the support of professor C. K. Omari for clearing my research permit, the Tanzania Commission for Science and Technology for providing the necessary clearance (no. 94–155 ER), the practical and administrative help provided by the regional and district authorities and the most tolerant help and companionship of the personnel of the RIPS programme. During a brief consultancy job for the RIPS programme, and during the numerous night sessions when my town visits were hosted by RIPS personnel, I was asked several times to pose one further question and to compare my findings with views from other locations. I would like to mention Lars Johansson, Tor Lundström and Timo Voipio in this connection.

The village studies are a result of cooperation with Hadija Maulidi, Hamisi Malyunga, Edgar Masoud, Ally Nangumbi, Akinai Msungo, Alex Nkane, Dorah Moomah and, last but not least, Manzi Makunula. I would like to express my sincere gratitude for their companionship and guidance.

Parts of Chapters 4–6 have been published in *Development and Change*, Vol. 27, no. 3, pp. 557–78 and we acknowledge the permission given to use that material again. An earlier version which develops the theme in section 6 has been published in Negash, Tekeste and Lars Rudebeck (eds.) *Dimensions of Development with Emphasis on Africa*, Nordiska Afrikainstitutet and Forum for Development Studies, Uppsala 1995 (pp. 200–220). The regional development of entrepreneurship has been a focus in the article "Informal Sector in Lindi District", pp. 233–262 in Pekka Seppälä and Bertha Koda (eds.) *The Making of a Periphery: Economic Development and Cultural Encounters in Southern Tanzania*. Nordic Africa Institute, Uppsala 1998.

Helsinki, July 1998
Pekka Seppälä

Chapter 1

Introduction

> In a universe characterized by the more or less perfect inter-
> convertibility of economic capital (in the narrow sense) and sym-
> bolic capital, the *economic calculation* directing the agents' strategies
> takes indissociably into account profits and losses which the
> narrow definition of economy unconsciously rejects as *unthinkable*
> and *unnameable*, i.e. as economically irrational.
>
> Pierre Bourdieu: *Outline of the Theory of Practice*

> Although villagers seldom conceptualize their standard of living
> in terms of aggregates such as monthly income, this does not
> imply that relative household living standards are not a matter of
> passionate concern to them or that judgments on this matter are
> apt to be seriously faulty.
>
> Polly Hill: *Development Economics on Trial*

During the last few years, rural development studies have advanced in their analyses towards locating complexity in peripheral rural economies. It has been increasingly observed that a rural economy can include very complicated mechanisms of interdependency even when the economy is very modest in monetary terms. Furthermore, the miniature webs of complexity have definite political and developmental consequences.

The recent studies deviate from the older pattern of the theoretical appropriation of rural society which tended to simplify rural terms of making a livelihood. A common line in old rural development studies was that the rural community was constituted as a fairly homogeneous and unchanging system. The peripheral economy was said to be based on undeveloped division of labour, rudimentary technology, partially monetarised markets and very limited innovativeness. In this setting the rural people all appeared fairly similar in outlook. They were peasants who toiled on their land. They shared parochial values and traits which suppressed any ideas of trying to be different. The rural people were said to be suspicious of government plans and lack initiative in the face of any external intervention.

The idea about this homogeneous population was held for a surprisingly long time. It survived because it was based on a specific perspective : the gaze from above. The perspective of control from above requires an objectification where the 'target population' is perceived as similar in terms of a key criterion, namely lacking development. The perspective from above was compelling because it was self-supporting and circular. Development, understood as modernity, was used as a yardstick to measure people. From this perspective they seemed to lack everything: tools were poor, harvests unreliable and the income level low. Indeed, seen from the perspective of modernisation the studied areas were truly peripheral and undeveloped.

Peripheral economies were approached by agricultural economists, anthropologists and political economists, among others. Each discipline constructed its own analysis of rural society. While the analyses were supplementary to each other, they still tended to convey the idea of rural folk as a group of similar people. For agricultural economists, they were a sample of similar households which varied in resource endowments but not in kind. For anthropologists they were exemplars of the shared culture. And for political economists they were the passive objects of the exploitation by capital and the state.

During the 1980s and the 1990s, the disciplines have started to converge with each through loaning ideas and concepts. The disciplines have also become increasingly sensitive as regards the variation and diversity in the rural ways of life.[1] Some new branches in the tree of rural development studies have opened visions where complexity is located where earlier studies located simplicity: fascinating studies have been conducted on the numerous ways that the peripheral people have developed to utilise their physical environment (e.g. Richards, 1985; Chambers et al., 1989). The studies show how local knowledge about the environment is utilised in combination with local organisational forms. When attention is placed equally on local knowledge systems and organisational forms we can observe unique production systems. Such production systems are entangled with detailed cultural explanations which anchor production in cosmology (Feierman, 1990; Richards, 1993; Moore and Vaugham, 1993). These recent studies show that the low level of technical sophistication does not mean a simple system. Instead, the harsh environment and lack of resources force people to construct complex arrangements to sustain their livelihood.

The resulting picture shows complexity in local livelihood strategies. What is even more important here is that the research orientation systematically observes differences between rural people. A high level of economic differentiation is observed in many peripheral communities. The economic differentiation enhances differentiation in value orientation. During times of economic insecurity and increasing differentiation, the cultural distinctions of religion, ethnicity, sex and generation are given new interpretations which underline differences in kind. Thus a peripheral rural community can be shown to be as multiplex in its cultural variation as in any other place—we just need to take close enough look to notice the variation. The relative poverty of the majority of the people certainly does not mean their cultural uniformity.

---

1. For an analytical review see Booth (1992); for studies with a multidisciplinary and sensitive approach see Hill (1986), Berry (1993) and Chambers (1993).

In this study, I follow the methodologically difficult but otherwise rewarding line of studying complexity in rural economy. I have a special entry point which, to my mind, is notoriously overlooked in rural development studies. This is the *division of labour* at a local level. There is a large amount of special skills even in the most peripheral societies. This division of labour is difficult to detect because the division of labour in a peripheral economy takes a special form. Rather than being a specialisation according to professions, division of labour takes place through *diversification*. Thus people have special skills which they can utilise for gaining income and respect but which do not require their whole labour effort. Instead these skills are applied in conjunction with other activities. For example, farming is often combined with trading activities or crafts. Teachers also have gardens and dairy cows. Local administrators tend to be engaged in trading or personal services. It is a rule rather than exception that a rural household has multiple sources of income. What first appears as a community of a mass of similar farmers, appears later to be a community with a mass of innovative diversification strategies.

Partial specialisation imports into social structure a feature which is unsatisfactorily developed in social theory. It has been given several kinds of structural-functional explanations. One view holds that people need to resort to multiple sources of income so that they can minimise risks. Another explanation starts from the seasonality of agricultural work and states that the other sources of income merely fill the slack periods. In some land scarce areas an explanation is offered that the land scarcity forces people to off-farm activities. Although these explanations are interesting and have a definite theoretical value, a common feature with them is that they are structural-functional which means that they aim to explain away the phenomenon, as passive reactions to external pressures. No effort is made to look inside the phenomenon and into its internal dynamics.

In this volume, I aim to study the logic and working of partial specialisation. I try to locate the dynamics that direct the *active strategies* to combine different activities together. A central observation of my analysis is that the partial specialisation enables a person to circulate resources from one activity to another. Money and labour power can be easily switched from one activity to another. This can provide comparative advantages in a resource-poor environment. Another observation is that linking two or more activities together enables a person to use resources simultaneously for several purposes. For example, teachers need to travel to town to fetch their monthly salary and these trips can be combined with some trading activities. Equally, respect accumulated through active involvement in a kingroup can be used simultaneously in local politics. These and other similar strategic considerations make diversification a complex strategy where resources are circulated back and forth.

Before we can observe the circulation within diversifying units, we need to know the diverse resource bases that exist in a community. In the beginning of the book the emphasis is laid on highlighting diversity. First, the variety of the sources of incomes and the complex networks of exchange that they create is emphasised. In order to find evidence, I have looked for aspects which look marginal or peripheral for normal studies on rural economy but which, when taken together, appear as a sizeable portion of human activity. In this quest I have explored petty trade, homecrafts, gift exchange and similar economic themes which I then present in ethnographic form. Second, attention is directed to the variety of householding patterns in the community. Some households are superior to others in their capacity to organise internal resource flows in a smooth way while others are more quarrelsome and unstable. The internal dynamics make a big difference to how effectively a household is able to diversify. Third, attention is given to the diversity of the cultural orientations—a type of variation which is so often lost in survey studies.

The next step of my analysis after mapping diversity is the analysis of the strategies of *diversification*. By diversification I mean active orientation to combine together different elements into a dynamic complex. A farmer can diversify to logging poles from forests and carpentry in the village, thus making the walking to distant forest fields more profitable. A village administrator can engage in trading, and thus use his connections in the district centre to serve several purposes. The examples show that diversification brings forward practical advantages through a rational use of resources.

However, the connection between different economic activities within a diversification strategy is more complex. It cannot be fully grasped with the straightforward argument of 'rational resource utilisation' as outlined above. The whole matter is further complicated by the co-existence of various cultural frames which lead into varying valuations of a single object of exchange. For example, a piece of cloth can be merchandise or a marriage gift. The trick of diversification is that through diversification, a person can acquire a valuable and then more easily convert it to a new cultural setting. In such processes of conversion, the value of an object of exchange is enchanted and disenchanted. In other words, a valuable can be assigned a new meaning, before it is used or passed forward. The operation is not a mystical or an exceptional feature but something that takes place continuously. However, it has a definite effect on how practices like entrepreneurship and trading are conducted and how processes like price formation work in practice.

The main thrust of the book is theoretical. I make claims on the practices of diversification. I also make further searches on the connection between diversification patterns and rural differentiation. If two households start with a similar resource base, what explains the accumulation in one household and a lack of accumulation in another? As I see it, given a similar resource base between two households, the management of exchange relations and the resource basket is a key to accumulation. I claim that the roads towards accumulation tend to include flexible specialisation, opportunism based on seasonal variation, exploitation of conjunctures and the circulation of resources at a local level. Accumulation requires complex strategies.

In this respect I challenge a conventional theory of rural entrepreneurship which can only locate what it expects to find, namely professional specialisation into one activity, or a lack of it.

Diversity and circulation are interesting themes as such but they also have definite implications on the pattern of the overall development in the society. I argue that the diversification strategies and consequent development pattern deviate significantly from the conventional view of modernisation. The local economy generates its own logic. Its logic is certainly dynamic but this dynamism is not necessarily 'progressive'.

Village economics

The analysis aims to give some tools for the understanding of rural development in Africa. Rural development is a term which first creates a fairly straightforward picture in the mind. It is people working on the field, following the extension officer, negotiating at a meeting of the cooperative society and despairing about price fluctuations. Rural development has generally a practical orientation. Things need to be improved but the right means are not that easy to find. So often the technologies which are well planned and tested prove to increase production but benefit less the poor sections of the population. So often the political processes intervene and disrail the well intended projects. Even when utmost care is taken to reach the village level, we are just confronted with yet another layer of differentiation within the village. Are there any means to understand these dangers beforehand and avoid these pitfalls?

This is the task which is placed upon the researchers engaged in practical rural development. The researchers are asked to give such a refined picture on the interdependencies so that the most obvious problems can be avoided or, at least, give a fair account of the past developments so that some lessons can be learned and some measures taken to lessen the negative effects in the future. Researchers set to this task with varying packages of tools. The field of rural development is multi-disciplinary and while agricultural economists have adopted a central place several other disciplines can give their contributions to the outcome.

In this book I shall present one toolbox full of concepts and ideas. This toolbox is one among many in the orientation which aims to capture the diversity and rural reality with all its colours and nuances. The recent research on rural development has emphasised the situated, local development potentials. The seminal works have opened new visions on local organisations, informal sector production, indigenous knowledge and specific regional adaptation patterns. Some of these themes are taken up here, although packaged into a new framework. My approach concentrates on a culturally guided appropriation of local production and exchange. I believe that the analysis on local level division of labour can provide new insights to studies on rural development. This theme has not received the attention that it should rightly deserve.

In general terms, I use *economic anthropology* as a toolbox for presenting a special type of analysis. I try to show how this tool set can be applied to make a different contribution within the framework of rural development. This approach does not provide the final word, or ultimate truth "in the last instance" but just a different picture. Although it poses itself as a holistic approach it is evident that many choices are made concerning what enters the analysis. When these choices are made, something is lost at the expense of gaining something else. There are trade-offs in every methodological approach.

In order to profile the book and its specific approach from other approaches I gave the book sub-title of Village Economics. The name is shorthand for a number of choices made on the methods and orientation. One method can be good for statistically accurate descriptive results while another can be useful for monitoring certain specific changes. Village Economics is an approach which limits itself to *understanding* socio-economic processes at local level. It gives neither highly accurate nor systematic specific information. What it provides is an understanding of the local processes that may, and are likely to, change the course of any external intervention in that local context. It is a special inter-pretation of the economic processes that loom behind the cold base-line data.

The term 'village' in Village Economics stands essentially for a setting which is wider than an individual household. This choice is indicative about a number of issues which are at stake. First, a village is a locus of public institutions and activities which concern most people in the location. These activities are common concerns which take people's time and effort and which cannot be understood if a village is presented merely through general geographic or sta-tistical background information as a random site for random data. A village is more than an aggregate of its constitutive units. Second, a village is also a set-ting for diverse economic activities and diverse cultural identities. There are several activities, like collecting herbs or being a musician, which may look totally marginal for an agricultural economist. However, when these marginal tiny activities are counted together, we end up with a profound level of occupa-tional specialisation and local production. These incidents of diversity are so numerous that they deserve special attention. In a village, each household has a package of different sources of income which partly overlap and partly differ from the packages of the other households. This difference is a precondition for exchange relationships. The numeric example shows the scope for diversifica-tion. At a village level it is easy to identify 50-100 sources of income. While one household may have diversified to, say, three different income sources, it still needs to reach a large variety of others through local exchange relations. Third, a village is shorthand for a set of interdependencies. It is a locale where things are produced and then exchanged, given as gifts and stolen, and finally con-sumed or sold. These chains of exchanges tend to lead into other localities through patronage or commercial links. Nevertheless, the complexity of the local setting provides a certain hindrance to overt external dominance and helps the villages to take an active role in such external relationships. I emphasise that local setting is a complex microcosm with active external links.

I have chosen to conduct the study in a part of Tanzania which is known to be a comparatively poor area. The studied people are often characterised as 'subsistence farmers' and the administrators sometimes refer to them as undifferentiated people, all alike and without initiative. One observer called the villagers 'the potatoes in a sack', using the famous metaphor of passivity. This view on 'peasants' does not hold on closer examination. I try to show that even in a distant village there is a developed division of labour and a variety of external linkages. A village is not a location to store people but a setting for complex economic processes.

'Economics' is the other code word which is central to Village Economics. I find the object of 'economics' as a very important but also difficult object to capture. Economics concerns the question how people give a value and compare different things. Economics is here first of all a language for a discourse which tries to answer how people manage a specific balancing operation between maximising individual interest and following a cultural pattern. I try to make this language transparent and clear.

The fascinating issue in economic phenomena is that people continuously do compare differences in kind. A hoe is compared with a tractor-drawn plough, maize is compared with millet and cooking food is compared with buying food from a restaurant. Since people have different perceptions on, and relations to, hoes, maize and cooking, they engage in a debate on comparative valuations. This debate is conducted all the time in homes, at the market places and during funerals. Thus economics is not the privilege of the scholars but a daily topic for the rural people.

It is often thought that countability is a precondition for economic analysis. Moreover, countability is often confused with exactness and thus so many researchers express their results in terms of numbers. These are the kinds of errors which keep rural development studies stagnant. We get numbers of the household sizes, calorie intakes and hoes owned. Naturally it is possible to make a correlation between such variables but here countability confuses rather than explains. What we would need to know is issues like who uses hoes and for what purposes. When these questions are asked, we proceed from facts to processes. And still we are within economic analysis. The crucial question is how to analyse economic processes.

When I opt to accept economics as a label for this approach I accept a set of questions but not the given answers. Economics is accepted as a set of questions concerning valuing, comparing and competing. When several items can be measured with similar yardsticks and compared with each other the discussion approaches the notions of optimisation and the rational use of resources—both questions so central for rural development research. However, it is a gross simplification to argue that when things can be given a single numerical value (or even be converted to monetary terms) the problem of comparing and opti-misation has been resolved. Rather, the social processes precede any act of price setting and intervene in any economic transaction that follows—as the *substan-tivist* school of economic anthropologists have stressed.

The trade-offs between using village economics or conventional economic analysis can now be summarised in several terms. What is lost in terms of exact numbers is won in terms of vivid descriptions. What is lost in neat generalisa-tions is counted in terms of diversity. If something is lost while avoiding con-ventional indicators perhaps something else is found in terms of locating important processes. And finally, if the analysis does not show interesting results in terms of an exceptional correlation between two variables, it can reach for something more valuable: it can explain the way the political and cultural processes intervene and modify expected causality.

It is good to be explicit as to what can be and what cannot be validly argued through this approach. It is possible to make a detailed analysis of the factors which are important for a rural economy. It is possible to show which parame-ters are likely to accompany wealth and which are likely to go hand in hand with poverty. It is also possible to indicate mechanisms of diversification and resource conversion which are likely to change a person's socio-economic standing. But it is not possible to point out which factors will inevitably indicate wealth or poverty. And it is also not possible to weight different processes of diversification and resource conversion and to measure their relative impor-tance for accumulation.

The order of the text

The paper advances back and forth between theory, conceptual analysis and empirical analysis. The attention to discrete economic processes has directed me towards the heavily empirical analysis of the diversity in its various forms. This may look like an empiricist project—what anthropologists call 'collecting but-terflies' and political economists 'surface appearances', with equal moral disgust—but which should instead be seen as a guided application of the actor-oriented approach. In other words, the theoretical analysis is based on empiri-cally grounded concepts with a degree of deductive and inductive reasoning.[1]

In the second chapter I outline the conceptual package for the Village Eco-nomics. Since the package is multi-dimensional, it is presented only briefly here. The individual methodological aspects are repeatedly discussed again in the following chapters.

---

1. There is much that can be said about the futility of the idealist reductionist theories and the usefulness of the more modest, permissive and adaptive approaches (cf. Rasmussen, 1988). Perhaps it is enough to recall the wish of Marx that we should not see an abstraction (which he defined as a separation of issues from their conventional con-text) as the final goal of analysis but the advancement from abstract back to concrete (i.e. towards a dynamic totality of internal relations and structures).

Chapter 3 brings forward basic elements of diversification strategies. Extensive examples are presented to give the sense of local conditions and actual options. The chapter creates a heuristic basis for the following, more technical chapters.

The following Chapters 4–7 analyse the economic, social and cultural dimensions of variation in Kilimahewa. In Chapter 4 I analyse the division of labour and ask, what kind of possibilities the variety of skills creates for diversification. In Chapter 5 I argue that the internal cohesiveness of a household, and its external openness, are two important (and analytically distinctive) criteria for a successful diversification. Chapter 6 analyses the importance of "cultural capital" in diversification strategies. I show how the village is culturally divided into several, partly overlapping fractions. I then postulate that several specific diversification strategies rely on an extensive combination of cultural and economic capitals. Chapter 7 is a summary in the sense that it combines economic, social and cultural factors in the analysis of differentiation in Kilimahewa.

In Chapter 8 the theoretically complex issue of the conversion of resources from one sphere to another is placed under closer scrutiny. I argue that the variety of cultural discontinuities crucially shapes the forms of exchange and the values/prices of items. Diversification is often a practical way to gain from the cultural discontinuities in the spheres of circulation and production.

Chapter 9 is based on a completely different set of material and analysis. In this chapter I analyse the development of the informal sector in rural Tanzania. I use national surveys and local studies to find indications of the degree of diversification. At the end of the chapter, I discuss the relationship between the concept of 'economy of affection' and the tendency towards diversification. I also ask whether the tendency towards diversification has an effect on the effectiveness of structural adjustment.

In Chapter 10 I synthesise the theoretical elements which have been hitherto discussed as methodological choices and ethnographic results. The theoretical discourse is supplemented with some comparative ethnographic evidence from different parts of Africa. The theory makes a major attack on the analyses 'from above' of the rural economic dynamics and differentiation in rural Africa. The last chapter is the only one where the argument is made with explicit linkages to theoretical discussions. For a reader who does not have the means or time to fully indulge the linear structure of the book, it is recommended to read Chapter 10 first.

Mental maps. The outlined analytical method needs to be communicated in an effective but flexible manner. In the following some graphic presentations are used to fully utilise our capacity to understand relations and processes as a part of the totality. Graphic presentation makes it easier to compress data into a defined frame—the reader is then left with the possibility to utilise this frame to the extent needed.

Another use of the graphic presentations is to lessen the problem of systematic presentation. Written text is linear. It requires a certain line of advancement to be intelligible. When graphic presentation is used as a device, we can present complex interdependencies which are not related through single causalities. The complex system can be presented through a mental map.

For the convenience of the reader, the notes on research methods and the presentation of the ethnographic site, the Kilimahewa village, are collected in Annexes I and II where they are easily reached.

Chapter 2

A Toolbox for Analysing Diversification

> The poorest are usually considered to be the most ignorant, those from whom there is least to learn. But how much do outsiders know about how the poorest cope? To enable the poorest to do better, the starting point is to understand how they manage at present. And on this poorest are the experts.
>
> Robert Chambers: *Rural Development—Putting the Last First*

An anthropological perspective on peripheral economy

As the sun nears sunset, the men gather around the market place where they do some shopping, walk about and exchange news. In Kilimahewa village, the market place is a centre of common activities, bringing together young and old, rich and poor. A *mbao* game is played every evening under a large mango tree. The game requires skill, the capacity to calculate different possible outcomes and a capacity to take risks. In this sense the game resembles many things that take place in the market place and in the local economy. In this book I present an anthropological account of the rural economy, viewed from a specific perspective. The central issue is the strategic circulation of the resources from one activity to another like the balls are circulated in the *mbao* game.

I shall present concepts and methodologies for analysing local economy which give room for local perceptions and values. The local perceptions in a peripheral community can vary in many ways from standard western concepts of economy. Words like entrepreneur, ownership, private sphere and accumulation can be given very different attributes. The perception of the whole dynamics of economy can be based on metaphors and values that are distinctive from what western economists cherish.

In Kilimahewa, the economy is an unpredictable and amorphous aspect of life. The economy is fully embedded within the web of social dynamics. The allocation of resources works through institutionalised patterns which, nevertheless, always leave scope for a choice between a few, fairly distinctive and known strategies. In this sense the economy resembles the mbao game. In mbao, the essence is the strategic behaviour.

The rules of the mbao game are straightforward: two players sit opposite each other in front of a wooden board. Each player has two rows of holes on his side of the board and some thirty small *kete* balls which he can move from one hole to another. A player starts by taking balls from one of his holes and then circulating through the set of his own holes, dropping one ball in each hole. If the last hole is empty he will 'sleep' there and the opponent takes his turn. If the last hole has some of his balls, he can continue by taking these balls in his hand and starting the circulating again from that point. The third alternative is an advanced version of the second one: if the player has some balls in the last hole *and* there are also balls in the opponent's hole adjacent to that of his own, the player 'eats' the opponents balls, adding them to his own numbers. He can continue circulating and eating until he ends up with an empty hole. In the game as in the economy, it is necessary to make continuous allocative decisions, weighing risks against benefits.

The analogy between *mbao* and economy goes even further. The very logic of economic behaviour can be seen through a parallel with the mbao game.[1] At the beginning of the game, it is important to collect a lot of capital in one hole and protect this hole as well as possible. When the time is ripe this capital is circulated throughout the holes and the extensive 'eating' of the opponents balls can be done in many different ways. This starting strategy, however, has apparent risks and it may lead to bankruptcy. For a less experienced and more cautious player, the defensive spreading out of the capital is better than concentrating all the balls in one hole. At the later stage of the game, it is useful for all the players to spread balls out safely in several holes and remember defence instead of concentrating only on aggressive 'eating'. The question of spreading out resources is also at the core of this book. It is not only a defensive strategy but also an offensive strategy. I ask in effect, how resources can be accumulated through their circulation between different activities, from one cultural sphere to another and between different groups of people. This is what I call diversification.

In economics, the courage to get involved is needed if one wants to win. In the mbao game a clever player may take up just a few balls, circulate them to the following holes, pick up again balls from the last hole, 'eat' the resources of an opponent and then continue circulating, finally even making up five full rounds. In the game, a player who does not have the courage to keep on circulating will not survive for long. The experienced and courageous player, on the other hand, can play his game with extraordinary speed, making long calculations in a matter of seconds and then carry out several rounds of 'eating', while continuously chatting (and sometimes cheating), thus distracting the opponent's concentration and morally forcing him to similar kind of quick game and, hopefully, forcing him into making mistakes. As the play continues, a skillful player 'eats' his opponent's balls and accumulates balls on his own side of the board. However, the situation can change dramatically within a short time. A person having relatively plentiful resources may lose everything in a few rounds. A person who looked destitute can score and the game con-

---

1. Actually, the lump of the balls in the game is called *mtaji*, a Swahili word which also stands for 'capital' in formal economics. It is likely that the mbao game is older than the monetary economy. Perhaps the analogy, which first seems an innocent play with ideas, has more to it.

tinues. The important things then are, within the margins set by the constrain-
ing rules, the courage to get involved, the right timing, a bit of luck and God's
blessing. Looked at from a close perspective, the rural economy works like the
mbao game.

The mbao game is an apt metaphor because it emphasises the importance of
circulating capital between different resource bases. This is the crux of this and
the following chapters as well.

Below I present some key concepts for the analysis of the village economy. I
draw a picture where low resource endowments are accompanied by complex
arrangements, a large variety in aims and a significant level of differentiation.
This view contrasts with a common view presented in rural development
studies. Consequently, some effort needs to be given to locating concepts which
enable the analysis of the complexity and locate the methodology in a theoretical landscape. I study concepts which describe the complexity of the peripheral
economy.

Diversification as a performance: an actor-oriented analysis of local economy

Complex, diverse and risk-prone economy

It is common to think that rural people are all alike, doing largely the same
things and sharing the same thoughts. This is an ideological bias which under-
lines, in one form or another, much of rural development studies. Alternative
observations on the economic behaviour guide my approach to the village
economy. My analysis is built on definite characteristics of the economy in
south-east Tanzania, yet my observations correspond with several otehr studies
conducted in the peripheral rural areas in variuos parts of the world. Robert
Chambers (1993:60–66) lists three major characteristics of the peripheral rural
economy: Complexity, Diversity and Riskprone (CDR). I have borrowed this
package from Chambers but I have also extended it to new uses. In the following, I first outline the concept with reference to Chambers's framework and
then adapt it to this study.

According to Chambers, CDR refers to a specific type of agricultural production system. It is a production system which governs much of the third
world where the green revolution or industrial agriculture has not rooted. The
production system is based on smallholder agriculture in different but often
marginal agro-ecological environments. The *diversity* of the system is apparent
in the diverse composition of households, in different labour arrangements and
conjugal contracts. Diversity is also apparent in different field systems and
cropping patterns, direct utilisation of various natural resources, in the variation of agricultural tasks and in the availability of resources over seasonal
cycles. The *complexity* of the system appears from the inter-linkages between
these factors. The interdependency of the components means that when one

aspect changes the other aspects also need to adjust unexpectedly. This makes it extremely difficult to locate simple causalities between two factors. The economic system which works on these terms is oriented towards optimisation among different aims rather than maximisation of the utilisation of a single resource. The economy works with small margins in an extremely difficult and unpredictable politico-economic as well as climatic environment and thus the optimisation equation needs to place great weight on dispersing resources against potential *risk* momentum. It is not good to carry all one's eggs in the same banana leaf basket.

Chambers utilises his framework to study farming practices. My modification is merely to extend the frame to non-farming activities. While analysing the non-farming activities we can notice a large variety of income sources. The diversity is again accompanied by complex patterns of labour arrangements, networking, forward and backward linkages and market segmentation. Stepping—metaphorically—outside the farmgate, diversity can be located in external economic linkages and common property arrangements and finally in the multiple patronage networks. The relative lack of sophisticated technology lulls us into thinking that a village enterprise works in a simple way whereas in reality it is a part of an extremely complex system of interdependencies. And again, the risks are part and parcel of reality for non-farming activities. The life-histories of the villagers show numerous cases where a non-economic factor like sickness in the family intervenes and destroys the resource base for the non-farming activity. Similarly, government policies and economic hazards may ruin a flourishing enterprise overnight. These are not just issues to be stoically accepted but they need to be included in the livelihood strategy and resource allocation in advance.

The CDR character of the rural economy is difficult to perceive because the economic resources are so meagre and the technology is based on such simple tools. Money and machines are items that shape the western conception of economy. In peripheral Lindi district, the complexity is based on numerous practical arrangements and transactions. For example, the production of maize porridge, with only maize and water as its ingredients, requires a long chain of transactions involving many people before maize is harvested and transported from a field, cleaned and dried, shelled and stored, milled and finally cooked. Moreover, every economic transaction can take a normal route but, when needed, it can be directed to follow the alternative path of socially constructed entitlements. In times of sickness, crises or any other misfortune the nature of the interdependencies becomes profoundly clear.

Diversification as a resource management strategy

There is a multitude of studies which note that rural folks are not just peasants. Instead, the studies expose a common engagement in 'informal sector' and other activities which provide 'off-farm income'. The expansion of these activities is often called 'depeasantrisation' or 'de-agrarianisation' (e.g. Bryceson, 1993b ; Pedersen, 1994b). The latter are descriptive terms for the change in a societal level. When this process is analysed at a household level, a term used commonly is 'diversification'.[1]

In my vocabulary diversification is a word for a process which is far more complex. Diversification is not the same as 'diversity'—a multitude in the different economic means, a multitude in social arrangements or a multitude in the cultural orientations. Diversification refers to an *active* strategy to diversify—to orient towards different directions simultaneously. Together the different element compose a *strategic* combination where different elements support each other.

The case of Mohammed, a 'pricoleur' from Kilimahewa, is illuminating. Mohammed has a tea-room where I used to sit in the evenings and have a cup of tea or a meal. The tea-room used to have very few customers and some of them just entered the tea-room to avoid rain. I first wondered how one could keep two persons always employed in a tea-room with so few customers. When I got more familiar with Mohammed and started to visit the private side of the tea-room, my view on his activities widened considerably. The backroom was a place for medical consultations, selling herbs and sacred scripts of Islamic verses with a healing power. All this was conducted in a seemingly off-hand manner with friends and relatives but amounted to a sizeable activity. Outside the tea-room business, Mohammed was engaged in running the mosque and he provided special meals for Muslim gatherings. He also disappeared from the village for the long spells of trading. The farm work was largely done by wives and children, with occasional help from outside labourers. If I had studied Mohammed and his wives as *entrepreneurs* in the catering sector, my analyses would have been narrowed to a small part of activities taking place in the public part of the tea-room. I might have argued that their bookkeeping is rather haphazard and the pricing of items is based on conventions. Or that the menu of the tea-room is too limited (the only meal was a bowl of rice served with one dried fish) and that he should profile the menu of his tea-room to attract customers. Finally I might have argued that the tea-room is an unprofitable enterprise. But there was so much more taking place there than just selling tea. Indeed, it does not make much sense to analyse the tea-room as separate from a complex diversification strategy.

Diversification is then the key word for my framework. Diversification means a strategy where a household accommodates several types of resources and employs multiple means to generate income. At the same time households

---

1. Rural economists make a further distinction between *horizontal* diversification within agriculture and *vertical* diversification from agricultural to non-agricultural income sources. See Chapter 9.

In the economic literature on external trade there is another meaning for diversification. Diversification is used to describe the expansion of the portfolio of exports from traditional exports to non-traditional exports.

specialise on some products or activities. This specialisation is a precondition for lively exchange relations between households. The research needs then to show, how these different elements support each other and create dynamic combinations.

The temporal element is always present in the diversification strategies. It is vital to time the activities in such a way that the seasonal and conjectural changes can be fully utilised. Diversification mean in this case the capacity to adjust to the changing realities. In order to emphasise the temporal element I define two ideal types of diversification processes: simultaneous and serial diversification. *Simultaneous diversification* takes place when several activities are conducted side-by-side. In *serial diversification* one activity is terminated before another one is started. I also talk about the seasonal diversification where the diversification pattern is based on the repetitive yearly cycle.

Diversification strategy is then a *management* strategy in which conventional economic resources are transferred between distinctive activities. The transferred resources are labour time, materials, tools, knowledge, logistical support and cultural capital. The management of these resources requires constant supervision and negotiation because access to them is socially conditioned.

The status of the concept of diversification should be clear now. It is a concept which is used for the analysis of strategic economic behaviour. But what makes people diversify? Some people say that it is a means to reduce risks. It has been postulated to be a characteristic manner of resource management for the middle-peasantry. Yet others have observed that rich people can efficiently use diversification strategies and create comparative advantage through combining e.g. wholesale business with farming and transport. Still others have made claims that the poor people seek extra income because they cannot survive through agriculture because of the small plots they have. In effect, some kind of valid reason can be found for all classes from rich to poor. Actually all these claims include something of the truth which does not invalidate the value of other statements (cf. Evans and Pirzada, 1995). There are different *motivational* issues which direct people towards diversification. There are push factors and pull factors. There are direct, utilitarian concerns and more indirect, cultural patterns which make diversification a compelling strategy of resource allocation. These motives are complementary to each other rather than exclusive. For this reason, the probing of motives is very difficult and such questions tend to always provide different answers—depending on the situation when asking the question and the relations between discussants. But here it is important to note that there are several significant motives to diversify. They are not exclusive to each other—they can work simultaneously.

One can always ask, whether 'strategy' is appropriate word to describe the process where that people make choices on the allocation of their time and other resources. After all, in many situations people may feel forced to act in a certain way due to circumstances. Only afterwards they can consciously take distance to the happenings and explicate their 'strategic' considerations. The discussion on the concept of strategy will be opened further in the last chapter. Here I merely state that the term strategy (in diversification strategy) implies a situation of choice which is mastered with a varying level of a conscious analysis of alternatives but which is almost *never* a matter of being forced to act at a certain way, without any alternatives.

Economy as a performance

Diversification is best understood as a combination of various economic activities within a social unit. We shall see that some farmers are also agricultural workers while others are craftsmen. A trader can mobilise his household to conduct agricultural work and provide assistance at the marketplace. A teacher is also a part-time farmer and a support for his wife who is a village politician. These examples show some simple types of diversification. They seem clear because they use *professions* or skills as conceptual categories. In my analysis I shall also separate different crafts and skills but I can see a danger of distortion in here. Professions are essentially categories of the western economy which is organised on the lines of the division of labour. Professions are far less significant in rural Tanzania. Some groups like teachers tend to emphasise their own professional distinctiveness because they have certificates which are deliberately created to make a distinction. But even teachers have little use of the certificate when they step outside the school compound. A trader does not have any advantage in being seen just as a trader by profession. A craftsman who works seasonally or when friends give orders is certainly a borderline case for professionalism.

I do not claim that people do not value distinctive skills as sources of special esteem and self-identification. A blacksmith may have inherited, through an experience of sickness, his skill from a dead grandfather and thus the skill has special importance. A trader may want to be known as a successful and reliable trader. However, behind every blacksmith there are a number of others who have laid their tools aside for the time being. Behind a successful trader are a mass of casual traders since most of the adults have engaged in trading at one point of their lives. And everybody is actually a farmer. Economic activities are things which one can be occupied with for some time but if they appear too demanding, or if money needs to be used for other purposes, the activity can be terminated. Years later, when a suitable time presents itself, one can continue with the activity.

Thus people shape diversification into a performance, where resources are managed according to the prevailing capacities and the constraints of the situation. A person needs to be continuously alert and ready to change behaviour according to the circumstances. Richards (1993) has aptly shown how agriculture in an African context is a performance which requires adaptiveness to confront the external changes in human and natural environment. A farmer needs capacities for an imaginative management of skills and labour power, used in various types of soils and slopes, in response to unpredictable weather conditions and market situation, to provide a variety of produce for a changing household. The equation is even more complicated when we include the various non-agricultural activities in the system. The non-agricultural labour tasks need to be conducted through a new set of economic linkages, and these are not necessarily easy to harmonise with the existing linkages and timing determined by the agricultural calendar.

Only an actor-oriented perspective can grasp the reactive—which is not equal to passive—strategy of a rural entrepreneur. A rural entrepreneur can seldom afford to stick to a professional orientation and concentrate on a certain type of activity, regardless of the changes in the environment. Instead, an entrepreneur must be flexible and adaptive both socially and economically.

While I dismerit the professional character of entrepreneurship I do not claim that just anything goes in an economy working as performance. There are always good alternatives and less useful ones. When I speak of performance I stress that no condition is permanent and the peasant intellectuals need to use those weapons of the weak that are available in order to survive and to prosper in the economy of affection.

Economic transactions: formalist and substantivist views

In the following I switch attention to a sphere of circulation. I make important—and speculative—claims on the working of the sphere of circulation. I emphasise the imperfect markets and gaps between different economic domains. I then proceed to claim that some villagers think of economy in social terms while others think in terms of abstract (economic) utility. The different value orientations generate different views and economic strategies. Finally I postulate that this difference in value orientations is one source of differentiation.

Diversification implies circulation of resources from one realm to another. Economists would immediately like to know the conversion rates (or prices) between different skills and things. The logic is that circulation brings things into a situation of comparison where each thing can be given a comparative value. Since some of the items within this circulation have a monetary equivalent, all products can be calculated in monetary terms. This view is held by the *formalist* school of economic anthropologists and echoes neo-classical economic thinking.

The opposite of the formalist view is a *substantivist* perspective on economic anthropology. The substantivist anthropologists argue that people carry out exchanges between skills and things which cannot be measured with a single scale. Each exchange has a conversion rate but the rate tends to change situationally according to the relation between exchange partners: agricultural labour has a normal piece rate but the work done at a sister's field may be valued as a gesture of attachment; the value of the words of a religious leader are usually not given any economic connotations but they take a commodity form when presented at funerals; a cloth left by a dead person cannot be sold for money to a living person but it can be given as a gift to a selected relative. These examples show that the value of the thing cannot be abstracted from the social relationship of exchange.

The ultimate substantivist view of economy states that the individual acts of production and exchange are merely means to express identity: people become engaged in many sorts of exchanges, not only to fulfil basic needs but because they want to communicate their existence and relate to other people. Making exchanges of things are, from this perspective, an outward oriented method to reach other people, comparable with talking. Looking from this perspective it seems that the different skills and things should not be understood as various ways to reach 'similar' money. The unifying, alienating power of the money form should not be taken too seriously. Instead, one should fully observe the special identities that are bound with different skills. In other words, the ulti-mate substantivist view counts even monetarised transactions within the sphere of substantivist, not formalist, logic.

The problem of the extreme substantivist perspective is that it ends with a descriptive analysis of the separate spheres of exchange relations. For example, a substantivist observer can describe the traditions that people follow when constructing houses, or when negotiating marriage payments, but he/she can-not place these separate processes in a single economic framework. Yet it is apparent that the economic resource base directs the choices that are available when both household construction and marriage payments are to be consid-ered, and that often the separate choices condition one another.

The appropriate interpretation of the economic transaction needs to have an element of *both* substantivist and formalist frameworks. This is so because what cannot be compared (on moral/cultural grounds) are still occasionally com-pared anyway: the cloth of a dead person does have a comparative price in the shop and the agricultural work of a sister can be valued through a shadow price. The duality of the economic logic continuously creates paradoxical situa-tions. The economic behaviour is actually a material expression of the discourse which continuously presents paradoxes to a person. A person is continuously pulled towards valuing things in social terms, on the one hand, and exchange value, on the other. This is not an exceptional feature of a peripheral economy—such contradictions are also common in western society—but in a semi-monetary economy the paradox is more apparent and striking.

The economic analysis of transactions is freed from its inherent methodolog-ical determinism when the researcher recognises social tensions among the studied economic actors and contradiction among the studied economic processes. One concrete step towards understanding the latent tensions and contradictions is the *empirical* analysis in the variation of the prices and non-monetary exchange rates. Furthermore, when one thing has different prices in different exchange situations, the motivations and reasons for variation can be placed in focus.

The appropriate interpretation of value formation lies usually between the extreme interpretations of formalist and substantivist theory. Any exchange is likely to have an element of calculation of relative benefits and taken-for-granted cultural practices. Having said this, a researcher still needs to approach the empirical reality of value formation with an open mind. The differences of prices may well have their origin in the differing frameworks of rural people in making value judgements. It is likely that *some* villagers focus on use values and social relationships, while *others* behave more like economists, focusing solely on exchange values and monetary accumulation. In other words, some think more like substantivists while others think more often like formalists. While some would like to maintain the different cultural spheres as distinctive, others violate the boundaries and take advantage of different value systems. The difference is not just between our theories, but between different views of the people studied.

Conversion

An interesting issue for value theory is the conversion of a valuable from one sphere to another. Here a conversion is largely a mental operation. For example, a shopkeeper reclassifies a bag of maize (a product of a domestic field) as a mercantile item in a shop. Or he reclassifies a maize bag (an item of merchandise in a shop) as a gift to a good customer. The conversion is done without any external exchange (although often prior to one). This kind of conversion of the referential meanings of items is done continuously. An item does not have any 'natural' social context (Sahlins, 1972; Sahlins, 1976). It loses its original value without pain and adjusts to new circumstances. A person has to deal with the double, or triple, value of an item.

The conversion within a diversification strategy is simple because the same actor plays the roles of both provider and recipient. He or she can remove an item from one social context and place it into another. When the conversion is done internally, it does not necessarily carry a value comparison. In other words, it does not require a direct equivalent transmission to another direction. The last feature is a definite advantage when business transactions are conducted. It enables one to allocate resources for one activity when there are extra needs, and to transfer them to another activity when the resources are more needed there.

The anthropological literature is rich with examples where exchange is based on delayed reciprocation, or through complex reciprocation (e.g. when several cycles of presentations and redistributions take place). The internal conversion of value within a diversification unit has similar features. The bond between two contexts is severed and thus the value formation is removed from the price mechanism. Naturally, this kind of move can lead to advantages but it can also result in impoverishment. It requires a certain self-restraint to be able to handle resource allocations between different economic domains. A common source of business failures is the use of all resources for private consumption, without making equivalent returns to another direction at a later stage.

Diversification and differentiation

My analysis leads to a complicated position on the dynamics of diversification. I am not making ontological claims on the nature of economic behaviour in general. I am not claiming that complex diversification is a *universal* pattern of resource management. All I am saying is that rural people can *potentially* use a complex pattern of diversification to take advantage of the imperfections, discontinuities and fluctuations that are characteristic of the rural economy.

In a village setting most people are engaged in a couple of different activities but many people use these merely as means of making a living. Some others see the world of transactions as a game, similar to mbao, where you need to be active and reflective. Diversification is a potential means to become engaged in this kind of active strategy. Even when resources are meagre, they can include several types of resources which can be strategically reallocated.

I am thus making a hypothesis that diversification is a potential means for accumulation. I argue that when two people start from a similar economic level, the accumulator is the one who takes a reflective attitude towards resource allocations and continuously relocates them for various uses.

This argument does not counter the fact that production is a major entry point to wealth creation and that access to the means of production is a crucial cause for differentiation. However, that argument is static in that it exposes differentiated access to means of production as a baseline fact. It does not tell, how it is possible that those starting from a similar productive capacity end up with different income levels. Here diversification appears as a factor worth considering.

In this study on diversification I emphasise the sphere of circulation. The sphere of circulation is very rich and incorporates several types of exchange. The market exchanges are challenged by the gift economy, barter exchange, ritual exchanges and a withdrawal from exchange. The social relationships of exchange partners tend to cast their shadow on each transaction. Thus transactions are pregnant with societal fabric—the memories of past exchanges. This is not romanticising the rural economy, or an idealist turn away from essential issues. The detailed analysis of the sphere of circulation, the working of the real markets, is very much on the agenda of rural development studies of today.

The imperfectness of the market situation is an obvious starting point for the analysis. Even if we accept the formal mechanism for price setting, we are bound to notice the lack of effective competition or price information in the rural setting. The prices of the skills and things vary enormously due to several factors. It is the major claim of this book that the clever and timely conversions between the various resources (rather than merely hard work, technological advancement or extreme specialisation) are the major road to wealth in the study area.

The theoretical approach and its mental cousins

I have briefly presented the approach without a detailed comparison with the other existing research traditions. There are several methodological orientations which could be utilised in a number of respects. In figure 2.1 I compare my approach with several other discourses which aim to capture the economic dynamics of households in rural Africa.

Figure 2.1. The theoretical landscape —a comparison of selected theories and orientations which deal with rural economy.

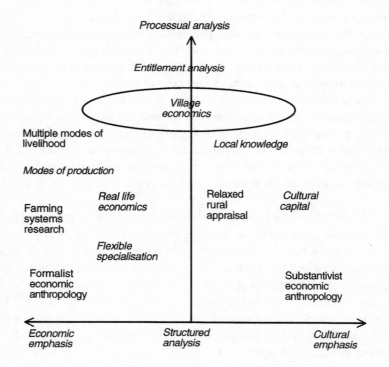

Dimensions:

Processual analysis: Qualitative analysis covering diachronic changes. Concepts are fluid and elements are seen to vary over time and space. Specific claims on specific cases.

Structured analysis: Quantitative analysis covering synchronic variation. Fixed concepts presented through operationalised indicators: Universal claims for comparative use.

Economic emphasis: Following the theory of the comparative, measurable utility.

Cultural emphasis: Following the theory of the culturally constructed meanings.

In figure 2.1 I have placed the approaches on two axes. The lateral axis runs from the emphasis of economic logic to the emphasis on cultural logic. The axis is defined by two schools of economic anthropology: *formalist* and *substantivist* economic anthropology. Most of the analysis of rural economy falls between these extremes. It is conventional that methods which rely on sample surveys tend to fall near the formalist end where economic factors have clearly identifiable causalities or, at least, patterns of co-variation. By contrast, the studies which rely upon qualitative methods tend to emphasise substantivist views which underline the distinctiveness of the different economic spheres, thus weakening or even eliminating causalities between independent and dependent factors.

The vertical axis separates the static, structural approaches from dynamic approaches. The structural approaches provide a synchronic picture of economic situation. *Farming systems analysis* is a research tradition which aims to be holistic and thus ends up being fairly static. Also discussions which primarily aim at critique of the liberal economic theory (e.g. *real-life economics*) succeed in distancing themselves from a formalist perspective but remain rather static in analysis.

I find more fascinating the economic theories which include processual analysis in their toolbox. There are several approaches which take such a view. *Entitlement analysis* is based on concepts which emphasise potential and moral claims on resources alongside with the direct claims of ownership. Thus the umbilical cord between things and people is broken and, instead, the negotiation between people appears as a crucial aspect. The question is, where do the moral claims come from? Marxist analysis of the *articulation of the modes of production* gives one definite view on the power relations in a rural society. The analysis shows how people organise their productive relations and how the competition forces those with less power to undermine the value of their labour. The analysis can show contradictions which induce changes in the local economy. Yet another research tradition is the discourse on *local knowledge*. This discourse emphasises the notions of practical knowledge that rural people have on their ecological and social environment. This knowledge, although difficult to articulate in terms of scientific language, plays a crucial role in how a local economy is organised. The local knowledge discourse tends to pay special attention to issues which are non-western and thus exotic for us. By contrast, the theories of networking (e.g. a theory of flexible specialisation) pay attention to modern market mechanisms and the possibilities that markets provide to rural producers. The dynamic element appears from a balanced combination of cooperation, competition and patronage between the producers. There are also several strands of analysis which are still embryonic but which could together be called *diversification theory*. These studies have used terms like 'multiple modes of livelihood' and 'straddling' as key concepts to analyse the complex patterns of resource allocation. I shall study them more systematically in Chapter 10.

In my analysis I have applied discourses which use local knowledge, embedded economy or diversification as a focal issue. These discourses are mutually supportive and, although they originate from different disciplinary traditions, can provide tools for an actor-oriented study of rural development.

The research methods in diversification analysis

The methodological agenda

Methodologically, this study emanates from two different aspects. First, it is a critique of the survey based household studies which try to place the African smallholders into quantitative estimations of causalities and, while doing this, simplify and distort the object of the economic analysis. Second, it emanates from the interest to study local economy as an organic whole, but characterised with a developed division of labour. I look at these two aspects in turn.

There is much to be said on the reliability of survey data as well as the validity of posing questions on issues/categories that are alien to the people studied. Surveys on income sources and household budget studies tend to give a picture of an object which is all time escaping from the categorisation. Nevertheless, there is a developing methodological discussion which includes the advanced versions of farming systems research and the subsequent exploration of the ways to grasp less noticed and more difficult sides of the local economy. The farming systems research has developed during recent decades and developed a capacity to analyse the diversity in agricultural production (Chambers et al., 1989) and the diverse types of farming 'households' (Moock et al., 1986). What needs still to be fully incorporated are the 'non-farm' activities and the forms of social interdependency and division of labour that make a farm integrated into its surroundings. In other words, the farming systems research has developed within certain limits—inside the farm gate. The important part of diversity in economy can only be understood if the farm gate is opened and the interaction with the surrounding village is also observed. There is much more outside the farm gate than the obscure 'market'. This kind of open, diversity oriented analysis I call 'village economics'.

The other side of the methodological agenda is empirical. I try to exhibit a detailed and fairly reliable picture of the village economy as a system. However, since a part of the economy is outside the monetarised sector and since there are many transactions which concern services and cultural valuables and where pattern of payment is indirect, the problem is to include these economic sectors within a holistic analysis but without distorting them too much. In order to reach this aim I have selected to utilise various rapid rural appraisal methods which primarily generate qualitative information. Given the use of the various 'rapid' techniques the reliability of the data is a weak point. In the text I supply information on the research methods and make their use as transparent as possible. I also give information on some earlier, extensive (and labour intensive) farming systems studies which have been carried out in the region.

The methodology does not aim merely to describe the diversity of the economic activities in a village. It aims also to explain why some people prosper while others are less successful. The causal explanations are not sought from the lack of some immediate conditions of production like skill, capital or market— there is an ample discussion on 'micro enterprises' from that angle. Instead, the capacity to circulate resources is seen as the most critical condition for success in the long run.

Combining economic and cultural analysis

Tanzanians are often masters in networking. As a part of diversification strategies I have also analysed concrete social networks in the village. The methodological postulate holds that active participation in a social network creates a reputation for a person. Over time, a positive reputation becomes established as a 'cultural capital', a resource which can almost be used like concrete material assets (see figure 2.2).

The economic and cultural issues are directly linked with each other. Economic resources are needed for obtaining cultural capital, and the other way round. I have separated various types of socio-cultural networks from each other. Each type has its own cultural capital. It is hypothesised that people benefit from certain types of 'cultural capitals' to succeed in certain types of economic activities. In other words, the economy is culturally embedded and culturally segmented. Another condition for success is that resources are transported from one activity to another. The accumulation is enhanced through surpassing cultural boundaries and exploiting existing discontinuities. This causal explanation is rather complicated and it needs to be linked with the methodological discussion: How can we get information on the social networks and 'embedded economy' in a certain location?

The "embedded economy" hypothesis claims that the social networks have a determining effect on the success of the income-generating activities but that they need to be combined with agriculture and cultural investments. The equation for the opportunity oriented analysis of the diversification strategy is described in figure 2.2.

The hypothesis is also a frame for the analysis. It outlines a culturally informed method for analysing livelihood strategies in rural Africa.

How may one observe diversification? While analysing diversification I have advanced through four major steps. The four steps are to:
- analyse the household level social, cultural and economic resources
- explicate the economic activities and processes taking place within a household

- indicate the pattern to combine serially or simultaneously different economic activities, to circulate resources between the activities and, after gainful conversions, to increase economic or cultural capital
- analyse whether the practised resource combination leads to social mobility from one wealth group to another.

Figure 2.2. The elements of a diversification strategy

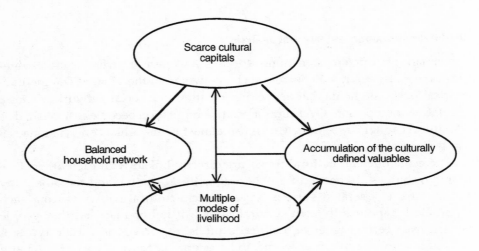

The research methods are described in Annex I. The characteristics of the studied village are presented in Annex II. When we proceed to analyse economic exchange networks within the village, we are confronted with a mass of idiosyncratic information—a sort of 'local knowledge' which is both essential for analysis and embedded in situated practices. Sharing this local knowledge, at least to some extent, is a necessary precondition for the understanding of the local diversification patterns. For the reader unfamiliar with the local circumstances, it will be useful to take a close look at the Annex before proceeding to the following chapters.

Chapter 3

How Diversification Makes Sense

> ... at this time of the year, if you have money, you should cultivate groundnuts. When you harvest groundnuts, you can use the money to cultivate some rice. And you buy rice. After two months, cashew is ready for harvesting. Now you sell rice, and you have money for trading during the cashew season... Cashew is the father. Cashew is the provider, groundnut and rice are its brother.
>
> A trader-cum-farmer in Kilimahewa

In this chapter I give examples of how diversification functions as an *active* orientation to combine different resources in a useful way.

One reason that makes diversification so common is that diversification makes sense. Diversification is an efficient strategy for resource utilisation. It makes it possible to use scarce resources where they are needed. And when a need decreases or disappears, the resources can be transferred to another activity. From the perspective of conventional enterprise theory, diversification is an unorthodox strategy of resource management. I try to show that what may look unorthodox from the narrow perspective of the conventional enterprise theory is perfectly practical and efficient from the perspective of a rural household.

Some of the patterns of diversification are based on fairly complex strategies. They could be perceived as performative strategies but this does not mean that a tendency to diversify automatically leads to profit. Rather, diversification has to be conducted through a skilful strategy which is geared towards optimal behaviour through mastery over an unpredictable environment. The complexity of the strategies is evident in situations where villagers utilise their social networks for economic transactions, where payments are delayed or replaced by gift exchanges, or where short and long time-frames are intertwined in economic calculation. In these situations, where the profitability of an activity is hopelessly dependent upon the factors beyond the tools of the conventional economic analysis, the measurement of profitability is extremely difficult.

Diversification can be performed using strategies which are exceptional and marginal for the village economy.[1] Yet these exceptional cases are a key to the

---

1. In Chapter 7 I shall use the concept of livelihood strategy to refer to the *systematic* analysis of the household level processes in a relatively static manner. Because of its wide focus the concept of livelihood strategy has a relatively descriptive and functionalist character. It can show at a very general level what kind of cultural, social and economic options are available for different wealth groups. However, it shows only what is normal or conventional. It is very difficult to place exceptional cases and conjuctural factors within such a framework.

understanding of the lively village economy. I use the diversification concept to highlight the importance of the marginal and exceptional strategies. These dynamic elements, when taken together, make up a sizeable portion of the economic life in a village. Case-studies show that diversification strategies vary from each other—and for each individual his or her exceptional behaviour may be a way to success.

The analysis of diversification strategies concentrates on the dynamic ways of combining together different elements for an opportunistic strategy. The variation between individual cases means that it is difficult to generalise at aggregate level (e.g. wealth group). In the following I present the main elements of the diversification strategies from an actor-oriented perspective. This presentation is followed by examples which show variation in diversification strategies. Thus I try to provide a heuristic picture of diversification which then, in the following chapters, will be placed under systematic scrutiny.

Combining activities—crossing the boundaries

Diversification means conducting several, qualitatively different economic activities within a social unit. The portfolio of activities is never dictated by economic necessity only, but is shaped in conjunction with cultural peculiarities and social networks. Thus the pattern of diversification varies enormously from one cultural setting to another. Since people are always reflective about their economic activities (even when this reflection is not 'discursive knowledge' but tacit knowledge on how to solve practical problems) one can speak of diversification as a strategy.

There are numerous economic activities even in a peripheral village. It is theoretically possible to locate almost an infinite number of combinations of activities. (One can make 4,950 different pairs from 100 activities. If we look at the possible combinations of three activities, we have 101,700 alternatives.) Rather than looking at theoretical alternatives, it is important to note those activities which are commonly combined, and for what reasons, in Kilimahewa.

Agriculture and trading are often conducted side by side, as mutually complementary activities. Agricultural crops provide employment and incomes seasonally. In agricultural communities like Kilimahewa, the economy runs in cycles where the agricultural period of weeding is a period of scarcity and hard work, while after harvesting money is circulating in plenty and work is minimal. It is convenient for a farmer to diversify to trading during the season of affluence. The combination of farming and trading is also intrinsic because practically all the crops produced for one's own consumption can be, when necessary, sold off. The practice of locating buyers, negotiating prices and selling his or her own produce gives a farmer experience in handling the marketing situation which is similar to trading. If one has some extra money, it is only a short step forward to start to trade, that is, to buy produce in order to sell it.

Agriculture can be combined with extractive activities with similar ease. This is the case because, in Kilimahewa, the agricultural plots tend to be scattered around the forested areas. While visiting fields it is possible to pick up several other forest products to sell. The difficulty with extractive activities is the necessity to deal with a forest environment which is inhabited by real and imaginary dangers.

Crafts are conducted with minimal investments in Kilimahewa. For this reason, crafts can be picked up seasonally and discontinued when there is a lack of orders. This character of crafts makes them a suitable addition for a diversification strategy. In contrast, an engagement in communal and personal services tends to be time consuming. In services, it may be difficult to draw a line between an economically profitable activity and a willingness to 'be around'. Thus engagement in common activities may be a source of respectability—the accumulation of cultural capital—or a sheer waste of time. In some service activities like Islamic astrology, the respected position may lead to considerable incomes.

Naturally, an integral part of diversification is the combination of the reproductive household chores with outward-oriented productive activities. It is of the utmost importance for a household that the reproductive activities can be run smoothly alongside the productive activities. Some reproductive activities like cooking tend to take several hours every day and thus give a rhythm for all other women's activities. In order to be able to stay away from cooking and child care for any longer period of time, the women create complicated systems of swapping labour. These swapping arrangements have similar features to diversification strategies.

This brief introduction shows how diversification functions through combining different economic activities into a coherent strategy. Thus intersectoral diversification is the basic type of diversification. It is very conventional to combine agriculture with trading, a craft or an extractive activity. Crossing sectoral boundaries is done continuously since sectoral boundaries are merely the creations of the external classification. For example, for a blacksmith, the production of a hoe may require a combination of craftwork and agriculture: a blacksmith producing a hoe first sells some sorghum to get money to buy pieces of scrap metal which he needs as raw material. In general, the backward and forward linkages are commonly a good reason for diversification. When a producer controls the access to raw material or the selling of the product, the risks related to mediators are diminished.

Making use of time and space

Seasonal and serial diversification: taking advantage of right timing

The temporal dimension is as crucial for diversification as it is for any strategic behaviour. The temporal dimension is a challenging object for research: it incorporates several layers (e.g. life-cycles, seasonal cycles, trading trip cycles) which operate in parallel. The temporal dimension has a capacity to generate systematic expectations on continuity and systematic expectations on change. However, all temporal matters are subject to unexpected ruptures.

In the following analysis I look at the ways of making use of temporal expectations for the benefit of a diversification strategy. I separate three types of diversification. When one activity is terminated to start a second one I speak of *serial* diversification. When the two activities are linked through a continuous flow of petty reinvestments, I speak of *simultaneous* diversification. Between these two models is seasonal diversification.

Simultaneous diversification is the basic type of diversification, a typical example of which is the diversification between agricuture and running a beer club. Agriculture does not only play a passive role of providing security. Instead agricultural produce can be sold (even in advance of harvest on credit) to fund the running costs of a club. Agriculture can also directly provide raw materials for the activity, like in the case of a beer club owner having coconut trees. The income from the beer place is then used to pay for agricultural labour, like coconut tree climbing.

The serial type of diversification means a major irreversible shift of resources from one activity to a new activity. The most typical pattern of serial diversification is ceasing employment as a labourer in the town and then investing in rural property. This pattern is not, however, easy to detect in Kilimahewa. This is so because the people returning from town are culturally not expected to present themselves as rich, modern or otherwise better folks. This contrasts with the praxis in Kilimanjaro region where many town-based officers and businessmen build expensive houses in their home areas and 'show off' their wealth. In Kilimahewa, the returning labourers are less inclined to 'conspicuous consumption' and showing off. Instead, they invest in urban property, rural land or rural wives—valuables which are not contradictory to rural values and which are difficult to measure. However, due to the low employment prospects and wage levels in urban areas, the returning labourers have currently less to hide. Many returning labourers come back nowadays with empty hands.

Another common example of serial diversification relates to trading. When a mobile petty trader has managed to accumulate profits, he often suddenly finishes trading and invests in a different kind of business. The mobile traders tend to invest—apart from the expansion of the trade—in land or a shop. These are perceived as the most profitable forms of serial diversification. They represent some security compared with the risky world of mobile petty trading.

A case between simultaneous and serial diversification is seasonal diversification. In the case-studies we have several examples where trading and agriculture are conducted seasonally so that the trading activity is kept at a minimum for several months only to shoot up when the demand is high. The labour allocation between the different activities is flexible and the total amount of labour varies as well.

In Kilimahewa, seasonal fluctuations are noticeable and they mark the economic strategies of all households. There are large differences between those households which can manage seasonal fluctuations and those that are the victims of seasonality. Making use of seasonality is a major feature for successful diversification.

Taking advantage of geographic variation

In some cases geographical dispersion is a strategic element in diversification. This means that a household has a person living in another location where he is able to conduct trade and occasionally give services, thus adding to the resources of the main part of a household.

I have already mentioned the networks that households generate in order to access different resources. In Kilimahewa, the households differ in terms of their capacity to maintain linkages to towns. Most households have contacts in the district centres nearby and in Dar es Salaam but only some households have the means to keep these contacts active. It is usually easy to send a message to town. One can also find ways to send small packets of food and other gifts to a distant town. It is more demanding to keep business contacts in urban centres. That requires an effort and resources to travel to towns and live there. Traders, teachers and administrators have a reason, due to their occupation, to travel to the towns. Consequently, they can also keep their business contacts with friends and relatives in town alive.

Every household has a number of rural-rural linkages. and these are equally important for diversification. However, the rural-rural linkages deal with different types of advantages. The flows of resources between rural locations are commonly the flows of agricultural products and extracted natural resources. The resources that are transferred between Kilimahewa and another rural site are items like vegetables, local tobacco and salt.

The geographic element in diversification strategies is important because villages, even when they produce a variety of services and products, are far from self-reliant autonomous units. The regional trade networks are dense. Historical incidents and geographical barriers have created pockets of specialisation which naturally generate trade networks. In other words, the production patterns are location specific and segmented, creating regional interdependency. The long-distance trade is partly hampered by the poor infrastructure. One consequence of the unpredictable infrastructure is that goods brought from Dar es Salaam tend to flood the markets occasionally, spreading from a larger junction to distant villages. Given unpredictable supply, the exceptional town connections may prove to be a high yielding asset.

The case-studies on diversification

The following case-studies are examples of diversification of economic resources and even wider conversions between different types of social contexts and different types of capitals. The cases are profiled as different strategies of diversification. The cases of successful strategies are followed by a less successful one. Some cases show serial diversification while others profile seasonal or simultaneous diversification. The case-studies start with a small presentation of the domestic group and its economic history. Subsequently, a more formal analysis of the diversification strategies is conducted.

The first case-study on a wealthy shopkeeper shows a commercial full-time commitment to an income-generating activity facilitated by a household division of labour. I call it an 'accumulation strategy' since it includes a dynamic growth-oriented combination of different activities and accumulation of wealth. The second case of a coconut trade shows a similar tendency towards commercial calculation integrating a combination of different trading circuits. The third case exemplifies an innovative woman who invests heavily in communal affairs. Finally, the fourth case exemplifies the income-generating activities of poor people and I call that diversification strategy 'survival strategy'.

Accumulation strategy: The case of the prosperous trader Rashidi Tambala

Rashidi is a prospering young shopkeeper who has managed to accumulate a sizeable amount of land. Rashidi has changed to new income sources several times as his means have increased. Rashidi is a 32 year old man with two wives. He has also been married earlier and the divorced wife has left him with one child. The present older wife has three small children while the junior wife has just given birth to her first child. Rashidi is also known to have fathered the child of a female village administrator. Beside this 'core family' Rashidi supports his father living in Mnazimmoja and two uncles and an unmarried sister in Kilimahewa.

Rashidi started his career by cultivating mainly groundnuts. When some capital was accumulated, Rashidi become a mobile trader and started to trade beans and maize from Songea. After a period as a mobile trader he traded at the Mtwara market in cooperation with a friend. This came to an end when Rashidi visited home to attend a funeral and, while he was away, the friend ran away with the money. As his next project Rashidi bought a camera and made a business of walking around the countryside taking pictures of people. At that time there were hardly any photographers in rural areas and the business prospered. Photography gave very nice profits but the camera broke down and Rashidi had to leave this business as well.

The years of trading had moulded the business skills of Rashidi. Rashidi opened his first shop in the old village in 1990. Unfortunately, the shop building was demolished by the floods. He then built a new house for his family and a new shop building. He has been trading merchandise from Dar es Salaam. He soon established a relationship with the Indian traders in Lindi. He can currently even command some credit facilities from his main supplier. With an owner of a petrol station Rashidi has a special arrangement for getting kerosene by the barrel. Kerosene bought in a large amount is cheaper than kerosene bought by *debe* (a canister of 20 litres used by normal traders) and Rashidi is able to attract a lot of customers by selling cheap kerosene in his shop. He is also the sole shopkeeper who is able to display and stock a large variety of bicycle spares, tools and other hardware items which have a very slow rate of circulation and thus require a major investment in stock. The hardware plays a minor role in the turnover of the shop but the items certainly make his shop a special attraction for men.

One of the major sources of income is trading with cashewnuts. Rashidi was also an early bird in this field. He started to trade in cashewnuts in 1991 when the liberalisation of trade was still at a formative stage and the setting was unstable. Rashidi had to sell his nuts at coastal towns but he managed to locate customers and organise transport. His earlier experience as a mobile trader was an advantage. Currently Rashidi buys cashewnuts directly through the backdoor of the shop from the petty traders who work under a loose contract with him. Rashidi can take advantage of these petty traders because the latter do not have their own capital to collect as large amounts of cashew as they have access to. Thus the petty traders sell quickly to Rashidi in order to receive capital for use in the following round of cashew nut collection. Apparently some of the petty traders sell stolen nuts but this is not Rashidi's concern.

Rashidi has managed to buy several pieces of land with the proceeds from his trading activities.

1. 1.5 acres of valley land
2. 4 acres of land bought in 1988 for Shs. 15,000
3. 1 acre of coconut and cashew in 1989 for Shs. 12,000
4. 3 acres of coconut bought for Shs. 53,000 in 1992
5. 2 acres of cashew nut trees bought for Shs. 9,000 in 1992
6-7. Two other plots in Luwale.

It is clear that Rashidi has no time whatsoever to engage in agricultural work. Rashidi has hired four watchmen for his fields. Besides these he uses labourers extensively to work on his fields. The crops which he grows are suitable for this kind of labour arrangement. Rashidi acknowledges that the value of land has increased considerably during the last few years and that this constitutes an integral factor of his economic strategy.

Rashidi has earlier lived in several places but currently his prosperity requires firm commitment to the village he knows so well. His strategy of accumulation is clearly geared towards the continuation of trading and large investments in agriculture. He has previously moved around but it is unlikely that he will establish shops in other locations. He still operates with the logic of petty trader, holding all the strings in his own hand. He is notoriously modest and keeps a low profile avoiding investing in cultural capital. This also makes him vulnerable to some envy and contempt. For example, in the case where a customer (who was angry because he was denied credit) stole from his shop, the villagers did not do anything to help Rashidi to catch the thief. Later on Rashidi belittled the whole incident. It was evident, however, that as a rich man he did not receive support from other people. Other similar incidents revealed that Rashidi was forced to tolerate many kinds of offensive behaviour and abusive language.

The pattern of diversification in Rashidi Tambala's household

Without question Rashidi has entered the accumulation path by means of first having diversified his activities and then straddling between them. Rashidi has engaged in serial as well as simultaneous diversification. His speciality is perhaps being at the right place before others. Thus he entered the cashew trade and photography very early and made good profits. He then invested in shopkeeping and managed to keep an edge against other shopkeepers. His shop is always full of people.

Rashidi's household lives in one location, a factor which does not facilitate spatial diversification. All his fields are administered from one homestead. A step towards spatial diversification is network building. Rashidi overcomes spatial concentration through social networks which he has established with other traders. These include a patron and several clients.

Rashidi has invested very little in cultural capital. In this respect he represents the new class of young money-minded businessmen.

Entering the accumulation path: The household of a young trader Hamisi Selemani

Hamisi Selemani is merely 28 years old. Even at this low age he has managed to make a career in trading. He has established various networks from the village level to the regional level.

The household of Hamisi is an interesting collection of young people. Hamisi has divorced his first wife but a child from that marriage stays with him. His present wife has not yet given birth. In addition he houses a younger brother and a sister, a child of his dead brother and a male trading friend. Hamisi runs his business with the help of his trading friend. His wife is responsible for housework and the occasional supervision of the day labourers. In addition to the resident members Hamisi says that he supports his parents and grandparents. He also contributes money to numerous funerals and attends some of them in person.

Hamisi was born in the old village. After finishing primary school he joined his brother who was running a restaurant in Mtama township. Besides the restaurant business the brother was also engaged in illegal business, smoked bhang and had very rough manners: he died from a bullet in a shooting incident in 1985. Hamisi inherited the restaurant and sold it to his brother-in-law for Shs. 20,000, and then started to trade in coconuts.

Coconut cultivation is very popular in the village. Trading in coconuts requires an ability to buy large amounts of coconuts for cash, hire a lorry and sell coconuts in the coconut deficient areas and townships. The real thresholds in the business are working capital and contacts. Hamisi buys the coconuts directly from the villagers at their farms, collects the coconuts with carriers and takes them to a storehouse which is protected by a watchman. He sends letters (using the drivers and passengers of the by-passing buses as messengers) to his potential buyers in town and agrees in advance the price and the amount of coconuts to be sold. Hamisi is well acquainted with some 12 buyers in four district centres. Two of them are 'brothers' and the others are friends. Hamisi collects 2–3,000 coconuts before transporting them. He joins with two other traders to hire a lorry. When taken to Songea the charge in 1994 was Shs. 180,000 (i.e. Shs. 60,000 per head). The buying price of the coconuts was Shs. 20–25 depending on the season. The wholesale selling price in Songea was Shs. 70. Deducting only the transport cost the gross profit was Shs. 30,000 per trip. In one year Hamisi made two trips to Songea, four to Newala, four to Nachingwea and three to Masasi, selling altogether some 30,000 coconuts. During the return trips he brought with him items like groundnuts and maize which he either sold immediately to local traders or stored in godowns to wait for a better selling season.

In a similar fashion Hamisi is engaged in cashew trading. At the early stage of the buying season he goes from house to house in the nearby villages. He buys cashew by using a cooking oil can as a measure. This way the price can be as low as Shs. 50–100 per kilo. After collecting 5–10 bags (90–100 kilos each) he takes a lift on a passing lorry and sells cashew to a trader in Masasi. The selling price is Shs. 210 per kilo (or Shs. 150 for second grade nuts). The transport charge is Shs. 800 per bag. During the previous buying season Hamisi managed to make four trips. The buying season is relatively short (2–3 months) but the cashew trade is more lucrative than the coconut trade.

Hamisi has managed to accumulate four plots for cultivation of which one plot of one acre was given him by his father. The valley plot gives rice and maize plus 1,800 coconuts annually. The second plot is the village government allocation of one acre. This is reserved for various food crops. Hamisi has bought his third plot of one acre from a villager for Shs. 12,000. It is a coconut plot in the valley with groundnuts interplanted with cassava. The fourth plot he bought from his father's brother for Shs. 9,000. It is a plot of 1.5 acres of cashew trees. The annual income from the fields amounts to Shs. 200,000 with cashew, coconut, maize, cassava and rice bringing the largest income.

Hamisi looks like a very modest man and his house and consumption patterns do not outwardly differ much from those of normal peasants. His reputation is dimmed by his late brother and he has a long way to go to establish himself as a respected man. However, he is currently quite content with his fellow age-mates and his business activities—the world of elders runs with a different sort of 'capital' far removed from his world.

Diversification in Hamisi Selemani's household

It seems that Hamisi Selemani has entered the accumulation path which can only be blocked by a series of misfortunes. His network of trading contacts is small but effective. He cooperates with youths of his age as a primary reference group. They occasionally lend money to each other, organise transport and spend time together. Hamisi also knows well a local elderly trader and a shop-keeper whom he trusts with his extra money. His external contacts are well established traders. Hamisi is an expert in networking.

The social networks of Hamisi Selemani are practical and utilitarian circuits of cooperation. When Hamisi makes profits he invests some of the money in land and some in trading. He has the usual aspiration of traders to open a shop and become a more settled trader. Selemani has taken the first steps in that direction.

Analytically we can conclude that Hamisi is engaged in inter-sectoral diversification between agriculture and trading. He is engaged in simultaneous diversification and money is continuously flowing between the activities. The pattern of diversification is facilitated by the hierarchical division of labour between spouses. So far the household has not engaged in spatial diversification in the sense that its members were distributed between several locations. However, the pattern of networking is a close equivalent to that. The pattern of diversification is strictly within the realm of the economic capital. He has not invested in any sort of cultural capital which would give him a higher standing in the village.

A case of a resourceful woman: Hadija Siri

Hadija Siri could be called a village activist because of her various commitments. She has lived most of her life in the village and she is well integrated in its social life. She has been involved in the women's organisation of the party, in village politics and traditional trades as well as small business. In terms of wealth her household ranks at the upper end of the middle group.

Hadija Siri is a 45 year old women who has divorced three husbands. Currently she lives together with an unmarried son and a daughter of her brother but she also often has two small grandchildren at her compound. Her own only child, an adult son, has a house in the same village. In the neighbouring house lives her sister.

Hadija's entrance to her income generating activities relates to her marital history. Hadija's first marriage was rather short and ended after the death of her second child. At this time of hardship she started as a female initiation expert—a skill which she still continues to master. Her second marriage brought her to neighbouring towns and even to Dar es Salaam where, because she was childless, she had an opportunity to engage in small-scale trading. Hadija returned to the village in 1982 after her second divorce. Soon she was involved in a political women's group, she was a member of a rotating savings group and was engaged in running a tea-room with other women. Hadija married Abdalla, the village chairman at that time, and stayed married until their divorce in 1993. Hadija and Abdalla had a similar orientation in village affairs as both were, and still are, active members and involved in running the mosque and organising Muslim celebrations. Both Hadija and Abdalla are still among the CCM elite in the village.

The diversification strategy of Hadija entails the use of cultural capital accumulated through formal institutions. Hadija is currently a member of the village government and on one of its committees. She was elected a section leader (for 50 households) by the section members. In the election she defeated two male candidates. Hadija is also one of a handful of people who have paid the entrance fee for the newly established primary cooperative. The official posts that Hadija holds mean very little actual power—village administration is run through a number of officers—but a lot of engagement in political events, discussions at the marketplace, traditional rituals and religious festivities.

The life-history of Hadija shows the typical swing of ups and downs in rural income-generating activities. Most of the women's projects in the village were destroyed by floods in 1990 and the women have only recently had the resources to start afresh. Two years ago Hadija started a tea-room with her sister at the sister's house. The tea-room has flourished during harvest time and it has been closed during the lean months. Hadija has recently joined another group of women who have started a tea-room in the valley where people work and where cashew and sugarcane buyers pass by. She has also reactivated a group of five friends to participate in a new scheme for bank loans targeted at women's groups. In addition, Hadija participated two years ago in a seminar for midwives. She learned the basic skill and nowadays she helps at two deliveries a month. She scolds her more

conservative fellow women who said that the seminars were nothing for women like Hadija who only read with difficulty if at all. Afterwards they were envious for her courage in taking part in the seminar and learning new things.

It is impossible to give a detailed figure for the economic benefits arising from Hadija's political activity. The village and party affairs have a very limited direct profit while religious commitments mean a net expenditure of money. The only activity with a likelihood for direct profits is participation in the primary cooperative. The tea-room has an estimated income of Shs. 60,000 a year. Together midwifery and initiation services provide her with an income of about Shs. 20,000 a year.

Beside being an entrepreneur and a village activist, Hadija is a farmer. Hadija has managed to get hold of four plots of agricultural land. She received a plot of one acre from her father. It has both cashew trees and various food crops. After her father's death in 1971 she inherited an acre of coconut trees. She bought her third plot of 1.5 acres for cultivating rice for a mere Shs. 300 in 1983. The fourth plot is the home plot of almost an acre allocated by the village government after the floods in 1990. Hadija does not find it profitable to engage in agricultural labour parties. Instead, she occasionally employs day labourers and also does some labouring herself. Her farm incomes are rather substantial reaching almost Shs. 90,000 a year, with cashew, rice and bananas giving the largest returns. The pattern of income and expenditure is presented in tables 3.1 and 3.2.

Table 3.1. The farm and off-farm incomes of Hadija Siri. (Shs. per year)

bananas	15,000
rice	12,000
papaya	10,000
pineapple	1,000
millet	9,000
cassava	4.500
pigeon peas	5,000
maize	4,000
cashew	24,800
coconut	8,000
groundnut	6,000
Sub-total: farm income	99,300
tea-room	60,000
circumcision	14,000
midwifery	6,000
Sub-total: off-farm income	80,000
Total	179,300

Table 3.2. The monetary consumption of Hadija Siri in one month.

Cloth (kitenge)	1,500
Lamp oil	1,260
Soap for clothes	890
Soap for washing	150
Body oil	200
Matches	80
Sugar	700
Tea	160
Vegetables	400
Flour	600
Charcoal	400
Frying pan	400
Social events	500
Comfort/partying	500
Fees	1,500
Total	9,240

The social networks of Hadija are several. First, she is active in women's groups with women she trusts regardless of their ethnic or social background. Second, she maintains a lot of contacts with her siblings and other near relations through gifts and visits. Third, she is engaged in private business and she runs her fields and tea-room with a certain commercial calculation on the value of labour. Fourth, she has an active role in village politics—a position which yields both respect and envy. It is fair to say that she has invested heavily in the mainstream 'cultural capital' of the village. This investment has provided her with a large safety net. Her income generating activities have arisen both through her marriages and her concern for women's situation.

Diversification in Hadija Siri's household

The diversification pattern of Hadija Siri's household is complex due to two reasons: first, the large number of economic activities in her portfolio of diversification and, second, the heavy investments in cultural capital. Both of these factors make the analysis of the household economy a tricky task.

Concerning economic diversification, the pattern appears as much adjustment to the whims of personal upheavals as premeditated consideration—Hadija has accumulated new tasks and skills as time has passed. However, her current set of activities is very sensible for one reason: the different tasks provide a steady income throughout the year. Together they compose a rational whole. I analyse at some length the relationship between farm- and off-farm incomes, and their seasonal variation.

In the case of Hadija, the two categories are neatly complementary. The incomes from the food crops peak from July to September, as can be seen from figure 3.1.

Figure 3.1. Hadija Siri: The agricultural income over a calendar year

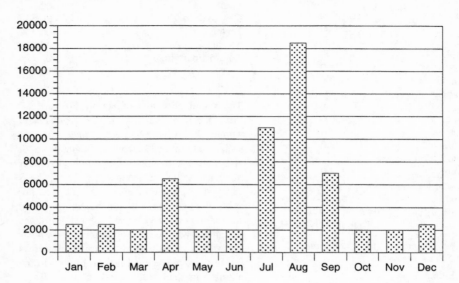

Besides the agricultural incomes Hadija runs a tea-room from November to February. These are the months when incomes from cashew have been received and business is profitable. Apart from the tea-room Hadija also has occasional incomes from her skills as a midwife and as a circumcision expert. The incomes from the cash crops and off-farm nicely balance the income during the rest of the year.

Figure 3.2. Hadija Siri: The non-agricultural income over a calendar year

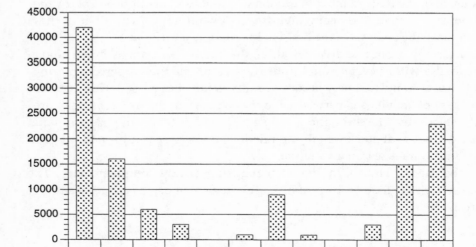

A study of the different income sources shows that diversification rather than specialisation is the pattern for Hadija's economic strategy. In her agricultural orientation, cashew appears as the most important cash crop. However, when all the agricultural crops are transformed into monetary terms it appears that no crop has a dominant position in the incomes. The relative importance of cashew decreases even further when the off-farm incomes are included in the calculation. The off-farm incomes amount to 45 per cent of the total income.

In the case of Hadija, the income from bananas amounts to almost 10 per cent of the total income. Bananas are economically significant to her. However, at the village level the income from bananas is almost insignificant. This example shows that when household level economic information is aggregated (i.e. transformed to few household or village level indicators), an important potential for local level exchange is wiped out from the analysis.

The consumption of this female-headed dispersed household has two important categories: business expenses (tea, flour) and the use of money paid for social activities. The social events, partying and fees (including hospital fees for relatives) account for a quarter of the monthly expenses. The high figure in spending on social events is partly explained by the fact that the recall questioning was done in August when the social village activities are especially hectic. Yet these expenses cannot be overlooked. They show that the creation of the position as a village leader has definite expenses. Moreover, the table of expenses does not show all the minor exchanges that take the form of gifts and loans and which are usually non-monetary. The recall method does not capture all these as well as the daily budget studies (e.g. Skjønsberg, 1989).

Survival strategy:

The household of the ming'oko seller Fatu Ismaili

Fatu Ismaili is a 55 year old widow. Beside farming, her only income-generating activity is selling *ming'oko*, a wild root crop. This is an unprofitable exercise and Fatu expresses dissatisfaction with it but she still prefers to continue with it, instead of offering herself more often for day labouring.

Fatu Ismaili was born in Newala district and she moved with her parents to Kilimahewa during villagisation in 1974. She has been married three times. During the first marriage she had three children which she raised. The second marriage was short and ended when the husband was imprisoned on theft charges. The third husband died two years ago. The youngest daughter got married recently, although within the village, leaving Fatu on her own. Currently Fatu receives gifts from her three daughters, a maternal uncle and her neighbours. Otherwise her support networks are negligible. Earlier Fatu used to support her own mother but the mother died a few years ago.

The death of the third husband left Fatu impoverished. Before dying the husband was ill for a long time and the payment for treatment drained all their savings. The parents of Fatu did not leave behind any land and now Fatu cultivates her only plot which she received from the village government. She takes part in labour parties and she has organised one land clearing party on her plot. She occasionally does day labouring.

Fatu has been collecting and selling ming'oko for two years. Ming'oko is a root crop which is usually eaten as a snack or combined with cassava to make a proper meal. The tools needed for collecting are very simple: a hoe for digging and a bamboo basket for carrying the roots. The work itself is hard. One needs to leave early in the morning for the forest. The walk to the digging place takes four hours. After a rest the group of women scatter to dig. After four or five hours they start the return journey. The forest harbours lions and if the women need to stop overnight they have to make a fire to protect themselves. At home the roots are peeled and boiled. The selling takes just a few moments but the income for the whole exercise is merely some Shs. 1,000.

Fatu Ismaili is a woman deprived of any position of authority that her age, kinship rela- tions and Islamic religion could offer her. During her third marriage Fatu was able to take part in communal activities like cooking for Islamic *ziara* gatherings. Now she has dropped even this activity. She does not pay for party membership and thus she is not eligible for joining the political selections which are still made initially through the party hierarchy. Fatu pays only the most pressing marketplace fee and the payments for obliga- tory public collections. In terms of cultural capital Fatu Ismaili is not openly defiant to the mainstream power hierarchies—she simply lacks such capital herself and she tries to cope within the limits of her marginal position.

The pattern of diversification

Fatu's pattern of diversification is definitely geared towards poverty alleviation. She is socially deprived and has limited means to put herself forward in the cultural arenas. As such her pattern of diversification is opportunity oriented economic diversification. Within the limits of her economic options, she strives along a path where income from gathering roots is preferred to agricultural day-labouring in order to maintain at least minimal respect and self-determina- tion. Nevertheless, it is clear that to her diversification itself is not an option of choices—it is a necessary means to stay alive.

Analytically we can observe the inter-sectoral diversification between agri- culture and extractive activities. The diversification is carried out seasonally and is spatially concentrated. The pattern of diversification requires knowledge about the surrounding forests.

The resource flows between activities

Diversification is sometimes seen as a static strategy of placing eggs in many baskets. I prefer to see diversification as a more dynamic strategy where resources are allocated from one use to another. Thus a household can have, say, three income sources and it needs to allocate its resources between these activities. It has to deploy available land, labour, skills, capital and contacts in a reasonable manner. Sometimes most of the resources are pooled and used for farming while, in another occasion, trading is given priority. Most of the resources are transferable.

Diversification makes sense when it is possible to move resources from one activity to another. There is a major difference in this respect between *finite* and *replenishable* resources. The difference between these categories is that the first ones are 'consumption' items. The resources which are finite are labour time, money and raw materials. Once labour, money or raw materials are expanded for one purpose, they cannot be used again. The second category consists of items like tools, information, contacts and cultural capital which, once used, can still be applied for another activity. These replenishable resources are infinite, since their use does not necessarily diminish their further use value.

The analysis of the reallocation of items makes concrete the understanding of how diversification can be a useful strategy. This concreteness can be deceptive if it is understood merely as an optimal use of scarce resources. In many cases, the reallocation of a resource means that the item is valorised from a completely new perspective. The item is given a new value and the value differentials are a source of profit. I shall come back to the 'conversion' of values in later chapters.

Reallocation of labour time. Labour time is a scarce resource in Kilimahewa. There are a number of reasons for this: the labour intensive technologies, the competing uses for labour time, funerals and other social commitments, the weather conditions which make physical work difficult at certain seasons, and the frequent sicknesses which decrease the productivity of labour. While labourers can be employed for a relatively low wage, the negotiation of the labour contracts and their enforcement is itself a laborious task. The household labour is still the most reliable source of labour but even that requires extensive negotiation. One of the crucial questions is then, how labour time can be allocated to the right tasks at the right time.

Diversification means making the best of the labour time. Here the case of craftsmen is illuminating. A blacksmith or a carpenter cannot afford to sit around and wait for orders. The alternative he has at his disposal is either to make items to store or engage in other activities when no work is pressing. Due to the scarcity of working capital the craftsmen tend to choose the latter alternative. They go on with farming, trading and other activities. When a person needs the service of a craftsman, he approaches the craftsman, and a contract is agreed upon. The craftsman then proceeds to produce the item at his convenience, for instance he can use a suitable slack period (from time-bound agricultural tasks) to make the item. This flexibility helps to keep the price of the work low.

A mutually supportive division of labour within a household is a precondition from which it is possible to venture into a flexible diversification strategy. The case of Juma Rashid, a fish trader, is illuminating. Juma has entered into something close to a contractual arrangement with his two wives. He has allocated each a portion of land and he also provides them with certain inputs. He then expects the women to conduct the farm work on their own, or helping each other, but in any case they are supposed to repay him all his initial costs. This arrangement was rather authoritarian and produced sarcastic comments from other villagers. Nevertheless, the system worked fairly well. The women could make their own arrangements so that one was taking care of children and cooking while the other was farming. Juma could run his fish trade and cultivate some crops on his own, allocating his labour time according to profibility during that particular season.

Reallocation of money. Notes and coins do not carry with them the history of previous transactions. For this reason, it is fairly easy to reallocate money from one activity to another. This is also how diversification is conducted in Kilimahewa. Money is transferred without any problems from one business to another business, from trading to consumption, and the other way round. The finances of single activities are not kept fully separate. People may have a system of financial follow-up which gives a rough estimate of how much a single field produced or the income of the sales trip to town. Money from one activity can be physically kept in a separate purse. But these calculations do not hinder a trader from deducting money from the purse and putting it to other uses when a need arises. Thus separate bookkeeping is certainly not a hindrance for diversification.

Reallocation of raw materials. The concept of raw material is a rather technical one and sounds strange when referring to the kind of very small scale economic activities that I am dealing with. Many of the raw materials are gathered directly from nature, or are cultivated, and it is the labour input which makes them valuable. If raw material is not a product of one's own labour it is obtained through local exchange. The transfer of raw materials to another activity then means that a labour input or a money input is reallocated to a new context.

A simple case here is the cultivation of rice. It is usually cultivated in a small field as a cash crop for urban consumption. However, some women, like Hadija in the earlier case-study, can 'reallocate' the rice into their catering business. They cook the rice and sell it as a dish at the market place or in the fields. When rice is cooked and served from a banana leaf with some flavouring, its value has doubled compared to in its raw form.

Reallocation of tools. Tools differ from raw materials in that they are not exhausted by 'productive consumption'. Instead, they can be used repeatedly for several purposes. Thus diversification creates in principle fewer problems of resource management. However, Kilimahewa is extremely poorly equipped with practically all kinds of tools. People need to borrow from each other even the basic items like hoes and watering cans. The borrowing of items takes place continuously and the same items can be borrowed repeatedly. The technological innovations have been very few and the distribution of tools from urban centres is hampered by the limitations in the availability of loans, spare parts and extension services.

From the perspective of diversification it is beneficial to pursue a strategy where the same tools can be used for several activities. These would be selected so that the important multi-purpose tool would be used most effectively. Access to a rare multi-purpose tool would then give comparative advantage. Currently there is limited evidence that some tools would be used in the described manner. If the idea is stretched a little, we could say that shop buildings are a multi-purpose resource. After all, a shop is used for many purposes. The trade in the front part is usually accompanied by an equally high rate of trade at the back door. There the agricultural produce is bought, loans are fixed and politics discussed. The volume of exchanges at the back door can be as important as the dealings over the counter. A car is another typical tool around which a diversification strategy could be constructed. It can be used directly for one's own trading or for the business needs of any other villager, it can be used for doing favours and enhancing respectability. Currently no person living in the village owns a car and some outsiders who have a vehicle can get extensive benefits from doing minor favours. An electricity is yet another multi-purpose resource. Electricity line was constructed through the village and, initially, some thirty households or shops applied for a connection. However, many of these were not able to pay for the connection costs and thus no household in the village was served. Electricity has the potential to become a central point for new diversification strategies.

Reallocation of information. General 'knowledge' on how to run a business is very widely applicable. Similarly, knowledge of different types of customers, their preferences and conventions, is a resource which can be applied in different business contexts. On the other hand, information on prices and the market situation is specific for each economic activity. Thus this information cannot easily be transferred to another sphere.

Relocation of contacts and cultural capital. It is one thing to know other people and another to be known by them. The accumulation of cultural capital means that a person becomes known and respected in his or her own right. Once a certain level of respectability is reached, it tends to increase rather than just be replenished when it is used. Thus the logic of social respectability is the opposite to that of the finite material world. The more the cultural capital is used, the wider becomes its referential power. This eases the relocation of cultural capital.

I have already referred to the importance of hierarchical patronage relations in trading. When commercial patrons are Africans (instead of Asians and Europeans) the patronage relations have a tendency to become multi-functional. One relationship swells into a form of general patronage, including political and religious dimensions. The wide interface may be dysfunctional in purely commercial terms but functional from a wider angle. The big traders need to have a positive relationship with the local authorities. They can enhance their position vis-à-vis the administration by directing their own clientage into the direction which pleases the administrators.

There are many situations where one type of cultural capital can be reallocated to another cultural sphere. The intermarriage of religious and political power is the most obvious case. I will show how the gerontocracy of respected Islamic elders also try to reach hegemonic positions in the local political arenas. The relationship between these two spheres is very strong.

The working mechanisms of cultural capital are always mediated and thus complex. It is not possible for a person to state that because he has accumulated a certain amount of cultural capital, he or she should automatically be obeyed as an employer is obeyed. Instead, cultural capital is always a negotiated and contested resource. A person with cultural capital has to do favours and then ask for reciprocation. But the other person cannot reciprocate in the same terms. For example, the services of a religious leader for conducting public prayers cannot be reciprocated just in terms of religion. Instead, he can be provided with tea, food, and all kinds of gifts on other occasions. The indirectness of the reciprocation enhances the tendencies of diversification. It is useful for a religious leader to be engaged in petty business because he will then have many people 'indebted' to him who are potentially good and reliable customers.

Case-studies on the complex diversification strategies

The following two case-studies show how resources can be circulated from one activity to another. The case-studies give further evidence on how diversification can be put into practice. The first case-study describes the history of resource allocations of an enterprising tailor-cum-farmer who enters trading. The second case-study provides information on the annual cycle of resource flow management for a farmer-trader.

From petty trader and tailor to a man of respect:
The case of Mussa Wanyama

Mussa is a 47 year old man. He has accumulated both property and a respectable position in the village. His outer appearance and manners are those of the traditional Islamic elder. His talk reveals him as a businessman with hopes for further accumulation.

The analysis of the households shows an extensive network of internal and external dependants and supporters. Mussa has currently two wives who are living on separate plots within the village. He has altogether eleven children with three women. Three of the children are grown up and live outside the compound. Mussa also supports a number of his relatives. As such the household is extensive.

Mussa moved to his maternal uncle after finishing four years of primary school. Mussa helped his uncle in his shop and the uncle taught him to use the sewing machine. Mussa continued with his uncle for six years. Then he got employment as a turnboy (i.e. a helper) on a lorry owned by a local businessman. After two years Mussa finished his contract and carried out petty trade for three years, while simultaneously continuing with tailoring. The profits of the income-generating activities he invested in cashew trees—he sold plenty of cashew in the year of the biggest harvest ever, 1974. Operation Vijijini forced him to move to old Mtua the same year. He continued with sewing until he lost the machine in the flood of 1990.

Mussa opened his shop only two years ago. A rich friend of Mussa from another village persuaded Mussa to sell him his old house in that village and invest in the business. Mussa sold the house for Shs. 200,000. Mussa invested the money in 20 bags of cashew and six bags of rice. The cashew he sold to the cooperative while the rice was sold from home. Next he started to build a house. He opened the shop with commodities worth Shs. 200,000. Mussa regularly visits Lindi town to get merchandise. He has managed to get loans of Shs. 30,000 from wholesale traders.

The shop was a very good investment in the beginning. Later on the shop has been less profitable because it is located a short distance away from the market place. New shops have lately emerged at the market place and together they have a large variety of items which makes them more attractive to the customers. The only advantage of the current quiet location is that sometimes women like to visit his shop because it is easy to do so without information on their purchases reaching their husbands. Mussa has already bought two plots at the market place and he plans to build a shop there when he has acquired enough capital. Meanwhile, Mussa has continued with crop trading and hoarding.

Mussa has altogether four agricultural plots and two commercial plots. The agricultural plots include a tiny plot at the old village acquired during villagisation, the home plot acquired after the floods from the village council, another plot bought for the second wife within the village, and a plot of 1.5 acres in the valley. The last plot was bought in 1979 and it has 130 coconut trees and some sugarcane.

The activities of Mussa are not limited to the economic plane. Mussa is a member of the mosque committee. He likes to appear in kanzu and take part in the prayers. As far as I know he does not command the Islamic astrology, direct prayers or present himself as a learned Muslim. His activity is more a commitment to common affairs. He is definitively younger than most other committee members and, having moved to the village at the time of villagisation, he does not belong to the core group of the wealthy farmers. All these attributes are reflected in his modesty towards elders—even when he sees them as old-fashioned traditionalists.

Mussa lives near the market place and is always present at village gatherings. He is a member of the village council and he is a leader of the village section which comprises two streets. The activity in the village affairs has benefited him a little. He managed to get one of the best plots during the last resettlement. (The plots which are still better are owned by a district planning officer and a town based businessman.) He has also managed to buy the plot at the market place from the previous village chairman. Mussa was also one of those few who both had an interest in and managed to fulfil the requirements when an international development agency extended a goat project in the village.

The pattern of diversification

The pattern of diversification can best be understood through the reorientations in Mussa's life-history. It can be argued that his life has always been geared towards trading but this is a simplification. Mussa has definitively changed his orientation and reinvested time and money into new ventures. These twists are illustrated in figure 3.1 below.

It is unlikely that Mussa will be able to fundamentally change his economic strategy in the future. He has passed many stages and entered a phase where family commitments and community responsibilities may pull him towards the path of the traditionalist village leader—a direction he both seeks and wants to distance himself from. The family demands are certainly pressing. Currently Mussa runs the shop with the help of his grown-up son who needs to be pushed forward. Mussa's external dependants consist of his parents, the parents of one of his wive's and two sons of his brother. Mussa used to help his wife's brother until the latter moved to his mother, and his wife's mother's brother until he died. Mussa also supports his son studying mechanics in Dar es Salaam and cooperates with his two married daughters. With family, community and all these other dependants there is less scope for new turns in his career.

Figure 3.3. The income sources of Mussa Wanyama

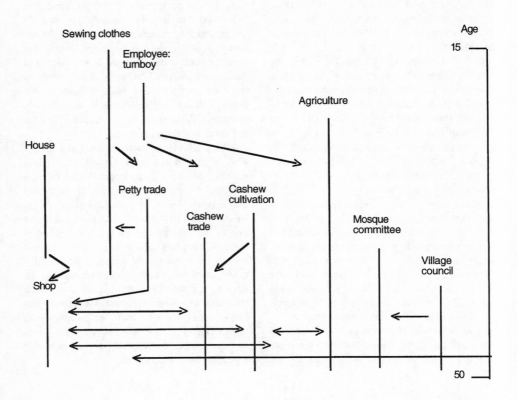

The adjustment to local culture: The case of Hassan Chikandanga

Hassan Chikandanga is a village cosmopolitan whose capabilities are very much wasted in the village environment. Because he is small in size and avoids distinctive speech idioms and clothing—features that would be very disadvantageous for a newcomer like him—it is difficult to guess that he has seen many places.

Hassan Chikandanga is a fifty year old farmer. He was born in the village but he has lived over twenty years of his life in other locations. He was schooled in a small town and later on he joined the army. During his career as a mechanic in the air force Hassan spent some years in Canada and Pakistan. Hassan resigned from the army before he had reached pension age and thus he was not eligible for an army pension. The property he

managed to accumulate was a flat in Dar es Salaam. It provides small rents but its capital value has increased. Currently Hassan contemplates selling it to thus end his current poverty.

During the years in the army Hassan was married but had no children and the marriage ended with divorce. Hassan tells that he left the urban milieu and his career because he was not happy with the way of life in town. He moved back to the south, got married again and moved to his natal village Kilimahewa. Here he has lived for some years with his wife and her younger sister. In this village he lives the life of the villager, with peace and sociability but also with the eternal problem of scratching together a satisfactory living.

The skills of Hassan Chikandanga are not of much use in the village. There is very limited demand for the mechanical skills that he commands. Hassan is one of the very few villagers who have learned English well but there are seldom situations where it could be used and where it would make a difference.

In the village Hassan shows some industriousness and interest to diversify. His home plot looks like a model plot with several crops grown interplanted and well spaced, various fruit trees making up an upper layer and a set of seedling benches arranged in front of the house. As a curiosity, Hassan experiments with a special fruit which he has imported from Zanzibar and which he tries to make productive in a different climate. His other two food fields are well situated in the valley but these are very small in size. Hassan has also a cashew field (too far away to take care of, however) and a field of coconut owned together with his two sisters and a brother. These fields are inadequate and Hassan has already opened a new *bega-kwa-bega* field in order to secure food availability.

Hassan has got involved in two types of activities which have provided him with some income. The first one is communal services.

Hassan worked as a leader for the land allocation committee after the floods in 1990. The task was difficult and provoked many quarrels and Hassan faced both respect and disrespect which led him to resign. Nevertheless, his modesty was recognised and he was later selected to a ward-level judicial council which settled legal cases excluding more serious criminal offences.

Hassan is also involved in trading. His major item has been fish but his engagement has been rather sporadic. Hassan has also traded in cashew. In both cases he has traded in Newala district or between Newala and Kilimahewa. Newala is where Hassan's wife come from and the wife's father has been supportive, providing some help and accommodation. Trading is a seasonal activity and the engagement in fish and cashew trading necessitates a reallocation of time and money through a yearly cycle. Fish trading is profitable at the time when the main agricultural harvesting period is over while cashew trading is linked to a specific agricultural season and takes place within those months. Seasonal diversification requires the rapid reallocation of resources. The pattern of seasonal diversification is explained graphically below.

The diversification strategy of Hassan Chikandanga

Hassan Chikandanga has engaged himself in seasonal diversification. Hassan has limited agricultural resources and a regular but tiny non-agriculture income. For this reason it is natural that Hassan is engaged in temporary trading activities where he can utilise his experience. Nevertheless, he has not been willing to fully commit himself to building the networks that serious trading requires. Instead, trading appears as an activity which can be tried and abandoned according to seasons and conjunctures. Hassan Chikandanga is looking for quick returns by trading with lucrative seasonal items.

The social basis for the diversification strategy is very narrow. Hassan's wife works in the fields and a young relative helps to sell fish at the market. The most important contacts outside the village are near relatives. Most important is a brother who works as a village leader in another village nearby. The brother can occasionally lend him money and in addition has access to valuable information. The other supporter is his wife's father.

Figure 3.4. The annual cycle of Hassan Chikandanga's economy

Diversification and accumulation

I have used case-studies extensively in order to illustrate the different versions of diversification. Through examples I have tried to show that diversification is not an exceptional pattern of resource allocation. It may be useful for poor households as well as rich ones. I emphasise the wide coverage of diversification through the following statements:

1. Different wealth groups have good reasons to diversify their activities. Poor households need to diversify in order to survive, the middle groups in order to minimise risks and the rich in order to locate niches of high profits.
2. Diversification strategies may look rather similar and often the difference between a successful and unsuccessful strategy is small. The difference can be a qualitative or quantitative difference, and it can be a difference of suitable timing or right location.
3. The diversification strategies are complex systems and it is not uncommon that successful households fail and less successful ones come up. Thus the individual households move from one wealth group to another.

I have postulated that different wealth groups have different ways to diversify. However, it is one thing to say that different income groups have different elements in their diversification strategies and another to explicate the dynamic use of such elements. The differences between the different strategies are often quantitative rather than qualitative, and the difference can be rather small. As a consequence, a household may well change upwards or downwards during its career, while its basic strategy remains practically the same. This may be interpreted as God's will. The *mbao* game gives another interpretation. It has taught the villagers that economic wealth is a perishable value. Most villagers have learned that diversification requires a constant effort to be alert and able to adjust to sudden changes in the natural and social environment.

The dynamic analysis focuses on allocative strategy, resource circulation and risk taking. Evans and Pirzada (1995) have argued that the allocative strategy and risk taking co-variate with wealth differentiation. The poor households make allocative decisions on the basis of 'survival' aim, which may mean being occasionally forced to take large risks. On the middle level, the households aim to minimise risks and sustain their level of income. The rich households have the different aim of maximising net income or profits in order to improve their standard of living. They can also afford to accept higher risks and venture into the fields which offer potentially greater returns. Evans and Pirzada emphasise the role of savings for the highest wealth group to have an edge over the others. "Perhaps, more than any other asset, the accumulation of savings enables the household to make the transition from a risk minimising strategy to a profit maximising one. The availability of liquid assets in the form of cash or livestock provides the household with a cushion to ride through rough times in farming and downturns in other entrepreneurial activities. As such, the household can then entertain the notion of undertaking potentially more rewarding activities that may also be riskier" (Evans and Pirzada, 1995:77).[1]

It is evident that risk calculation plays an important role in economic decision making. Paradoxically it drives different wealth groups for different reasons towards diversification. Whether diversification increases or decreases the riskiness of portfolio, depends on the characteristics of a new activity and its linkage to the existing activities. Whether the risk is worth taking, depends on the level of resources in the household. Perhaps it is not important to emphasise the motives ('survival', 'sustainability' or 'growth') behind this strategic decision making. It is less speculative to say that most households find it rational to diversify but that they have different resources to mobilise for their diversification strategy.

The risk calculation then includes a self-evaluation of the social networks and entitlements that can be used as a safety net. Only one should note that there are large differences between economic activities in terms of whether they tend to generate safety networks. If the activity is such that it yields limited moral support in case of failure, it is utmost important to have diversified to more reliable activities. When the household has diversified, and the needed resources (skill, tools, contacts) are easily convertible to the use of another activity, the risks are likely to be manageable.

---

1. Evans and Pirzada do not take the crucial step of analysing the combinations and linkages between the different activities. Instead they confine themselves to the analysis of the separate activities side-by-side with each other.

Chapter 4

Variety in Means—
Economic Activities in Kilimahewa

> Outsiders tend to undervalue the capacity to keep going under dif-
> ficulties, and to treat the coping strategies as 'muddling through',
> not skilled achievements. But in truth—at the appalling, and
> rapidly deteriorating, environmental and economic conditions
> faced by many small-scale farmers in the African tropics—even to
> reproduce the status quo is oftentimes a brilliantly innovative
> achievement.
>
> Paul Richards: *Cultivation—Knowledge or Performance*

In this chapter I present an overview of the division of labour in Kilimahewa. In
Kilimahewa village one can identify up to one hundred different sources of
income. In the following I shall look at the variety of possibilities for 'sidelining'
within agriculture to minor crops, forest products and the like. I also study the
variety of 'microenterprises', also called income-generating activities. Finally I
look at the more formal sources of income.

This variety of the economic activities that I depict is in stark contrast with
the image that many administrators and foreign visitors have about the
southern regions of Lindi and Mtwara. Their common impression is that all the
villagers in the area are just farmers plagued with a lack of economic thrust and
initiative. They call the area the bottom of a sack, a Cinderella region from
which no economic development will emerge. Statistical analysis tends to
confirm this view. The World Bank with its authoritative voice has named Lindi
region as the second poorest region in the second poorest country in the world
(World Bank, 1993).

How is it possible to bridge these two contradictory views? It is obvious that
the World Bank, with a quick survey of some 16 households, is unable to see the
variation between the households and the villages. Yet its analysis can have its
own truth. Measuring with the monetary indicator of purchasing power converted into U.S. dollars, the income of an average villager is obviously negligible. She does not have money to buy western consumer goods. Nevertheless,
she has money to buy several kinds of goods and services which are produced
locally and which satisfy a wide variety of needs. The local products also contain more than their exchange value. They reproduce and carry onwards the
social relationship between the exchange partners. They create social and economic safety nets.

This chapter introduces themes and ideas which are taken up in the following chapters. Thus I show production relations which are complicated and yet

not subjugated to capitalist relations of production. I show monetary exchanges which do not rest on the commoditisation of goods. I show wide local exchange networks which are as efficient as any formal retailing systems in the area. The analysis depicts an economic context which is more than a closed autarchy and yet is not equal to an open capitalist market.

The resulting division of labour is dynamic, complicated and oriented towards culturally diffuse aims. The division of labour creates 'development' which is not similar to modernisation and does not necessarily lead to growth. Neither is the resulting 'development' a way of life in a harmonious village where equality and similarity prevail. We need categories of different kinds to localise the dynamics in this type of economy. I put a lot of emphasis on local knowledge. It is a factor of production which makes it possible to create economic niches in a harsh economic environment. Local knowledge is knowledge of the local social systems, ecological resources and capacities to use them in acceptable and efficient ways. Again, culture intrudes into the analysis of economy.

Analysing the spectrum of economic activities

How should one analyse the division of labour in a rural community? Since agricultural production has a dominant position among the economic activities of the villagers, I could approach the division of labour from the perspective of diversification and ask: What do the people do apart from agriculture? This question is logical but it turns out to be unsuitable for two reasons. First, there is an enormous scope for diversification within agriculture (i.e. 'horizontal diversification'). Many agricultural activities are conducted with similar outward oriented logic as the non-agricultural activities. Second, several non-agricultural sources of income are intimately connected through backward linkages to agriculture. The borderline between the categories is very fluid in peripheral community like Kilimahewa. Due to these two reasons, one needs to be cautious while classifying economic activities. In order to grasp the full spectrum of economic activities it is useful to start from the minimal question: What do the people do for their living except cultivate food crops for their own consumption?

This is the question I set out to answer.

The identification of the economic activities

The domestic economy is hard to follow even for a household member—the current flow of resources is difficult to count and the future incomes are unpredictable. In order to make it intelligible, people make their own 'folk models', i.e. functional ways of categorising events and resources into meaningful entities.

For a researcher, domestic economy looks even more complicated. The necessary and painful analytical step to freeze the economic interaction and the concomitant flow of resources into definite components has an effect on the results of a study. Therefore, sensitivity is needed while selecting the entry points and key concepts. For a researcher it is useful first to work through the hermaneutical spiral and locate the 'folk model' of an economy, before advancing to its analysis.

When it comes to conventional methods of analysing economic activities, some of them distort the object of research totally while others use more adapted categories. Each has its advantages and disadvantages. For example, the analysis starting from the household budget tends to emphasise the monetary economy. The study utilising the time use analysis does not have that bias but is, instead, blind to exploitative social relations. The gender analysis of the resource flows reveals the major unequal distribution mechanisms but undermines the entitlements that exist as potentials in an economy shaped by uncertainty and high risks.

There is no simple solution to the classification problem. Whatever the selected method of analysis is it is important to note that the identified economic activities are partly overlapping and interdependent. The exclusive categories are only required by the statistical method for its additive operations. Exclusiveness is a hindrance in any qualitative study. In processual analysis, it is often helpful to follow the categories and analytical frameworks of the studied people as far as possible.

In the following analysis I have taken up only one theme as a point of entry: the advancement of partial specialisation in the local economy. This means the celebration of the marginal income sources which hardly enter the conventional economic analysis but which, for a villager, provide a large variety of essential use values. The provision of services is an example of a cluster of income sources which are normally excluded in the essentialist economic evaluations but which have a paramount role in the well-being of people. The utilisation of the natural resources is another cluster of activities which are often also underrated or simply omitted from the economic studies.

The major question for the economic analysis is still paradoxically this: When do we leave the realm of the sources of income? The answer is that it all depends on the perspective. I have often come across the folk model of economy which does its best to mystify, enchant and distract the interpretation of income sources as 'normal' social activities. Thus, for example, the making of mats is perceived as just a pastime and a matmaker does not 'remember' that a mat might be sold afterwards. Similarly, the payment for an elder after the settling of a dispute is perceived by a giver as a token or a gift that has nothing to do with the economy. Indeed, the payment in these transactions is far removed from direct counting of the labour effort. However, these small streams of transactions amount to a major pattern of the economic flows in the village.

There are still other, related methodological choices which have both fundamental theoretical and practical methodological repercussions. They have a stake in the balance between maximal research effort, optimal ignorance and outright bias. One choice is the value given to the monetised economy. I have largely followed the line that what is locally perceived as a transaction to be compensated has entered the 'economic' sphere of exchange. However, I have consciously avoided counting its monetary value, in terms of value added or as a share of the gross local production, because I see the price ratios as an inadequate criterion (i.e. a narrow explanation because it is removed from social context) for economic valuation.

In the Marxist literature, the major division of labour is posed to exist between those who are employers because they own the means of production and employees who own just their labour power. In my analysis of the income sources I place less emphasis on the control that people have over the means of production. This is partly due to the selection of the entry point. It is obvious that the control of the means of production divides people structurally into different groups in Kilimahewa. The ownership of land and trees is still the most secure way to accumulation. Yet there are numerous reasons why one should not take for granted that a formal ownership of land or other capital goods necessarily means also being richer than other people. For one thing, the level of productive investments is very low. The major item is still land and it is seldom used as a capital investment for speculative purposes. When land is used for agriculture, one always needs to have access to labour as well. In Kilimahewa, the access to another person's labour power is easily perceived as a relation of dependency which, if enduring over a longer period of time, commits its usurper to a relationship of entitlement. Thus the ownership of land creates relationships with people who make demands, directly and indirectly, on its produce.

Non-agricultural work is also occasionally conducted through relations of production where one person employs another. This is common in crafts, although it does not mean high differentiation between the employer and employee. The labour contracts tend to be temporary or based on fixed shares. In Kilimahewa, the employer craftsman has not reached his position because he has invested in tools or machinery. Rather, he has reached a superior position because he has his skill and he is trusted by customers when making deals. He has reached a position where he can organise the work process and he needs helpers.

It is not uncommon in Kilimahewa that a person shifts to and fro between positions as an employer and an employee. This takes usually place between sectors. Thus a person can be a government employee for a period and then shift to become a trader with his own employees. It can also happen that a person holds the two positions simultaneously. I shall come back to this theme in the analysis of 'straddling' in Chapters 9–10.

The sectors of income sources

Any strict sectoral division of the village economy is an artificial construction. In order to make my analysis of sectors a step nearer the life situation I locate three overlapping sectors, namely agriculture, income-generating activities (also called microenterprises) and formal sources of incomes. The sectors and their sub-divisions are presented in figure 4.1.

Figure 4.1. The sectors of economic activities

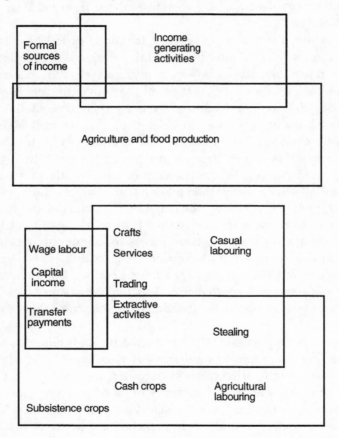

The detailed division of labour into single activities is presented in table 4.1.

Table 4.1. *The diversity of the sources of incomes in Kilimahewa*

Income generating activity: (only monetarised or partly monetarised activities)		Agriculture	Other incomes
Extractive activities	*Trading/services*	*Agriculture/Livestock*	*Wage labour*
Hunting	Tembo beer club	Mixed food cultivation	Teacher
Gathering	Selling grain beer	Rice cultivation	Administrator
Fishing	Selling local softdrinks	Groundnut cultivation	Coop. secretary
Selling firewood	Selling doughnuts etc.	Cashew nut cultivation	
Making charcoal	Selling root snacks	Coconut cultivation	Watchman
Selling building poles	Selling cooked food	Vegetable gardening	Climber
Pit-sawing	Selling cigarettes	Fruit trees	Tapper
Making bricks	Selling local tobacco	Spice and drug gardens	
Grass for thatching	Selling fruits	Tree seedlings	Day labourers
Leaves, fences/roofs	Selling coconuts		Agricultural labourer
Crafts	Selling kerosene	Keeping goats, sheep	Carrier
Making ropes	Tea-room	Keeping cows	
Making local beds	Kiosk	Having chicken, guinea fowl	
Carpentry	Shop		
Masonry	Hoarding food crops		*Capital incomes*
Building houses	Trading vegetables		House rental
Building latrines	Trading fruits		Selling land etc.
Pottery	Trading dried fish		Interests
Making mats	Trading used clothes		
Tinsmith/blacksmith	Trading coconuts		
Services	Trading cashew		
Tailoring			
Cutting hair			*Transfer payments*
Repairing bicycles			Gifts
Repairing shoes			
Ironing clothes			
Traditional doctor			
Circumcision expert			
Midwife			
Musician			
Community administrator			
Relig. teacher/administrator			

Households differ very much in the *extent* of diversification. There are a few households which are engaged in an extensive strategy with as many as five different economic activities. There are also a few households which allegedly rely on basic agriculture only. The extent of diversification is a crucial factor in my analysis. Annex 1 lists the activities outside agriculture for a sample of 39 households. On average the households listed 2.4 activities. If the cases of agricultural specialisation (people usually mentioned having goats, vegetable gardening and having fruit trees for selling fruits) were included the households had in average three economic activities in one year (in addition to food production). This table, combined with qualitative information on agricultural (i.e. horizontal) diversification is a sound basis for arguing that diversification is a common practice in Kilimahewa. The annex also shows the obvious result that there is a *high level of differentiation in the extent of diversification strategies*. Some households tend to engage in more extensive diversification than others.

Diversification within agriculture and food production

The analysis of agriculture aims to answer one question: What are the patterns of sidelining/partial specialisation within the agricultural sphere like in Kilimahewa? The hypothetical starting point is that a household cultivates those few staples which form the main part of food consumption. The possibilities of diversification are then:

– the cultivation of minor crops for local trade,
– the cultivation of cash crops for external trade,
– working as an agricultural day labourer on others' fields and then buying food,
– accessing food through hunting, fishing and gathering, for one's own use or for exchange,
– stealing food from fields,
– stealing cash crops for trade.

The options for food related diversification are presented in figure 4.2.

Figure 4.2. The diversification options within agriculture and food production

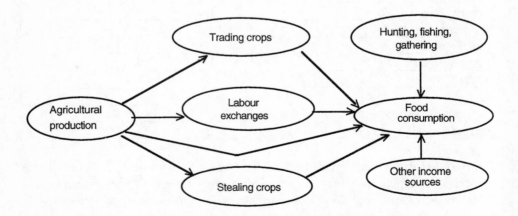

I hope to give a picture of agriculture where cultivation is not determined directly by ecology or technology but by their socio-cultural appropriation. Food production entertains a variety of options for both rich and poor households. These options continuously place rural households in the situation of making choices. The households do on-farm trials and modify their crop selection every year. In this respect, agriculture is carried out as a performance rather than a profession in Kilimahewa.

The vulnerability and complexity of agriculture in Lindi region

Agriculture is the main source of income for all wealth groups in Kilimahewa village. The agricultural production is supplemented with gathering and hunting which are supportive systems of food production but which play a minor role in the total food intake in the village. Agriculture has also indirect dominance in the economy because several of the other sources of income are based on the processing and trading of the agricultural products.

The southern regions are commonly seen as an area where little change in the agricultural scene has taken place. Of course, this is a superficial picture. History reveals major colonial plans to boost cotton cultivation, then groundnut and still later on cashew nut cultivation. These campaigns have influenced the whole area of land tenure, agricultural prices and marketing systems. Nevertheless, these large efforts have largely had a temporary impact. Only cashew nut propagation has been successful in the longer time perspective: due to the planting in the 1950s and the 1960s, cashew nut covers large tracts of land and more than half of the smallholders are cashew nut growers. The problem is that currently the cashew trees are overaged and unproductive. Instead of providing income they cover land and prevent a sustainable rotation of other crops. Yet only a minority of farmers can afford to pay for the inputs and labour needed to make cashew cultivation a profitable venture. (See Seppälä, 1998b, for discussion on cashew cultivation.)

The agro-ecological system has changed during this century so that the impenetrable thicket has given way to the expanding population and more permanent field systems. The thicket is still a major force to reckon with and using fire is still the most efficient means to combat it. When the burn and slash method is used, some shrubs can easily remain alongside bigger trees in the fields after burning and soon the weeds and grasses grow up again. Thus many fields look like a forest to an inexperienced observer. It requires an experienced eye to see the crops among the weeds and bushes. This distinction is not made easier by the fact that the leaves and roots of wild plants growing in the fields can also be used for consumption.

Crop rotation takes place between whole fields or sections of fields. Fallowing is also practised but the fallowing periods have decreased in the areas where population density is high and fallowing has practically been abandoned within Kilimahewa and nearby villages. The increasing permanence of the field systems has modified the patterns of crop rotation. Crops are commonly rotated from the most nutrient demanding to less demanding crops and, given the limited options to give up exhausted fields, these fields are used for prolonged periods for crops like cassava.

The local agricultural research station carried out a major farming systems study on the cropping patterns in Lindi region in 1980. The study concluded that (in monetary terms) the most important crops in the region were rice, sorghum and pigeon peas followed by cashew and sesame (URT, 1985:114). Within Lindi region there was a lot of variation from one area to another. This is evident from the observation (cf. Annex II) that the variability between villages as agro-ecological systems is considerable and each of them has its own micro-environment. (One consequence of the variation is that it enables crop trade between villages.) The farming systems study also showed that farmers tended to have several crops in various fields and agricultural specialisation took the form of sidelining/partial specialisation. In other words, different households cultivate different special crops for exchange but this specialisation is not done at the expense of major food crops.

The cultivation of crops is based on hoe agriculture in a complex field system where each household usually has 3–5 plots. Typically the fields are distributed according to different altitudes and soils and thus produce different crop mixtures. One or two fields are devoted to gardening and the most important staples and pulses. These fields are tended carefully and the crop mixes are well planned. The other fields can provide a smaller mix of food crops and cash crops. The lowland fields are intensively cultivated while the upland fields are cultivated rather casually. The upland fields can be left untended due to labour constraints and not just because of planned fallowing.

The difficult agro-ecological environment sets limits for the agricultural development. Rains are modest (with an average of 1000 mm per year) but, what is more important, highly unreliable. The mean temperature is also high and, combined with humidity, makes it very difficult to work during the middle of the day for most of the year. The other hazards that may compound the difficulties of a farmer are pests and wild animals. Wild pigs and monkeys are an intolerable problem in the distant cassava fields while birds come to feed on grains like rice.

Socio-economic factors also induce changes in the selection of the crop mix from one year to another. Especially the availability of labour and seeds at the critical time of planting and the fluctuating relative prices affect the selection of crop mixes. The farming system studies have identified access to labour as the major constraint for agricultural production in the region. The different crops have different returns to labour, the major difference being between upland crops and lowland valley crops.

When it comes to upland crops, Brown (1985:53) estimated that cashew and cassava had rather similar returns to labour in 1980. Oates (URT, 1985:115) calculated that cashew in pure stands gave the highest return to labour in the

uplands in 1980. In those years when the cashew price has been down the farmers have simply abandoned the cashew fields or allocated only limited labour to
collecting the harvest from the untended trees.

The soil fertility decline has increased the role of cassava as the main staple.
Cassava is also sold to traders who take it to international markets.[1] There are a
few pockets within the southern regions where upland land is used too intensively and the exhausted land can be used only for cultivating cassava with
diminishing returns. These pockets (situated primarily on the Makonde
plateau) are still exceptional. It can be generalised that the field systems and the
crop mixes in the southern regions provide a large variety of food through
smallholder agriculture. The agriculture is characterised by diversity rather
than the dominance of either cashew or cassava.

Compared with upland crops, the valley crops yield a more reliable harvest
and there is a possibility for still higher returns to labour. The most productive
was coconut which gave ten times higher income than cashew per labour unit
in 1980. As a slowly maturing tree crop coconut gives permanence to the otherwise changing cropping patterns.

Apart from coconut, the labour allocation between different crops is subject
to continuous competition. The labour allocation depends on the field system of
the household, the availability of labour and recent changes in the relative
prices.

The complex crop combinations, the diversity of the micro-environments,
the unreliability of the rains and the hostility of the pests compose together an
agricultural system which Robert Chambers (1989) calls a CDR system: a complex, diverse and risk-prone agricultural system. This is a system which has
developed to be responsive to changes in the environment/rainfall. The system
is not, however, fully resistant to interventions which can potentially destroy its
delicate balance of sustainability. While the technological breakthroughs have
not made—and are not likely to materialise—any major impact on the production, the changing price ratios (between crops, and between land and other
prices) and the following exploitative cropping patterns could turn the agriculture from sustainability to land mining.

Land tenure, crop mixes and differentiation

In the following analysis I relate the options of agricultural diversification to the
differentiation of households. The question is whether horizontal specialisation
in agriculture works as a barrier against differentiation or whether it enhances
differentiation. The evidence shows that, on the one hand, the partial specialisation to minor crops and the gathering of wild species creates exchange between
poorer primary producers and that this specialisation provides income which is

---

1. Cassava export from the region increased substantially in the early 1990s but then
ceased soon afterwards. The reason behind this pendulum was changes in cassava production in Asia.

an alternative both to agricultural proletarisation (i.e. becoming an agricultural labourer) and to agricultural peasantisation (i.e. becoming a producer of one cash crop catering for an unstable world market). On the other hand, there are certain circuits of cash crop production open for wealthier farmers which enhance exactly the opposite development: the tendency to separate between capitalists and agricultural labourers. These crops pave the way for a pronounced differentiation. The crucial question is then which of the tendencies has a greater effect on the crop mixes and resource allocation patterns in the poor households.

In Kilimahewa all households grow a relatively large variety of crops. Yet there is consistent variation in what crops are cultivated by different wealth groups. One explanation for the variation in cropping patterns is that different households have access to different types of land. This does not mean that the poor people were not implementing conscious strategies to experiment with more valuable crops. It only means that such a strategy is more complicated because one first needs to have access to the right type of land.

Kilimahewa is situated between two uplands near a river valley. The agricultural profile of the village is influenced by the division of land into valley land, upland fields and home plots. Most people claim that access to land is a relatively minor problem. This is also proved with the cross-tabulation of the general wealth ranking with the household's access to land. Even wealth group 3 has on average over four acres of land. This is an adequate amount for a normal sized household to till. However, what is problematic is the access to good alluvial soils near the river and the village area. The co-variation between wealth ranking and the household's access to valley land is very strong.

Table 4.2. Agriculture in Kilimahewa

(mean values by wealth)

Wealth group	Land (acres)	Land in lowland	Annual value of three major crops	Total number of the crops	Months buying food	Number of cases
WG 1	12.5	7.0	110,000	9.0	0	3
WG 2	5.6	2.0	61,000	10.0	0.5	15
WG 3	4.6	0.5	30,000	8.2	2.0	21

The different wealth groups[1] report a fairly similar number of the various crops: the middle income group reports ten different crops while the poor report eight crops on average. The difference comes from the variation in the average number of fields. The richer households have fields in a larger variety

---

1. The random survey had very few cases in wealth group 1. The PRA studies on agriculture included more rich households but that data is not included here. Cf. Chapter 7 for a more detailed analysis of the village elite.

of the agro-ecological micro-environments. There are some poor households which do not have any access to lowland fields.

Another way to describe the importance of the valley crops is the listing of the most important crops. The richer households tend to have valley crops as their most important crops. The fertile river valley is suitable for several cash crops: rice, groundnut, sugarcane and coconut plus different vegetables. In addition, the rich grow all the typical food crops, namely cassava, pigeon peas, maize and millet. This is shown in table 4.3.

Table 4.3. The three most valuable crops by wealth group

(Percentage of the occurrence within the three major crop in terms of monetary income.)

	WG 1	WG 2	WG 3
Cassava	33	33	76
Cashew nut	33	60	29
Coconut	33	20	5
Millet	0	40	66
Groundnut	33	13	5
Pigeon peas	0	20	33
Rice	100	33	24
Maize	33	60	66
Sugarcane	33	13	0
Banana	0	7	0
Total	300	300	300

The result gives a clear indication about one element in the pattern of differentiation, namely that the agricultural specialisation towards major cash crops is the possibility which is more readily available for wealthier farmers and that it is not carried out at the expense of food crop production. The security of food crop production is given priority. But looking inside the category of the food crops a certain differentiation emerges. The poor people rely mostly on cassava, pigeon peas, millet and ming'oko root. The rich can afford to eat more rice and maize.

Specialisation on major cash crops in Kilimahewa

In Kilimahewa it is easy to observe that crop specialisation takes the form of diversification. The analysis of the household budgets shows that specialisation towards a certain crop is seldom done at the expense of food crops. It is very uncommon to see that the monetary value of the most important crop is more than half of the household budget. If looking for candidates for specialisation to major cash crops, the possible crops are rice, coconut and cashew.

Rice cultivation is a fairly reliable exercise if one has access to good valley land (whereas rainfed rice is a more hazardous crop in Lindi district). Rice has also a steady market and although imported rice has entered the market people prefer to eat local rice because of its better taste. The import of rice tends to slightly stabilise the price fluctuations over the year but it has not meant a large drop in price. The disadvantage of rice cultivation is that it requires a lot of work. The rich farmers use agricultural labourers to break the land. During the following phases of cultivation they are directly involved in supervision and actual work. Rice is threatened by occasional floods. Rice is also threatened by birds during the months before harvesting and thus the scaring of birds is a major labour task on top of the normal agricultural work cycle.

Coconut is a second candidate for a specialising farmer. It requires very little labour and it is also a reliable crop: coconut trees are largely a local variety which has been grown for decades and which is relatively free from diseases (whereas diseases are a major problem for new varieties cultivated in Coast region). The problem with cultivating coconut has been that it has been associated with special types of soils (existing in valleys) which are limited in availability. Only recently the villagers have tried to cultivate coconut trees in different environments and they have been surprised by their success. Another special feature for coconut is that trees take at least eight years to mature. It requires careful and long-sighted planning to become involved in coconut cultivation.

Cashew is a third alternative for a specialising farmer. Cashew is very visible in the terrain and covers huge areas of land. However, cashew has historically been a risky investment. First, the price fluctuations have been enormous during the last two decades. Although the cashew price was high during the study period there is no guarantee that it will stay at the same level.[1] Like coconut, cashew is a tree crop and thus it takes several years for a producer to respond to the changes in the market situation with new productive trees. The risks are high because cashew is sold to the international market and if the international demand decreases, the producer has very limited alternative outlets—the local consumption of cashew is quite low. Secondly, the fungus disease of the trees has decreased the level of production. One needs to make a fairly sizeable investment in sulphur to keep the trees productive.

To sum up, no cash crop has reached the position as the single major cash crop in Kilimahewa. Instead, different wealthy households have a tendency to cultivate different cash crops.

Diversification to exceptional minor crops

As far as major crops are concerned, the poor households rely more on the typical food crops and cultivate only small amounts of major cash crops. They may have small rice fields in a very distant place or a cashew field which is not tended properly. The poor households also produce less food than they con-

---

1. The real producer price has decreased during 1996–8. This was partly caused by increased crop taxation by the Cashewnut Board of Tanzania, the cooperative and the district councils with their auxiliaries. Cf. Seppälä, 1998b for background.

sume. If they sell food crops it is likely that they are forced to buy a similar amount later on.

These results based on the cropping pattern of the major food and cash crops need to be evaluated with caution: there is still a variety of *minor* crops which have limited commercial value but which can occasionally provide a means for diversification for a poor household. Fruits are a good example. They are commonly cultivated without major thrust and commitment. Mango trees are usually not planted and the shade of the tree is perceived as as important a benefit as its fruits. One or two papaya trees are often grown at the homestead. Yet there are few farmers who harvest exceptional numbers of fruits. Thus seasonally fruits emerge among the most important crops sold out of Kilimahewa.

Some of the minor crops are forest products or domesticated wild species. For example, the *matili* fruit trees grow totally wild in the bush. Children perceive themselves as the rightful harvesters of most fruits. In some other villages, the picking of wild fruits is conducted in quantity and the fruits are sold to traders who sell them as delicacies to Dar es Salaam.

Another group of crops which is used for partial specialisation on a small scale is vegetables. Vegetables are underrated in the people's own agricultural evaluations because vegetables are either grown seasonally, produced as a by-product (cassava leaves) or likened with the picking of wild plants for making relish (some spinach-like varieties are wild). Nevertheless, there are a few villagers who grow and trade in vegetables, even in the face of the competition of the specialised growers from other locations.

Cassava is also a potential crop for cash crop specialisation. In some neighbouring districts it has been seriously asked whether cassava monoculture is appearing in the farms of some poor farmers. Cassava is the last crop which can be cultivated when the fields are devoid of nutrients. Instead of leaving the land to rest, the poor farmers have been obliged to abandon crop rotation and continue indefinitely with cassava. Since cassava is also sold both on local and international markets, it can be used to replace not only other food crops but even cash crops. This is certainly an alarming tendency but I did not locate a similar process in Kilimahewa. Some home plots seemed to lose all the nutrient content of the soil but often their owners could solve the problem by moving to another plot in another location.

In general, the farmers show both interest in and caution towards specialisation. Everybody knows a person who happens to grow onions, lemon or red pepper on an exceptional scale. This kind of experiment is well known and noticed. There are also the individual success cases of some fruit cultivators. What makes people cautious is the need for extra work and the problems of marketing perishable products. There have not developed any sustained systems of marketing vegetables to the urban markets because there are several other locations closer to towns and/or better endowed with soils and rains. Thus competition and specialisation take place on a wider regional scale as we shall see in the following chapters.

To sum up, the agricultural diversification related to a non-food crop on a large scale is a luxury of the wealthy households who can afford to fail. The poor households have less scope for experimentation. They can cultivate small amounts of the most profitable cash crops. Alternatively, they can specialise into minor crops. This 'low road' to horizontal diversification can also entail elements from additional sources of food: gathering, hunting and fishing. I shall return to these income-generating activities later.

Diversification from cultivation to local trading

Cultivation is often classified into the categories of cash cropping and subsistence cultivation. In Kilimahewa, the line between these categories varies from one household to another. Practically all crops are also traded within the village. Only two crops, cashew and simsim, are cultivated for the purpose of export out of region but even these crops can be consumed locally if the market fails.

From the perspective of diversification it is interesting to ask whether partial specialisation to certain crops by certain households generates trading within a location. The answer can be given through an indirect deduction. The normal diet includes up to thirty locally produced food items while the normal household cultivates some ten of them. The remaining twenty food items are sourced through local exchange networks. Actually the rate of exchange is even higher because people also buy most of the crops that they produce; one can, for example, buy a coconut because one's own nuts are not yet ripe. The following month the same person appears in the market as the seller of a coconut. Thus the level of local agricultural exchange and interdependency is high.

Diversification is pursued by combining cultivation for sale with the trading of other people's crops. Naturally every farmer needs to sell his or her cash crops. Some farmers, however, make a special effort to sell their produce directly at the urban market to get a special price. Among women, a few are engaged in selling their spinach and onions in towns. Men sell coconut, groundnut or oranges at the town markets. When a farmer makes the effort of starting a marketing trip, it is common to buy a little more from other farmers to have a load which is large enough to cover the travelling expenses and to generate profit. Thus incrementally, through several minor steps, a farmer also becomes a trader.

The rich trading households are increasingly involved in hoarding food. Rice and maize have good storage capacities and very fluctuating prices. A wealthy household can combine its own rice or maize cultivation with some buying and place the stock in a good store. The crop is sold with a large profit at a later time of scarcity or during Ramadhan. The systems of hoarding include barter arrangements (maize against more maize, cassava against rice etc.) where the cash-poor household can be trapped into a dependency relationship.

Agricultural labour exchanges as a diversification option

The poor farmers have a possibility to diversify from own farming through exchanging their labour to access food. There are two alternative ways to do this. First, they can engage in communal labour parties. Second, they can make day labouring contracts as agricultural labourers (cf. Berry, 1993).

A proper labour party is organised by an open announcement and the participating people are provided with food and beer. Alternatively, only relatives and some other selected people can be asked to help in a specific task. Historically the labour party was a system of reciprocating and thus each participant himself organised a labour party at another time. With the advance of differentiation, it has become more common that the poor people participate in labour parties, while the rich either organise them or withdraw totally from the whole institution. In any case, the reciprocity has broken down.

The labour parties have earlier been common for several tasks (cf. Wembah-Rashid, 1975:66–68). Currently labour parties are organised to accomplish heavy agricultural tasks like weeding. A practical problem with *mkumi* labour parties has been that some people join them to contribute labour later than others and still take full part in the eating session in the afternoon. This opportunism has lately made the institution more unpopular. Another natural cause for the decline of labour parties has been the impact of the monetised economy. In neighbouring (densely populated) Newala district it is possible to organise a labour party where participants are paid in money. In Kilimahewa this is seen as inappropriate and instead one can observe the institution slowly dying.

The alternative to participation in labour parties is getting involved in agricultural wage labour. The normal arrangement is that an employer announces in public the task to be done. An interested person approaches the employer. The work is counted as a piece work so that a field is measured and a payment is made by the are (i.e. ten times ten steps). The payment is around Shs. 150 for hoeing an are of land and Shs. 100 for weeding an are. A labourer can earn over Shs. 500 a day. The work is usually paid for in money but it can also be paid for in food. The employer often works alongside the employees to check the quality of work. The employees tend to work sporadically, having a rest period of several days for spending the money earned before commencing the next contract. Very rarely a person works continuously for a single employer. The few exceptions are special workers with definite responsibilities. The coconut climbers and coconut tappers tend to work on permanent contract with a fixed share payment. Children are employed to look after goats where a few goat owners combine their herds to attain an adequate flock. Regular employees are paid after every week or month in cash.

Access to and use of labour power are a crucial factor for differentiation. It is also a major cause for differentiation within a household. The household head can try to control the sales of a harvest and thus indirectly control labour. However, household labour is not a resource which is readily available to the household head. Instead, different persons retain control over their own labour directly by having individual fields or indirectly by making demands on the priority of tasks to be conducted and on the access to the product.[1] It is quite possible that a household member sells his or her labour power outside instead of working for the household farm even when there is work to accomplish.

The combination of the three labour categories—own cultivation, agricultural labour parties and agricultural labouring—gives different wealth related labour profiles as shown in table 4.4. In the *mkumi* labour parties the poorer people are currently the main participants. They are also active in day labouring. There are only a few rich households which employ day labourers extensively for various tasks.

Table 4.4. *The agricultural labour exchanges (percent of household within a wealth group)*

Wealth group	Participated in labour parties	Organised a labour party	Did agricultural labouring	Employed agricultural labourers
WG 1	0	0	0	100
WG 2	57	29	21	71
WG 3	55	22	33	16

The number of days that people take part in labour parties is generally low. The poor take part on average two days a year in the labour parties. By contrast, the variation in the participation in agricultural labouring is higher. The highest level of participation is around 60 days a year which can provide a living for a maximum of half a year. Thus agricultural labouring is not used for conscious proletarisation but as a supplement for one's own agriculture and other activities. Both women and men take part in agricultural labouring and also employ agricultural labourers.

The stealing of crops

Stealing of crops is very common in Kilimahewa. It is likely that stealing has reached higher levels in this village than in the neighbouring villages. To some extent, Kilimahewa has acquired a reputation as being a place where the normal social control mechanisms have lost their hold (cf. Annex II). One explanation for the high rate of stealing is the distance to the fields. Whereas the settlement was earlier near to the most valuable valley crops and people could closely observe each other's movement, the new settlement is away from the valley and people can roam around the fields without being observed. Other reasons are the mixed ethnic population, roadside location, bhang cultivation (which has been largely stopped by the police) and the recent flood disaster. Thieves can

---

1. The exchanges of labour between households take place even when there is no disagreement within a household. Both women and men find it inconvenient to work alone and thus a friend of the same sex is asked along to work, taking turns first in one's own fields and then in the friends.

also enter houses in the middle of the village. Often the thief may be known but the other villagers do not take any action against the person. The *ngambo* village guards are unable to protect property and crops. The government has tried to form new *sungusungu* [1] self-protection groups in villages but to no avail.

Stealing of crops is done mostly during the night and practically all the crops are subject to this practice. Women have commonly chosen groundnuts as their private cash crop because it is difficult to steal groundnuts at night. The most valuable coconut fields are protected by the watchmen who live in the coconut field. In contrast, cashew fields tend to be large, far away and thus impossible to guard effectively. The possibility of stealing is a major reason for farmers to leave their cashew fields untended. Thus stealing has an indirect adverse effect on the production level of cashew.

It is equally common to blame thieves for most misfortunes in crop production. Most villagers share the view that the most sophisticated forms of stealing involve witchcraft. Witchcraft makes it difficult to detect the thief because a person can employ muted ghosts [2] to steal from the fields of others and to work on the fields of their masters. Another method is sending snakes to steal rice grain by grain. Because the stealing takes place incrementally it is very difficult to detect and, therefore, it is necessary to protect the fields using garden magic. The medicine-men provide small parcels which can be buried in the fields. There are also Islamic specialists who provide Koranic scripts for the same purpose.

Stealing of the crops has an equalising effect on the income distribution. It counterbalances the equally immoral practice of the rich to hoard crops and speculate in a fluctuating price. The young people are normally targeted as the main group who steal in the village. Stealing gives the youth access to crops which they cannot cultivate themselves. However, the youths state that crop stealing is practised by people of all walks of life: men and women, young and old.

Agriculture, diversification and differentiation

The discussion has followed the logic of locating rather than measuring the ways of agricultural diversification. The analysis shows that agriculture is oriented towards subsistence needs but with a scope for partial specialisation. The purely agricultural way of specialisation is focused on certain major or minor crops. Other ways are engaging in agricultural labouring, trading with

---

1. *Sungusungu* is a traditional form of conflict management in cattle-rearing areas of central Tanzania. Later on, the term has been used by the government in other regions for different conflict management strategies. Cf. Ishumi (1995).

2. Muted ghost is called *ndondocha* in Kimakonde. An evil person can steal the body of a dying person and convert it to his or her personal slave. The evil person removes the soul and tongue from the body, thus making it an obedient, silent and invisible slave.

agricultural crops, stealing crops or producing food through gathering, hunting and fishing.

The listed methods of diversification give a number of options for poor and rich farmers. The analysis shows that even when people cultivate normal food crops it is far from evident that they are working in their own fields or that they will consume the food themselves. Instead, there are a number of methods for diversification within the agricultural sector which complicates the process.

In the discussion I have shown that some methods of agricultural diversification increase while others decrease differentiation. Agricultural production figures (i.e. crop mix and amount of production) give only the initial estimate of the household's relative capacity to generate food related income. This initial estimate needs to be checked with four other diversification factors. First, the labour costs are a major expenditure in agriculture. Between the wealth groups, the payments for labour exchanges tend to have an equalising effect on income distribution. Second, speculation with seasonal price variation increases differentiation between households. Third, the supplementing of crop production with gathering, hunting and fishing reduces food related differentiation. Fourth, stealing has again an equalising effect on income distribution. The end result is often quite removed from the original production figures.

The final level of differentiation is difficult to estimate because part of the food production (collecting roots, mushrooms and cassava leaves) never fully enters a commercial calculation and, secondly, because some of the activities (stealing, hoarding) are morally suspect and thus not revealed to other people. In statistical analysis, they are usually omitted completely.

Diversification to microenterprises

In the following section I analyse the diversification to economic activities outside agriculture. The analysis includes even marginal economic and rare activities. The issue of diversification versus professionalisation is most pertinent in the analysis of these activities which fall outside agriculture and which are borderline cases when it comes to payment. I argue that several of the activities have a special identity worth taking into account—even when those who practise them may themselves give them a limited value. In this way I want to emphasise the complexity of production and the great variety in terms of produced items and services.

I use the terms income-generating activities and microenterprises interchangeably to describe skills like being a herbalist, a trader or a brickmaker. The category is defined in a residual way as all the sources of income which are outside agriculture, formal wage labour and transfer payments. There are several borderline cases which could be classified either as an income-generating activity/microenterprise or as one of these other categories. Sometimes the formal employment provides so small an income and takes such a marginal share of total labour time that it could be best conceptualised (from the actor's perspective) as one income-generating activity among others.

My approach is very critical to the axiomatic and categorical idea of professionalisation which governs much of the literature on microenterprises. Many microenterprise studies describe, say, blacksmiths or shopkeepers, as if they were professionals with a plan to enhance their business over the coming years. However, less 'applied' research may locate a lack of professional orientation and long-term commitment.[1]

An overview on the income-generating activities

The income-generating activities are divided here into natural resource extraction, crafts, services and trading. The extractive activities mean the collection/processing and marketing of natural resources. These are mainly forest products. The crafts include tasks of processing which can be carried out in the village and which involve heavy physical labour. Services are such economic activities which can be carried out in the village without major physical effort. The last category of trading involves buying and selling without major processing. Many activities could be classified in several categories or their production includes backward linkages into some other categories. That is why the classification need not be given much emphasis.

Extractive activities

The extraction from nature engages a wide section of villagers. Even relatively well-off women like to take part in some gathering trips. Herbalists, musicians and carpenters also venture into forests to find materials they can use. The link between nature and the village people is strong and complex. The difference among the villagers is whether one exploits nature casually for one's own good or seriously as a source of extra income.

Many extractive activities are economic activities which are undertaken because of pressing poverty: when agriculture does not provide a living one needs to engage in some other tasks. However, not all poor households engage in extractive activities. There are also other values like respectability which have an influence on who is actually engaged in extractive activities. Some extractive activities like hunting and gathering have a negative reputation as if they were the skills of backward people. In Kilimahewa, the Mozambican Makonde are a special group who are seen as backward people. These people are a relatively

---

1. This point is exemplified by Kenneth King (1977). He shows how artisans in Nairobi shift many times during their career between self-employment and employment, between this and that activity, and between urban and rural residence. A certain opportunism is a precondition for survival for these artisans. Similar patterns can also be found in rural Lindi.

small group with a distinctive dialect and culture. The Mozambican Makonde are most active in hunting and gathering.

For the Mozambican Makonde, hunting and gathering provide a monetary income although usually on a minor scale. Yet the Mozambican Makonde are keen on these economic activities because they see them as a means to separate themselves from the social hierarchies of village life and to generate income through their own local knowledge. They deliberately distance themselves from the village leaders who maintain the prevailing values of village—including a special geographic order where the forest is placed at the bottom of the hierarchy.

A similar 'bush' reputation is shared to some extent by all the activities which are carried out in the forest. The villagers rationalise the value statement through highlighting the dangers in the forests. They emphasise that forests accommodate lions, snakes and other dangerous animals. Every now and then one hears stories about people being killed by the wild animals. In addition to normal lions there are 'paper lions', which are actually witches in lion form. These lions are so fast that they cannot be captured by any ordinary means. They are allegedly able to disappear through a trick of being, when looked at from up front, as thin as paper. The people engaged in forest activities need to struggle with natural and unnatural forces of the most severe kind. It is natural that when Mozambican Makonde frequently visit the forests, they are exposed to witchcraft accusations by their fellow villagers.

People who frequently go to the forest acknowledge the dangers but they handle them by avoiding staying overnight in a forest and by moving around in groups. They tend to complain that the forest trips are physically arduous and that thorns make moving around very difficult.

Hunting. Hunting is done by a few men, mostly those who are Mozambican Makonde by origin. It is mostly done for subsistence but there are many who also sell their catches. They hunt mostly small animals like rabbits using traps

Animal	Means of hunting	Price
Guinea fowl	nets	800–1,000
Porcupine	gun, bow, trap	3,000
Gazelle	gun, bow, trap	1,500
Bushbuck	running, trap	5,000
Wild pig	gun, bow, trap	5,000
Rabbit	trap	500
Rats	trap	25
Birds		
- small birds	slingshot, trap	20–30
- fungo	trap	500
- nenje	bow, trap	800
- noda	trap	200
- nkuli	trap	500
- chitavala	trap	200

and nets. Slingshots are used to get small birds. It is also possible to use a certain sticky liquid from a tree which is placed so that the bird gets stuck. Hunting parties using fire and comprising a large number of people take place in some other villages in the region. The hunting of large game is prohibited. Nevertheless, there are some people who own guns, bows and arrows and who hunt large game. Hunting is always dangerous because the forests accommodate increasing numbers of lions spreading out from the national parks in Liwale district.

Gathering. Gathering is done in a collective fashion by women. The gathering trips can take several days and require a major physical effort. The items gathered are root crops, fruits, herbs and items for medical purposes. The most important root crop is called *ming'oko*. It is a thin small root which can be eaten either after being boiled or dried. The peeled roots are sold by the bucket (at Shs. 1,000–1,200). It is also common that men buy the ming'oko load, boil the roots and sell them in small bunches as a snack. Ming'oko is an important variation to a cassava diet for poor people because it is tastier. The rich people use it mostly as a snack. There are also other yam varieties which are domesticated some of which are larger than cassava. These roots are sold for up to Shs. 500 per kilo. The other food items collected are climbers and small fruits. *Matili* fruit which resembles an orange is very common. Another common wild fruit is *vitoro* which is smaller than an orange. Children like to collect wild fruits but they seldom trade with them.

Fishing. Fishing is conducted with nets and wickerwork fish traps by small groups of men while children use fish hooks. The *madema* traps are constructed by fishermen from bamboo and coconut sticks. Some women use a cloth or a small-sized net which is prohibited but which yields small fish called *dagaa*. The catch is sold to friends or brought to the market. The neighbouring river has some fish but the fishing faces competition from the cheap fish imported from villages near the sea. Elsewhere in the region there are inland lakes which provide fish. In those locations the fishing has developed into a hierarchical institution where boat owners and net owners are separate from fishermen while the drying and trading of fish are yet other special tasks.

Selling firewood. Firewood is not a major problem in the village and the market for firewood is limited. The collected wood is sold in bundles for Shs. 200. The customers are rich people, school and restaurants.

Making charcoal. Charcoal burning takes place on a small scale for local customers like the restaurants, the dispensary, and for irons used to iron clothes. The charcoal is made in large kilns which produce up to a hundred bags. The selling price is Shs. 300 per bag. The roadside selling of charcoal is difficult because of the stiff competition from other villages with access to wood in a more suitable location.

Selling building poles. There has been a good market for building poles and several men earn a good income from this activity. The good straight poles need to be carried from some distance away and the price is Shs. 150 for a large pole. A bundle of small sticks can be sold for Shs. 30. Different types of poles are needed for wall poles, plaiting walls and making the roofing. Poles are sold directly from home or at the market-place.

Pit-sawing. Falling trees and making planks is an activity which requires a licence and which is totally prohibited on Rondo plateau. Yet sawing takes place for the needs of the local builders and carpenters and for the export of the valuable hardwood. Sawing is conducted seasonally and the labour arrangement is either as self-employed or as a kind of piecework. In the latter alternative, the wealthy entrepreneur owns the tools and employs the workers. The entrepreneur also supervises the work on the spot and arranges the transport of wood. The prices of the hardwood boards (1 1/4" x 1' x 12') are around Shs. 1,200–1,500 depending on the wood species.

Making bricks. A brickmaker needs access to soil, water and firewood. There is only one person in the village who concentrates on brickmaking on a larger scale. He employs labourers and sells the bricks even as far as Lindi. The major problem in making bricks is transport. In Kilimahewa, the use of bricks is limited to a few wealthy households. A cheaper alternative is to make unburned bricks in the village during the dry season.

Collecting grass for thatching. Women collect grass from nearby hills and sell the grass in bundles for Shs. 50 from their homes.

Coconut leaves for fences and roofing. The poor people ask permission to collect coconut leaves from the fields. The leaves are sold at Shs. 10 per bunch and used to cover harvested crops or make toilets and fences.

Crafts

Crafts are mostly practised by men and women of advanced age. Blacksmithing, carpentry and pottery are very much the affair of old people and it is difficult to get young people interested. The old people have often learned the skill from the preceding generation or through apprenticeship and can have an emotional attachment to the craft for this reason. There is no definite cultural hindrance for getting an apprentice from another kin group; craft skills are seldom governed by a mystical force which would need to be inherited before becoming a craftsman.

Crafts have always incorporated a means to express identity and belonging through special ways of ornamentation and decoration. This is most obvious in pottery where ornament can even repeat the themes of the facial scarrings. The unique character of the produced items is enhanced by the practice of producing to order. The specifications of a product can be modified to suit the needs of the customer. An exception is pottery where several pieces can be produced without a predetermined customer. Pottery work is also the skill where barter exchange is used as a common means of selling the product. The exchange takes place with the pot being filled with grain, then emptied, after which the pot is exchanged for the grain.

Making ropes. Making ropes is a special skill and ropes are usually bought on order from specialists living in the neighbouring mountain village. There are also ropemakers in Kilimahewa. Ropes are mostly used for local beds.

Making local beds. The beds are actually simple frames made of poles which need ropes instead of mattresses. A bed with ropes can be bought for Shs. 700–1,000.

Carpentry. The carpenters make chairs, doors, window frames and roofing. They work to order and a customer may be requested to provide the wood.

Masonry. Only a few houses are made of bricks. The bricklayer works with a labourer. The payment is Shs. 4–5 per brick which makes up to Shs. 30,000 for a normal sized house.

Building houses. It is common to employ a builder to carry out the major tasks of construction for Shs. 5–7,000. The builder makes the wooden frame and roofing. The placing of mud can be done by the customer or it is possible to organise a labour party to accomplish the task. The total cost for the house is up to Shs. 20,000.

Building latrines. A labourer can be employed to dig the large hole and make a construction above it for Shs. 1–2,000. There is only one expert in the village who can construct a reliable wickerwork cover for the hole.

Pottery. Mainly old women of Makonde and Yao origin make pots. The pots are made of suitable soil from within the village but some special clay is needed for hardening which needs to be brought from the Ndanda area. The pots are sold locally by barter arrangements or for money. Women carry out most of the activities on their own. (In comparison, the women in Mnazimmoja township can buy clay, firewood and colour plus pay for a labourer to transport the pots from the place of burning.)

Small pot	Kikaango	50–150
Larger pot	Chungu	250–300
Big pot	Mtungi	700–1,000

Making mats. Mats are used both indoors and outdoors as a place for sitting and chatting. Hard mats called *utefu* (made of *matefu* fibre) are sold for Shs. 300–400. The soft *ndulu* mats are sold for Shs. 500. The same materials can also be used to make storage baskets. The more decorated *mkeka* mats can cost up to Shs. 3,000. The colour used for decoration is factory made and brought from the towns. Again there are other villages in the district which display their products at the roadside and sell a large amount of mats. The renowned specialists at basket making are located in neighbouring Masasi district.

Tinsmith. Tinsmiths tend to work in small groups of a few people. A tinsmith can produce and repair several kinds of items for villagers. The items produced are buckets (Shs. 500–1,000), cooking stoves (Shs. 500), watering cans (Shs.

2,500–3,000), kitchen kettles (Shs. 1,700–2,200), kerosene lamps (Shs. 70), bangles (silver coated Shs. 100 and gold coated Shs. 150), bicycle carriers (Shs. 1,000) and bicycle stands (Shs. 800). The materials used are aluminium sheets and iron rods.

Blacksmith. Blacksmiths are usually elderly men who work with a younger man as an assistant. Blacksmiths produce hoes, knives and sickles on order or to store. The locally produced hoes are favoured to the hoes produced in the factories.[1] The material is usually scrap metal. The demand for new tools is high but the work is hard and time consuming.

Services

Services provide either immaterial products or products where the 'servicing' is coupled with a material product. In any case services require only a small amount of physical effort. This 'sweat' criteria is a major local dividing line which allocates people to different categories. Heavy physical work is downgraded by the elderly Muslim gerontocracy as an unsuitable type of work. Services, by contrast, are light work which can be done without getting one's clothes dirty. Services tend to have the second advantage that they are either provided at the market place or in other places where lots of people gather. Thus they are the opposite of the more solitary forest activities. In many times the 'work' of offering a service is inseparable from the general interest in staying around, hearing the news and just being available in case a customer turns up. When there are several persons offering the same service, the practitioners try to minimise the business side of the affair and stress the social proximity with the potential client. These kinds of considerations make it sometimes difficult to see where the greetings end and serious enquiry about the potential service starts.

The practitioner-client relationship varies between different services. Some services are offered to individuals while a kingroup is the client for some other services. The services which relate to life cycle rituals are likely to be conducted by a person from a similar background: same ethnic group, same Mosque or neighbourhood. In any case, the process of how a practitioner and a client find each other is directed by the social considerations of belonging.

Tailoring. Tailors work to order and do both repair work and sewing new clothes. There is no further specialisation but some tailors are preferred more by men or women because of the special cuts and decorations they can handle. The customers usually provide the cloth. The rates are negotiable but a sizeable job of making trousers costs five to seven hundred shillings while a shirt is four to five hundred. Some of the retired tailors have rented their machines to other

---

1. Locally produced hoes are smaller one-hand hoes. They are a major enemy of the extension officers who propagate heavy hoes for more 'efficient' cultivation.

tailors. Some tailors have trainees to help but this is rare because of the limited market and the relative lack of work.

Cutting hair. A few men do the haircutting with minimal implements and without any premises. The payment is Shs. 50 shillings per cut. Women also do haircutting and plaiting from home but this is a service done without any monetary payment. In other locations there are special rates for shaving beards and the pubic hair.

Prostitution. Rural prostitution is carried out under subtle rules of some respect. The women may take initiative but the payments are preferred in terms of gifts and a prostitute is not supposed to be called as such. Payments vary from a hundred shilling upwards.

Repairing bicycles. Bicycles are used for heavy load transportation although they are not meant for it and then often break down. Consequently, they tend to be in appalling condition. Bicycle experts can repair all parts of a bicycle. Bicycle repairers mend a puncture for a hundred shillings. The spare parts are not easily available in the village and occasionally tinsmiths make new spares.

Ironing clothes. Washing and ironing clothes is a service which is sold visibly at the market place. The practitioner does not have premises but works at the shop front. It is most common that people wash clothes themselves and bring them only for ironing. The prices for washing and ironing are fifty shillings for small clothes and a hundred shillings for large clothes.

Traditional doctor. There are different types of herbalists, doctors and spirit mediums. Since these are often overlapping skills I present them here as one activity. A traditional doctor has broadly three different ways of healing. First, a doctor knows which plants have a medical effect. Some of them are planted in the compound but most are collected from forest. One doctor could identify twelve different plants which she collects. The parts utilised are roots, leaves or twigs and they can be applied either as a powdered drink or rubbed on the skin. There are also several items which can be bought at the market-place in Mtwara or Lindi towns. The second way of healing is a communication with the dangerous sea spirits (*pepo* or *jini*). The items used at the healing sessions are special clothes, sunglasses, drums and rattling instruments. The diagnosis is made under possession by talking in languages and writing with special colours which then can be diluted in rose water and drunk as a medicine. The third method is the prevention or identification of witches. A practitioner can go around the compound or field of a customer and locate items that a witch has placed there. Alternatively, the doctor can prepare amulets with scriptures and medicine inside. The amulets can be placed inside clothes, under the floor or even at the doorside where it hangs openly.

The traditional doctor works with a family member or an apprentice as a helper. The work is fairly regular excluding the Ramadan period when the spirit possession activities halt. The payments for the different treatments vary according to their efficiency and the ability of the customer to pay. The payment for simple medicines is Shs. 50–100. The payment for complicated treatment including possession can run to thousands of shillings. Payment is fixed in advance but paid only if the medicine works.

Circumcision/unyago expert. The circumcision of boys and the seclusion of girls is very popular nowadays and even young people have taken up the skill of being a circumcision expert. The circumciser is paid Shs. 300 per person. There are other experts specialised in ritual teaching (*unyago*) of girls. The experts of the girls' ceremonies are more aptly called ritual advisors because female circumcision is not practised and the major part of the teaching is to advise children on their future responsibilities as women. Both the rituals are currently performed for small children between five and ten years of age and the whole ritual, including seclusion, is carried out within a week.

Midwife. The traditional birth attendants provide their services against the payment of Shs. 700 per birth. Most birth attendants have received some training from a mission hospital.

Musician. There are several kinds of musical groups which perform at different types of occasions. Groups of dancers can be asked to perform a dance at a circumcision ceremony but they receive only food as payment. By contrast, a group of drummers may ask for an advance payment (up to Shs. 1000) and during the playing they show clearly whether the audience has given enough additional contributions. The drummers are employed for circumcision ceremonies, weddings and the spirit exorcism rituals. The other village musicians include a harpist, a guitarist and a group of bamboo tube players. The latest method of providing music is through tape records.

Community administrator. The village has several administrative posts which are unpaid but which may provide minor income occasionally. The posts include village chairman, district councillor, village committee member, village section (vitongoji) leader, ten cell leader, village peacekeeping task, party official and cooperative officer.

Religious teacher. A religious teacher is commonly a learned youth who has the vigour and interest to educate students in the Koranic scriptures and the proper behaviour of a good Muslim. The students make a monthly payment of Shs. 50 each. The four schools each have one or two teachers and some 20–40 students. The classes take place during the morning and weekends and the students tend to be very young.

Religious administrator. The category of religious Islamic administrators includes a variety of different, partly overlapping, skills. *Kadhis* are officials who know the Islamic law and officiate at marriages and funerals. The *imam* leads the prayers at the mosque. Alongside these categories there are the amorphous categories of *shehe* and *mwalim*, which denote an Islamic leader and a learned person, respectively. There are several persons who are referred to by these titles even when they do not have an official position in a mosque or a madarasa. Either they have previously had such a position or they have shown their commitment in the rituals. Some of the learned persons have special skills of making amulets, making predictions through Islamic astrology, curing sicknesses and using their powers to harm their enemies. The most powerful persons almost have a monopoly on the healing of distressed persons because they can cure but also harm the spiritual power (embodied in so called 'stars') of a client. The payments for these experts can run to several thousand shillings.

In comparison, the administrative structure of a Christian church is very narrow. At the same time the services that a church provides to its clients are very few.

Traditional administrator. The traditional leaders are male elders recognised by an ethnic group or its section as the local leaders and carriers of the tradition. The leader makes a special appearance when a wider problem has appeared in the group and a communal ritual needs to be carried out. The elder will be provided with items for sacrifice which he spills on the sacrificial ground and tree. It is also said that these leaders representing different ethnic groups may be called together when rains are not behaving as they should. The only occasions when the elders are entitled to a contribution are for officiating at funeral procedures (excluding the burial which is the task of the kadhi) and solving disputes.

Trading and food related services

I have classified together trading activities and such services where processing precedes selling the food. Sometimes the distinction is vague because the labour input in processing may be small compared to the labour input in buying and selling the food item.

Trading with food includes backward linkages to agriculture and extractive activities. Tea-rooms and beer clubs, for example, work mostly as the trading places where the owner of the premises purchases cakes and beer in bulk to be sold onwards in retail. This practice is more common than selling only one's own produce. In the case of tea-rooms it is also possible that a sort of sub-contracting arrangement takes place: the tea-room owner provides a corner for a private doughnut seller who then does her business inside the tea-room and later pays for using the premises.

Trading interests men and women, from the very young to the very old. It has the same advantages as services, but, in addition, trading is definitely seen as the most lucrative means of getting rich. Money transactions are more frequent and immediate (and thus more reliable) than when one starts other, more laborious tasks. Everybody can observe that the rich people in the community are engaged in trading. What additional proof is needed?

Trading has a mixed reputation as a source of livelihood. The coastal Swahili have been active in trading for a long time. Trading is perceived as a means of making a living for a clever person and the mobility that it includes has been understood as a positive way for a man (but not necessarily for a woman) to actively take grasp of the wider world. The problem appeared from the direction of the past national ideology. The national leaders, the government officials and the radio nicknamed the traders *walunguzi* (speculators) who engaged in unproductive activity at the expense of the hardworking peasants. The ideology led to several administrative measures including closing the private shops and forcing the urban traders to move back to the rural areas. During the later part of the era of the Ujamaa policy, the traders were equated with criminals. This trader-hostile policy was difficult to implement on a local level because it made access to basic necessities difficult for the ordinary people. The study of Don Hassett (1985), carried out around 1980 in Mchinga village in Lindi, shows that the local officers had to 'adjust' the official policies and employ a less strict interpretation of the regulations so that villagers had access to the necessities of daily life. Currently the regulations inhibiting trade are either revoked or inoperative but a certain element of the negative attitude on traders prevails among some ruling party and administrative officers.

The items which can be traded are stratified so that some items can be traded with a small initial investment over short distances while others require substantive investment, planning and selling over long distances or over a long period of time.

The fish trade provides a good example of the risks associated with trading. In Kilimahewa there are several fish traders. They pursue different diversification strategies but usually their diversification portfolio includes agriculture and other forms of trading. Fish traders work through simple cycles of trading where a trader travels by bus to the selling point, buys fish for the amount he can afford, returns and sells all the fish himself at one or several market places. Once he has sold the stock he can start a new journey to buy fish or he can start to do something else. Many traders like to operate seasonally, and they plough all their resources into other activities in between. After a pause, a trader starts to collect capital again and then resumes the fish collection trips.

Trading fish has risks which can fundamentally change the way operations are carried out. Just prior to my field-work, the fishermen of the coastal villages increased their fish prices drastically without prior warning, thus causing great problems for traders. The traders tried to pass on the price increase to customers and faced fierce protests. Later on, the sea fish found a new competitor; dried lake fish was transported by plane and lorry all the way from Lake Victoria to Newala. (It was the Rwanda war and the stories of corpse-eating fish which probably reduced consumption in northern Tanzania.) The sudden influx of new fish species caused a stir in the market. Suddenly, the fish traders started to make their trips to inland Newala, instead of coastal Kilwa, for their supplies. A competition started between two fishing communities, between two fish trader networks and the competition changed consumer preferences. In this complex situation, a trader needed a sound mind and a capacity to adjust if he wanted to survive in the business. Some of the traders were quick to adjust and made good money with the new types of fish. Some tried to combine fish trading with other types of trading in the Newala direction. As it happens, some traders found the new situation beyond their control. They ceased to trade and shifted resources to other, more reliable ventures.

Running tembo beer club. The coconut beer clubs are run through several kinds of arrangements. It is possible that different persons divide the tasks of owning the club, running it, providing beer, transporting it to the club and selling the beer to the customers. The beer clubs are also known to town based traders who visit clubs to buy beer in big containers.

Beer clubs work fairly steadily throughout the year with a slight drop in attendance during the rainy season and during Ramadan. During the months of October and November the beer clubs also sell cashew beer (i.e. the juice of the cashew fruit). It is widely preferred because of its taste and nutritional content. Many people have access to cashew beer even without visiting a club.

Selling grain beer. Selling grain beer is run at a comparatively low level and the beer is mostly available on ritual occasions. Selling grain beer does not compete with selling coconut beer and the village government is officially against using the grain for beer making. The production of liquor is a profitable but rather rare enterprise. The production of hard liquor (called for example, *mrema*, after a famous politician) is very rare in this village.

Selling togwa softdrink. Togwa is a product of the coconut which is available seasonally as a refreshment.

Selling doughnuts, chapati etc. This is a trade which several woman undertake occasionally when they need cash. The tools are the same as those needed for daily cooking. The required investments are just cooking oil and wheat flour. The common practice is that a woman makes doughnuts at home and then enters a tea-room to sell inside to the customers. The baker gives a hundred shillings to the tea-room owner as payment for using his premises. Others sell the product outdoors.

Selling snacks. The most common snacks are cassava, sweet potato and ming'oko. They can be sold cooked, fried or roasted. The selling takes place at the market place and other gatherings. Sugarcane is a also sold as a snack seasonally.

Selling cooked food. The selling of proper meals takes place both at the places where people gather and in the fields. The food is usually cooked at home and carried around in a large pot until it is finished. Commonly the food is cooked rice with minimal relish and the price of a plate varies from Shs. 70 to 150 depending on the season. The sellers are a mixed group of women (called *mama ntilie*) and the selling is perceived as respectable work.

Selling cigarettes. Selling cigarettes is the most simple way for a youth to enter the magic world of trade. It is enough to buy two parcels of cigarettes from town and start selling one by one. The profit is almost ten shillings per cigarette and up to a thousand shillings a day. During the early eighties, when the avail-ability of cigarettes and similar consumer goods was limited, the commission trade was practised. In that system, a shopkeeper gave cigarettes to a retailer who paid the normal shop price for those cigarettes he managed to sell during the day.

Selling local tobacco. Tobacco is sold either as loose snuff or cut from a large roll of tobacco. The tobacco sold is very strong and it is preferred only by the old men. Tobacco originates either from a neighbouring village or from as far as Songea.

Selling fruits at the market. Fruit selling is a petty business with minimal entry requirements. The market place trader has most likely bought or stolen the fruits rather than produced them himself.

Selling coconuts at the market. This is a petty business which is again done sepa-rately from owning coconut.

Selling kerosene. Selling kerosene is a family trade which is carried out from home. It is common that a man collects a canister of kerosene from town and then it is sold in small quantities by whoever is at home. This activity is often the first step in history of a business before starting a kiosk which is operated from home.

Tea-room/restaurant. Both men and woman have a great interest in establishing a tea-room. The tea-rooms tend to have very minimal equipment and be poorly constructed. The gossip, music and prostitutes are attractions for some customers and a distraction for others.

Kiosk/shop. A kiosk is a small shop which is run from home instead of a separate building. In contrast, a shop is a separate building which requires a watchman for a night and a more expensive license. Shopkeeping is the dream of most of the villagers and shopkeepers are thought to be among the richest villagers. However, shopkeeping is also tedious work which requires travelling to provide the stocks and a lot of diplomacy to handle the clients with needs above their means. The reported profits are several thousand shillings per day.

Hoarding food crops. Hoarding is an activity which shopkeepers and other wealthy people do increasingly. The hoarded items are maize, pigeon peas and rice. Profit (excluding inflation) is well over a hundred per cent if a crop is bought immediately after the harvest and sold during the hungry season. The profit can be still higher when payment is demanded in the form of future crops.

Trading with vegetables. Vegetables are brought by lorry from distant villages to Kilimahewa. The popular items are tomatoes, onions and okra.

Trading with fruits. A trader buys fruits when they are still on the tree. An orange tree costs five hundred shillings. An agricultural labourer is then employed to harvest the tree. The trader takes fruits to the urban market by lorry and sells them wholesale. A mango bought for ten shillings will be sold for thirty shillings in Songea.

Trading with dried fish. Dried fish has most commonly come from Kilwa district. Recently the price of fish has doubled. At the same time the fish originating from Mwanza but transported to Newala has entered the market and conquered a sizeable number of customers because the fish varieties are new and very palatable. Dried fish is either sold by the trader himself at the market or sold to a person with a market stall. Occasionally smoked fish is sold at the market while the locally caught fresh fish is sold from home and does not enter the market place.

Trading with used clothes. Trading in second-hand clothes is a lucrative business but it also has its pitfalls. The clothes come to Lindi town in bulk where a wholesaler can buy a whole bale of trousers or shirts. The wholesaler then distributes it onwards selling clothes at piece rate to the rural traders. It is necessary for a rural trader to have some control of the type of the clothes so that they are suitable for the climate. Swedish bales have the highest price because they have the best quality. The traders report profits above a thousand shillings a day.

Trading coconuts. Trading coconuts is a large business. A trader buys coconuts when they are still on the trees, pays for the climber, the carrier and the person who splits the coconut. He then organises transport. A lorry can take several thousand coconuts which is usually above the handling capacity of one trader and it is common for traders to join together for transport. The coconuts are sold wholesale to urban traders. While profits are sizeable, there are also risks involved. The coconuts are very bulky to transport and they need roofed storage so that they do not rot.

Trading with cashew nuts. The cashew season is a short and feverish season for traders. The cashew trade is the most profitable type of income generating activity for a person who has a lot of capital to be invested for a short period of time. Cashew is bought directly from farmers soon after harvesting. The normal pattern is cash buying for a local measure of a margarine tin (a volume of slightly over one litre). The buying price is about fifty per cent of the selling price at the major cashew collection points. The trader needs to organise bags, a carrier for the bags and, if cashew nuts are sold in another location, transport. Earlier the traders graded the nuts on buying them but recently the competition for produce has meant that grading has become more superficial or ceased altogether. The early season is very secure for the traders whereas at the end of the season, when prices are reaching the highest levels, the trader takes the risk of prices collapsing.

The practitioners of the income generating activities

The characteristics of the various people involved in income-generating activities in Kilimahewa are shown in table 4.5. I study the columns of the table one by one. The first line shows the number of people engaged in each activity. Only a few activities are practised by more than 50 persons. These are activities like mat making which are practised by women and only partially monetised.

Table 4.5. The income-generating activities in Kilimahewa

1	2	3	4	5	6	7
Income Generating Activity: (only monetarised or partly monetarised activities)	Number of persons: * <10 ** <50 ***>50	Sex: Male / Female	Wealth Group: 1= rich 2=middle 3= poor	Time allocated: Main / Complli- mentary/ Marginal/ plus Seasonal	Labour arrang: Individual/ Family/ Partner- ship / Wage labour	Change in last year: Increasing/ Stagnant/ Decreasing
Extractive activities						
Hunting	**	M	3	M	I	S
Gathering	***	M/F	2-3	M-C, S	I	S
Fishing	*	M	3	C	I/P	S
Selling firewood	*	M	3	C	I	S
Making charcoal	*	M	3	C	I	S
Selling building poles	**	M	3	C	I	I
Pit-sawing	**	M	3	C, S	I/W	D?
Making bricks	*	M	2-3	C, S	I+W	S
Grass for thatching	***	F	3	M	I	S
Leaves, fences/roofs	***	F/M	2-3	M	I	S
Crafts						
Making ropes	**	M	3	M (C)	I	S
Making local beds	**	M	3	M (C)	I	S
Carpentry	*	M	2-3	M (C)	I (P)	D
Masonry	**	M	2-3	M (C)	I+W	I
Building houses	**	M	2-3	M (C)	I+W	I
Building latrines	*	M	3	M	I	S
Pottery	**	F	2-3	M	I	S
Making mats	***	F	1-3	M	I	S
Tinsmith/blacksmith	*	M	2-3	MA/C	P/I	S
Services						
Tailoring	**	M	2-3	MA (C)	I	S
Cutting hair	*	M	2-3	M	I	S
Repairing bicycles	*	M	2-3	MA/C	I	S
Repairing shoes	*	M	3	MA/C	I	I
Ironing clothes	*	M	2	MA/C	I	S
Traditional doctor	*	M/F	2-3	MA/C	I+FA	I
Circumcision expert	**	M/F	2-3	M, S	I	I
Midwife	**	F	2-3	M	I	I
Musician	**	M/F	2-3	M, S	P	S
Community administrator	**	M/F	1-3	M/C	I	S
Relig. teacher/administrator	**	M	1-3	C/M	I	I

(*Table 4.5. Continued*)

1	2	3	4	5	6	7
Income Generating Activity: (only monetarised or partly monetarised activities)	Number of persons: * <10 ** <50 ***>50	Sex: Male / Female	Wealth Group: 1= rich 2=middle 3= poor	Time allocated: Main / Complli- mentary/ Marginal/ plus Seasonal	Labour arrang: Individual/ Family/ Partner- ship / Wage labour	Change in last year: Increasing/ Stagnant/ Decreasing
Trading/services						
Tembo beer club	*	M	2-3	MA(C)	I+W/F	I
Selling grain beer	*	F/M	2-3	M	I, P	S
Selling local softdrinks	*	F	2-3	M, S	I	S
Selling doughnuts etc.	**	F	2-3	C	I, P (S)	I
Selling root snacks	**	M/F	2-3	C	I	S
Selling cooked food	**	F	2-3	C (MA)	I, P	S
Selling cigarettes	*	M	2-3	C	I	S
Selling local tobacco	*	M	3	C	I	D
Selling fruits	*	M	2-3	C, S	I	S
Selling coconuts	**	M	2-3	C	I+W	S
Selling kerosene	**	F/M	2-3	M	I/FA	S
Tea-room	*	M/F	1-2	MA (C)	I+ FA	I
Kiosk	*	M/FA	2	C	I+FA	I
Shop	*	M/FA	1-2	MA	I+FA	I
Hoarding food crops	**	M/F	1-2	C, S	I	I
Trading vegetables	**	M	2	C (S)	I	S
Trading fruits	**	M/F	2	C, S	I	I
Trading dried fish	**	M	2	MA	I	I
Trading used clothes	*	M	2	C	I	S
Trading coconuts	**	M	1-2	MA (C)	I+W,P	I
Trading cashew	**	M (F)	1-2	C, S	I+W	I

Explanations:
1. The income-generating activites are classified so that they make sense in local terms. However, the activities related to agricultural and animal husbandry as well as different forms of casual labour are omitted although their function is similar from the local perspective.
2. The numbers of the practitioners refer to the number of people who have been engaged in this IGA within a calendar year. The numbers exclude all kinds of helpers and workers. Thus 'shop' refers to the number of people running a shop and excludes the number of family members working at the shop.
4. 'Wealth group' refers to the three ranked groups presented in table 2. Wealth refers to the household status and not the individual status.
5. The income-generating activites vary considerably in terms of time use. 'Main' activity refers to a nearly full-time engagement, for example running a beer club or a shop. A 'complementary' activity has lower returns and it is set aside when agriculture becomes dominant. 'Marginal' refers to an occasional engagement and characterises many crafts which depend on demand by order. Regardless of the overall time use several activities are 'seasonal' due to availability of raw materials and/or market.
7. The change in the number of the practitioners refers to the change in the time perspective of one year.

The rest of activities are practised by smaller numbers. The small number of people involved in the beer business is exceptional on the Tanzanian scene. One explanation is that the Islamic culture does not encourage beer drinking. Another explanation is that many households have continuous access to their own coconut beer and seasonal access to cashew liquor. Yet another (but rather weak) explanation is that the village by-laws prohibit the use of grain for beer making in this village which is prone to hunger.

When counting the numbers one should note the large turnover of people. Although the current figures can be low it is common that several people have practised the activity earlier and then abandoned it. The village accommodates, for example, several craftsmen who have practised their skills in town but who do not bother to continue in the village setting. Similarly, many women have been active in income-generating activities when the childcare and household situation was more suitable and they are ready to take them up again when the situation once more becomes suitable.

The gender analysis of the income-generating activities is based on the stereotypical profiles and the importance of the gender division should not be overemphasised. It is clear that men take up women's tasks when they notice that the women make high profits. Similarly, a woman can sometimes take up a typically male task when she wants to get higher profits or when she has learned the skill elsewhere. Women can enter several 'male' tasks as auxiliary labour or take part in specific work but they do not run the business. Both men and women take part in, at least, gathering, fishing, collecting leaves, traditional medicine, music entertaining, community administration, selling grain beer, running tea-rooms, hoarding food crops and trading fruits.

When it comes to time allocation most of the income-generating activities are relatively marginal activities. They are carried out when there is less agricultural work or when there is some evidence of demand. Crafts are usually priority work for men but the work is often done by order and it is difficult to receive orders. Thus crafts shine as marginal work in terms of time allocation.

The labour arrangements vary greatly from one activity to another. The major problem in all forms of cooperation is the lack of trust in financial affairs. Every so often people tell about how they started a common project with a friend who then disappeared with money. The same lack of trust also plays a part when the quality of work is considered. The workers are thought to be unreliable and to require constant supervision. This holds also for some family members—for this reason the shopkeepers often use children as their assistants as the children are dependent upon them and directly under their control.

The partnerships among men exist in fishing, playing music, carpentry and blacksmithing. Men also pool resources while hiring vehicles for trading with coconuts. Women do several activities as a group but without division of labour. A proper partnership is established for selling grain beer and selling doughnuts. Women have also had several formal women's groups. The UWT (an organisation for women of the ruling party CCM) was earlier active in promoting these groups in the fields of gardening, pottery, grain milling and sewing. These groups have practically died out because the organisation of the

UWT is very weak. Women have also had several rotating saving groups in the village which died out when the village economy was destroyed by the floods. Currently new women's groups are being formed to draw resources from the special loan scheme targeted at women's groups.

Several income-generating activities include wage labour arrangements. The wage labour is *kibarua*—piece work with varying lengths of contract. A barmaid and a lumberjack are employed permanently but on commission. Those engaged in making bricks and building houses employ casual labour for the time of the contract while those trading with bulky coconuts and cashew employ carriers occasionally.

The last column of the table shows the change in the number of people involved in each economic activity. The change in the number of the people involved in income-generating activities was evaluated only in the short time perspective of one year. The activities attracting new entrants are related to building work, traditional services and trading. There are indications that the same sectors are also growing in the whole of Tanzania (cf. Chapter 9).

Differentiation and income-generating activities

The relationship between the income-generating activity and differentiation is extremely complex for a number of reasons. Many activities are heavily *seasonal*. Although income-generating activities can provide good returns during the best seasons they may provide next to nothing in the off-season. The average income can only be worked out by first comparing the total yearly income with the total yearly expenditure. Villagers are not accustomed to counting the returns on labour at this level of abstraction. Consequently, their estimates are likely to be distorted towards the short-term gains during the busy season.

The seasonality of the income-generating activities is presented in table 4.6. Many crafts take advantage of the dry weather and reduced agricultural work and prosper during the agricultural slack period from July to October. The trading activities are also practised intensely during the same months. The seasonality has a considerable effect on the calculation of the income. The relationship between the length of the effective season and the total income is not, however, straightforward. Some activities like trading cashew have a short season but high potential income. Some other activities are both temporary and yield a low income.

Furthermore, the handling of expenditures and income from an income-generating activity can only with difficulty be separated from the household economy. In many cases, there is no reason for the separation. We can make an indirect guess on the profitability of an income-generating activity when we classify the activities according to the respective wealth groups of the operators. This analysis shows that the poor people dominate the extractive activities. These activities are easily accessible and demand almost no investments. Crafts and services are practised by poor and middle income groups. Trading shows

Table 4.6. The calendar of labour input on income-generating activities

Income-Generating Activity	Calendar Months											
	Jan	Feb	Mar	Apr	May	Jun	Jul	Aug	Sep	Oct	Nov	Dec
Extractive activities												
Hunting	**	**	**	**	*	*					**	**
Gathering	*	*				**	**	**	**	*	*	*
Fishing	*	*	*	*	*	*	*	*	*	*	*	*
Selling firewood	*	*	*	*	*	*	**	**	**	*	*	*
Making charcoal	*	*	*	*	*	*	*	*	*	*	*	*
Selling building poles	*	*	*	*	*	*	**	**	**	**	*	*
Pit-sawing							**	**	**	**	**	**
Making bricks				*	*	**	**	**	**	**	*	*
Grass for thatching				*	*	**	**	**	**	**	*	*
Leaves, fences/roofs	**	**	**	**	*	*	*	*	*	*	**	**
Crafts												
Making ropes	*	*	*	*	*	**	**	**	*	*	*	*
Making local beds	*	*	*	*	*	*	*	*	*	*	*	*
Carpentry	*	*	*	*	*	*	*	*	*	*	*	*
Masonry	**	**	*	*						*	**	**
Building houses	*	*	*	*	*	*	**	**	**	**	*	*
Building latrines	*	*	*			*	**	**	**	**	*	*
Pottery	*	*				**	**	**	**	**	*	*
Making mats	*	*	*	*	*	**	**	**	**	**	*	*
Tinsmith	*	*	*	*	*	**	**	**	**	**	*	*
Blacksmith				*	*	**	**	**	**	**	*	*
Services												
Tailoring	*	*R	*	*	*	*	**	**	**	*	*	**
Cutting hair	*	*	*	*	**	**	**	**	*	*	*	*
Repairing bicycles	*	*	*	*	*	*	**	**	**	*	*	*
Repairing shoes	*	*	*	*	*	*	**	**	**	**	**	*
Ironing clothes	*	*R	*	*	*	*	*	*	*	*	*	*
Spirit exhortation						*	*	*	*	ı	*	*
Traditional doctor	*	*	*	*	*	*	*	*	*	*	*	*
Circumcision expert						**	**	**	**	*	*	*
Midwife	*	*	*	*	*	*	*	*	*	*	*	*
Musician	*	*					**	**	**	**	*	*
Community administrator	*	*	*	*	*	*	**	**	**	**	**	*
Relig. teacher/administr.	*	*	*	*	*	*	*	*	*	*	*	*
Tembo beer club	*	*	*	*	*	**	**	**	*	*	*	*
Selling grain beer							**	**	**	**		
Selling local softdrink							**	**	**	**		
Selling doughnuts etc.	*	*	*	*	*	*	*	*	*	**	**	**
Selling root snacks							**	**	**	**	**	**
Selling cooked food	*	*	*	*	*	*	**	**	**	**	**	**
Selling cigarettes	*	*	*	*	*	*	*	*	*	*	*	*
Selling local tobacco	*	*	*	*	*	*	**	**	**	**	*	*
Selling fruits						**	**	**	**	**	**	**
Selling coconuts	*	*R	*	**	**	**	**	**	**	*	*	*
Selling kerosene	*	*	*	*	*	*	**	**	**	**	**	**
Tea-room	*	*	*	*	*	**	**	**	**	**	**	**
Kiosk	*	*	*	*	**	**	**	**	**	**	**	*
Shop	*	*	*	*	**	**	**	**	**	**	**	*

(*Table 4.6. Continued*)

Trading/services	Jan	Feb	Mar	Apr	May	Jun	Jul	Aug	Sep	Oct	Nov	Dec
Hoarding food crops												
Trading vegetables	*	*	*	*	*	*	*	*	*	*	*	*
Trading fruits	*										**	**
Trading dried fish	**	*	*	*	*	**	**	**	**	**	**	**
Trading used clothes	*	*	*	*	*	*	*	*	*	*	*	*
Trading coconuts	*	*	*	*	*	*	**	**	**	**	**	*
Trading cashew	*	*							**	**	**	**

The asterisks refer to the relative amount of time needed for each activity. The stars refer to the variation of time need for one activity. Thus the table can be read only horizontally. Due to the qualitative research method it is not possible to compare the time need of, say, trading cashew and trading coconut, by counting the number of the stars.
The letter R stands for Ramadan which does not have fixed a date. Ramadan increases sales for some income-generating activities.

the biggest variation. There are many categories of trading which can be entered easily. It is more difficult to enter trading with coconuts, cashew and merchandise because these items require larger amounts of capital. These items provide larger profits and, consequently, the rich are specially interested in these trading activities. To sum up, the category of the income-generating activities is very wide and it includes anything from the most lucrative forms of trading to a partially monetised seasonal craft.

I have now described the relationship between income-generating activities and wealth groups. It is a different question to ask whether the existence of these activities increases or decreases differentiation. There are serious technical problems associated with measuring whether the income-generating activities as a whole increase differentiation compared to a situation where this income is missing.[1] This question is also hypothetical and the answer is bound to be circumstantial. *If* the village did not have all these activities, would it be more equal? The likely answer is that the narrower production base would mean higher dependency on external actors. The dependency would most likely increase the opportunities for the town-based accumulators to enhance exploitative relations based on land acquisition and low crop pricing (cf. the argument of Hydén in Chapter 9 on 'captured' vs. 'uncaptured' peasantry). These exploitative relations would then make their inroads into the village, polarising people in terms of access to the means of production. This is a likely scenario but it is hypothetical.

---

1. Adams (1994) has compared different differentiation indicators in a decomposition analysis of the various income-sources. A proper index should take into account the effect of symmetry (people swapping positions while income values remain the same), the effect of the equal proportional increase of income over time, the effect of the change in population size etc. His analysis also shows that the way the classification is made between different income sources (in his case, non-farm, agricultural, livestock, rental and transfer, and the further decomposition of the non-farm income into self-employment, unskilled labour, government employment and private sector income) has an effect on the results. In my own analysis, the more problematic twist is the unsuitability of monetary equivalent as an indicator of a value for several products and services.

Other sources of income

The sources of income outside agriculture and income-generating activities are wage labour, transfer payments and capital incomes. These three categories are relatively rare sources of income but they tend to make up a significant portion of total household income when they occur. A rough estimate is that all households have some agricultural income, about eighty per cent have some of the income-generating activities while only ten per cent of the households have formal sector wages or regular capital incomes. When it comes to the transfer payments, the definition of 'transfer payments' dictates the results. I have used a threshold criterion that a household has transfer income/expenditure when a residential unit gives or receives gifts worth over two thousand shilling a year.[1] If this definition is accepted practically all households have positive or negative transfer payments.

Wage labour

The salary levels have dropped drastically in Tanzania during the last two decades. Until recently, the primary school teachers received a salary of ten thousand shillings per month which is the amount a male agricultural day labourer earns if he works twenty days a month. The teachers felt that the pay was far too low and that the low pay had a demoralising effect on work performance. According to teachers, the educational merit should be marked more clearly through higher wages. The problem of the teachers was amplified by the habit of the district council of 'borrowing' the salary allocation for long periods which meant that the teachers could remain without any payment for several months. The salary problem was greatly alleviated when the teachers' salary was almost doubled in 1994 and increased again in 1997.

Teachers are the major group in Kilimahewa with a regular salary. The other wage earners are a few administrative persons employed by the district council who experience the poverty of the district council through irregular and low payment. The major part of the salary of the higher authorities is paid in terms of various kinds of allowances but the village and ward level officers do not have such advantages. They also lack operational budgets and indeed any kind of support services that would make it possible to actively work in their field of expertise. Instead, they keep a low profile and avoid disturbing the villagers.

Transfer payments

Transfer payments take different forms from a small gift of a bucketful of groundnuts to a new corrugated iron roof for a house. In the analysis I have concentrated on the number and type of the relationships between persons making the transfer payments and largely omitted the quantitative amounts

---

1. Two thousand shillings is a little more than the price of the most common gift, a kanga cloth, given to a woman.

because the latter information is usually unreliable.[1] I have only set a minimum level of two thousand shillings per annum in order to root out petty gifts. This does not imply the lower limit for a single item—gift giving can and often does take place through small occasional gifts which together amount to over this value. Indeed, for the household reproduction the petty gifts, when occurring in a repetitive manner, may be a major source of support.

The analysis shows that the flow of resources between rural and urban areas is a *two-way flow*. The idea that the rural areas are a net receiver of the transfer payments may well have vanished along with the collapse of the salary levels during recent decades. The idea was based on the male breadwinner moving alone to an urban milieu but retaining his commitment to the rural area. In Kilimahewa there are very few families where the male head is absent for this reason. The typical migrants to the town are single male and female youths who do not have the means or commitment to support those left in the village. The 39 households interviewed reported altogether eight persons as Dar es Salaam based supporters.

The analysis of the transfer payments shows that rural-rural payments are as common as the urban-rural payments. Moreover, the rural base poses itself as often as a provider as a recipient of the transfer payments. Naturally, the items used for payments reflect the local specialities in production.

Rents and other capital incomes

The most valuable type of capital is urban property. The monthly rents may be relatively small but the increase in urban property values means that the benefits at the time of the sale are considerable. The urban property has often been acquired at an earlier stage of life when staying in the town but it is not impossible for rural people also to invest in urban property.

The other types of capital income are rental income from village plots, houses, bicycles, sewing machines and similar items. These are 'modern' property and the rental agreement can be made without creating conflicts with the relatives and other potential benefactors. On the other hand, agricultural land is still subject to different kinds of claims. It is very rare for a wealthy man to receive considerable income through renting out agricultural land or coconut trees.

The effects of the division of labour on the pattern of rural development

What kind of rural development does the locally oriented, culturally informed division of labour that we have described, generate? Does the development

---

1. This data is rather rudimentary because people tend to underreport the external flows or keep them secret. I suspect that survey data on transfer payments gravely underestimates the gift flows.

pattern differ from the basic pattern of modernisation—a model that is always the implicit point of reference? I shall discuss two effects of the rural division of labour. The first one is that the small, relatively independent production units tend to dominate the scene. The second one is that the small production units produce a majority of the rural consumer goods and services, thus giving rural society a certain political independence.

Large number of the small production units. I have outlined the diversity of income sources within agriculture and income-generating activities. This shows the remarkable degree of the division of labour. One effect of the pattern of diversification is a large number of small specialised production units.

The high number of competing units can be explained in many ways, all explanations relating to labour costs and labour arrangements. Rural households can reduce their labour costs by laying down tools when the season is over and the majority of the villagers have exhausted their purchasing power. Rural households can also provide a part of the reproduction costs of labour from the farm income. The small enterprises do not invest much in tools or materials and thus the entry requirements—at a low technological level—are usually quite small.

The employment effect of the small production units is difficult to value because most of the units are temporary, seasonal income-generating activities. I would like to underline the broad scale of the labour tasks that the diverse economic activities provide. There are tasks for men of all walks of life: old people, crippled people, widows, businessmen, churchmen, thieves and farmers. All categories of people can find an economic activity which suits their cultural orientation and economic resources.

The wide coverage of basic needs —self-reliance in key issues. The major effect of the large number of specialised production units is that the major basic needs can be covered with local products. The construction of a house is an excellent example. It is possible to construct a good quality house without using any items brought from outside the village. Even nails can be substituted, and are usually substituted, with ropes of a special kind. Yet the construction of a house requires a large number of exchanges. One needs to buy at least three different types of poles, sticks, two kinds of ropes, grass, loan tools, employ masons, thatchers, carpenters, organise work parties and so on. All this can be done locally.

Looking systematically at the common consumption baskets we see that the major manufactured items are second-hand clothes, medicine and some consumer items (soap, body oil, kerosene, matches and cigarettes). Many services and goods are available both as manufactured and locally produced items but it is only the wealthier households which buy manufactured items above these necessities.

Chapter 5

Variety in Agency—
Households with Soft Boundaries

> The problem in our family is how my husband handles our incomes. All my incomes are taken by my husband who leaves me only little for my expenses.
>
> A young villager

> It is good to have two wives who cooperate well together. One wife can cook and take care of children while the other works on the fields. They can help me and I can help them.
>
> A village trader

> Reconstruction of family relations over time in Africa poses difficult problems of documentation and therefore demands particularly self-critical interpretation. ... Intentional pursuit of sectional interest certainly offers the most tangible subject matter for study. In the long run, however, it needs to be combined with a theory of motivation which includes the power of cultural definitions and ideological goals.
>
> Jane Guyer: *Family and Farm in Southern Cameroon*

Methodological considerations

One of the most intriguing and complex issues in the analysis of diversification strategies is the question, what is the actor/agency that is responsible for conducting these strategies. There are, at least, four possible options as an appropriate agency for a diversification strategy. These options are an enterprise, a household, an individual and an amorphous network. In this analysis I use household as a unit for diversification strategies.

There are solid reasons for using the household as a starting point when locating an agency of diversification strategies. After all, there are numerous small transactions which take place within a domestic group and which help the group to integrate its various resources into a functional system. The household concept has, however, been repeatedly attacked by the economic anthropologists and for good reasons. It has been forcefully argued that the concept tends to hide rather than reveal social *relations* within a domestic group. If used unreflectively, it is taken for granted that household membership is clear-cut and that, within the group, the resources are simply pooled together. Neither of these unreflective suggestions can fully stand an empirical investigation and be taken as given facts. There is much fluidity and scope for negotiation in the domestic arenas.

I shall contribute to this debate by emphasising the variation between households in their patterns of internal cooperation. I shall not claim (like some economic anthropologists) that households do not exist or, if they exist, they are merely sites of exploitation. Neither shall I claim that households are united and harmonious wholes. Instead I claim that *some* households are full of conflicts and *some* are united. I then make a further hypothesis that, from the perspective of accumulation-oriented diversification strategy, *good cooperation* within a household makes it much easier to apply a complicated and successful diversification strategy.

Good cooperation means a kind of 'domestic contract' whereby decisions on resource allocation are respected by all household members; money is given or lent to a person needing it for an economic activity; work tasks are divided in an acceptable way and adequate compensations are made to guarantee future cooperation. The opposite of good cooperation is struggles for resource allocations, egoistic motivations, hiding wealth and general mistrust. Thus the situation at home makes a difference for the management of economic projects.

Now this perspective may sound banal but it is crucial and often overlooked. This perspective has been neglected because the dominant gender perspective, while emphasising a distinctive women's sphere, does not have room for identifying cooperation. When I emphasise cooperation and good internal relations, I do it from a certain economic angle. The emphasis is placed on the overall accumulation. It is worthy of note that when I speak of good cooperation I have not made any statement on the equality within a household. Good cooperation can be reached broadly through two ways. Either there is a democratic pattern of decision making and resource allocation which guarantees equality. Or there is an authoritarian but benevolent 'head of household' who has reached the consent of the other household members. Thus good cooperation does not necessitate equality. Therefore the agenda is different from normal gender-oriented household studies. When gender studies concentrate on (the lack of) equality within the household they tend to overlook the value of cooperation for accumulation.

From this perspective I also challenge conventional progressive views on the domestic division of labour. Domestic division of labour is always there in the African rural households. Again, it makes a huge difference whether the division of labour is a functional division based on agreement/consent, or whether the division of labour is a divisive force, fragmenting the household into separate hostile sections.

My perspective is special but, naturally, I am still confronted with the normal methodological problems of classifying and evaluating domestic processes. There problems are formidable because a domestic group is a realm where social, cultural and economic processes are completely entangled with each other. Domestic patterns of resource allocation are notoriously difficult to pin down and observe in a consistent manner. A major reason is that the delayed and indirect patterns of exchange and distribution take place also in the domestic sphere; the division of tasks and the patterns of remuneration are not linked directly with each other. That is why the empiricist reasoning seeking only direct domestic exchanges can create significant distortions.

The variation between individual households is high where both the composition and the dynamics are concerned. It is not possible to elicit a culture-specific pattern of division of labour, or culture-specific role models and authority patterns, without undermining the variation. The study of the domestic groups can, however, locate the key parameters which define the range of choices that a household is facing. Moreover, it is possible to locate important domestic dynamics and tensions that each household is likely to face.

There are several other studies on rural economy which use an enterprise as a unit of analysis. I shall return to that discussion in Chapters 9–10. The advantage of the enterprise perspective is that the conceptualisation of the economic processes is more specified. I still hold that the enterprise is a misplaced and inoperative unit for many of the issues which concern micro-enterprises.[1] Marginal economic activities are totally dependent on the wider household economy, especially on its labour arrangements and agricultural resource base. This is the case even when the relations of cooperation are severed within the household and a person running a micro-enterprise first seems to work on his own.

Household studies: from units to processes

It is challenging to analyse household economy in a society where the group formation is constantly fluid. There are several reasons which make it rational and beneficial for some people to move in a household and for some others to move out of a household. The very idea of relating the identity permanently to one house only can even be seen as a sign of narrow-mindedness in Kilima-hewa. For example, the trading men need contacts in different localities as a part of their mobile business strategy. Women for their part build up safety networks through knitting together connections in different localities. Thus the openness towards external attachment is a sign of social richness. Moreover, it can be an avenue for 'straddling' between different social positions. I make my analysis of the household dynamics from this 'permissive' point of view.

Since my study concerns primarily economic processes I approach the household in such a way that the membership is valued in terms of economic contributions. In other words, a person can be counted simultaneously as a 'member' of several households if he has an important economic role in all of

---

1. Cf. Pedersen (1994b) for illuminating analysis on the differences between categories of rural enterprise.

them. A person can be counted as an 'external member' of a household other than where he resides.[1]

The fluid external boundaries of a household (i.e. partial membership) is a problem only if we want to make it a problem. More precisely, it would be a problem if we needed one exact figure for counting the household size which would then be used as a divider to calculate per capita figures. Any national survey needs to make such calculations and thus the people need to be allocated to the stipulated household units. In many other studies the enumeration of household size gives very little relevant information and actually dislocates the interesting social processes from the focus. Instead of units, a household analysis should concentrate on the social processes.[2]

I divide domestic social processes into two groups: those which are dispersing (centrifugal) and those which are uniting (centripetal). There are always dispersing processes which generate fission of the united groups into smaller units. There are other, uniting processes which help to keep people united so that they can share the resources they have available.

The following dispersing processes take place on the domestic scene:

a) Division of labour. The internal division of labour may split a household in several sub-units of individuals or groups, even when it continues as a co-residential group.

b) Multiple location. A household may reside in several locations and change the location several times.

c) Generational change. Households face different phases of fission when children move out.

d) Divorces. Divorces split households permanently.

The dispersing processes are difficult to pin down properly because of the ideology of the superiority of permanent families both among researchers and the people studied. This is a major source of confusion for household studies. Any analysis which aims to tackle processual issues properly would need to have a time-frame which is at least a calendar year and preferably longer. In such a time-frame, the dispersing processes are more likely to enter into the analysis.

---

1. The official definition of household used in the government surveys is fully exclusive (URT 1992, appendix 6). It is important to note that the non-exclusive counting is not possible in official surveys for two reasons. First, the demographic studies need to have exclusive households because no person can be counted twice or the demographic statistics would be distorted. Second, when household size is an important indicator, it is not possible to include qualitatively different types of members—a person cannot be said to be a member of the household A with twenty percent and a member of the household B with eighty percent. By contrast, a semi-qualitative study can explore fully the different degrees of the household membership.

2. One way to approach the continuous change in household membership is to study it as a surface variation of the other, more general and predictable social processes like generational cycles and residential patterns at marriage. It can be argued that each of these processes have their own logic—it is just their combined effect which creates the multitude of changes at the surface level.

The uniting forces are the forces of attachment, belonging, interdependence and love. Although they have a material basis, the ideological element of sharing is central for them. However, it is difficult to point out social processes which enhance the uniting forces in domestic dynamics. Instead, interdependence increases slowly as the social interaction and the load of shared history within a household accumulates. There are also different interpretations on the level of the unity. Domestic groups show much more unity when ideological or cultural elements are studied than when economic cooperation and wealth distribution are placed in focus. These are two complementary views on the integrity of the domestic groups.

To sum up, I have argued that the group formation and unity vary from household to household.[1] In this chapter my purpose is not to study the domestic group composition as such but its effect on rural diversification strategies. I hypothesise that, when studying diversification, the domestic dynamics have an important explanatory role. More precisely, people can make decisions on group inclusion and commitment which are motivated by, and have effect upon, the combination of the forces and the relations of production within the group.

In the following I shall highlight three types of domestic dynamics that have an effect on diversification strategies. These are marriage stability, migrations and the developmental cycle of a household.

Domestic dynamics

Marriage and divorce

Marriage is a major institution for group formation but in Kilimahewa it permits an astonishing level of variation. There are many ways to get married, stay married and end a marriage in Kilimahewa. Because of its vulnerability marriage is a very much debated and joked about institution—a medium for positioning and grading fellow villagers. Marriage does not have an undisputed prestige as the cornerstone of an orderly life and certainly marriage does not have a hegemonic position as the most important personal attachment—a relationship with an age-mate of the same sex may be more rewarding in many ways. In this society with mobile people and multiple identities, marriage is just one way of relating to other people. Marriage as an institution is respected at the general level for the sake of moral order but the actual norms do not require a person to keep one single marriage as a life-long bond.

---

1. The household member can also give, when provided with different cues, varying interpretations on the level of their unity. Domestic groups show much more unity when ideological or cultural elements are emphasised than when economic cooperation and wealth distribution are placed in focus. These are two complementary views on the integrity of the domestic groups. For the sake of simplicity I have omitted the level of different interpretations from the analysis.

The first marriage of a woman is normally agreed at a low age and, if formalised properly, sealed with the payment of the bridewealth which amounts to Shs. 10–30,000. The bridewealth is paid by the bridegroom or his parents to the parents of the bride. The first marriage is supervised by an Islamic Kadhi, a marriage certificate is not given and the bridewealth may be paid only partially before marriage. In the following marriages the bridewealth tends to be very low or non-existent. At an advanced age both men and women tend to have attained a degree of economic independence and the marriages can be contracted and dismissed without external intervention.

At marriage it is most common that a woman moves to the man's village. There are several cases, however, where a man has moved to his wife's (parents') village or the wife has insisted on moving there later on. These cases are usually cited by the men as a cause for trouble. Men feel themselves oppressed by the wife's relatives who always have the option of forcing the man out of the family if he has misbehaved.

The fluidity of the marriages is apparent from the statistic of divorces. On average, the spouses have together over three divorces or widowhoods in their past. Given that some of the observed households are still young it is likely that the average number of the total divorces/widowhoods over life-cycle per household is still higher. Divorce is culturally acceptable for many kinds of reasons.

At divorce the wealth which was accumulated during the marriage should be split between the spouses. In a few cases I recorded that the man was ordered to pay his wife a lump payment of Shs. 50–100,000 (in 1994 currency) which corresponds to half of the value of crops and the house. This amount of money is very high for many men and it is doubtful whether the payment can be enforced in poor families. If a dispute occurs, the divorce case is settled by kinsmen or a case is brought to the village secretary for filing and processing at higher instances. The deficiency of the legal system is that the local settlement mechanisms lack the means to enforce decisions while the town based settlement forums are perceived as distant and unreliable institutions.

As a livelihood strategy option, serial marriages are a means to spread social networks. Although the relationship to the previous spouse can be very strained, the past marriage still generated an accumulation of kinship ties to the relatives of that spouse. After all, marriage is perceived as a uniting institution and, even when the marriage fails, the intention towards unity and mutual respect may linger. There is nothing exceptional in this. The rules of greetings, social identification and economic circulation all emphasise the interest to generate and maintain kinship ties between people who otherwise only come casually in contact with each other.

Another way to expand the scope of social relationships is naturally polygamy. Polygamy is mostly practised by wealthy men and it is often a conscious part of a diversification and accumulation strategy. When a wealthy man is engaged in business he usually needs several wives to accomplish tasks on the home front. It is common that one wife takes care of household chores while the other works on the fields and/or supervises the agricultural labourers. The division of tasks is possible when the wives are living near to each other so that they can help each other in child care and cooking.

The maintenance of the children is a minor economic burden but over time it has its bearing on the diversification strategies. Usually maintenance becomes an issue at divorce when the children need to be allocated to one of the spouses. In Kilimahewa, flexibility and situational factors dominate in this matter. Most often children are first weaned by the mother and then taken over by the father. Yet many women want to keep some children and have the resources to maintain them. There are also families where some children move to their grandparents' place or join the mother's brother's family. In this way a child can be brought up to balance the dependency ratio of the household of ageing people who are alone—today's supporters are tomorrow's dependants.

One should also add that several children do not have a named father in the first place. A child may have been born to a young girl who has been impregnated by irresponsible boys, or the child's mother is a divorced/widowed woman who has had several boyfriends.[1] The repeated occurrence of these cases indicates that social parenthood is perceived to be separate from biological parenthood.

On the basis of the previous description it can be generalised that, from the perspective of diversification strategy, it appears that a marriage bond does not automatically form a sound basis for good cooperation in Kilimahewa. Here I have stressed that the ideological emphasis that the villagers place on the marriage bond is much weaker than, for example, in Christian villages in Kilimanjaro region. However, the villagers are not all alike in Kilimahewa. There are many households which have found their own way to organise internal division of labour which allows for a sufficient amount of respectability and responsibility for each member. These households are examples of stability and continuity. These households differ starkly from those households where the continuity is broken by repeated divorces. Certainly marriage stability and commitment is one factor which divides the villagers in Kilimahewa into different categories.

Migrations and multi-local households

Migration takes place continuously in south-east Tanzania and complicating the studies of rural sociologists is not the main reason for it. Migration can be divided into rural-urban migration and rural-rural migration. Rural-urban migration is largely labour migration and it is the male youths who move most eagerly to towns. Young men migrating from south-east Tanzania are so

---

1. Cf. Shuma (1994) on the permissive attitude on the pregnancies of schoolgirls in Lindi district.

numerous in some parts of the Dar es Salaam that they are nicknamed *Wamachinga* with a pseudo-ethnic name (Mihanjo and Luanda, 1998). The migration decisions tend to be a very private affair, even to a disturbing extent. Instead of planning their moves openly, men tend to 'disappear' into towns and then, after several months or years, reappear in the village as if nothing had happened. Communication during the stay in town can also be left at the barest possible level. If the disappearance lasts several years it is quite possible that the returning man finds his spouse remarried to another man.

The labour migration does not mean that the part of the household remaining in the countryside will continuously benefit from its urban members. Two decades ago the urban salaries were much higher and it is likely that the remittances used to be higher than what they are nowadays. Currently it is more appropriate to speak of gifts. Household members who live in the nearest regional capitals and maintain contacts with their rural base receive gifts as often as they give them. Urban members give clothes and processed food as gifts while rural members give mainly food. Money flows can take place in a rural to urban direction when the urban members are still attending school, or when they are women with poor husbands.

Rural-rural migration (or the extension of rural base) takes place when people get married and look for a place to settle down, when witchcraft or other social reasons force a household away from its village or when the land becomes exhausted. The new house is usually built in another village with the support of, or gift from, a relative. The migration does not necessarily have to be complete or permanent. Several households have kept their plot at an earlier dwelling place and extended visits are made to plant and harvest this plot. Some household members or kinsmen are left to guard and utilise the plot.

Another alternative for acquiring land is reclaim land from the forest near a new, emerging village. Several poor households have opened a new plot in a distant river valley which is far away from the road and the luxuries of village life. The river valley is difficult to reach and an uncomfortable place to live. Many villagers from Kilimahewa have solved the problem by building a small shelter there. They can stay in the shelter for 2–3 months during the most arduous period of rice cultivation. There are a few exceptions to this rule, people who have settled more permanently in the off-shoot village. These people tend to be Mozambican Makonde by ethnic origin. They are used to living in harsh conditions and they want to avoid the hassle and social control of the village life.

In addition to voluntary migrations, most households in Kilimahewa have faced two forced resettlements. The first resettlement was the villagisation programme in 1974. During villagisation the nearest villages were forcibly moved to Kilimahewa. The village was built in the middle of the existing inhabitation in a rich valley area. The village was densely settled but each immigrating group was placed on its own street, thus giving some continuity. Each ethnic group had its own leading elders and own burial grove.

The second resettlement took place after the flood in 1990. It is widely held that the flood was a result of the conflict between an Islamic lay priest and the village youth. According to the story, the priest visited the village speaking the words of God. However, the youths received him scornfully, exclaiming that he was a drunk and smoked bhang. In response, the priest cursed the village—and only a matter of months later the flood suddenly took place. The flood came totally unexpectedly and it swept over the whole village, killing many people and destroying most houses. In addition, most of the domestic animals were killed and most of the valley crops destroyed. The government and the mission organisations started emergency aid which rescued the villagers (and several other villages sharing the same fate) from massive starvation.

When these migratory movements are combined, we get a picture of people who have faced several migrations. The migrations have created a dispersed household structure. However, from a perspective of a diversifying household, the dispersed structure can be an advantage as well. Households from all wealth groups have some members in urban centres, although it is mostly wealthy households which have material property and important business links in the towns. Again, the dispersal/division is not a crucial issue in itself. The crucial issue is whether there is ideological unity and practical commitment between the dispersed household members. If there is unity, the resource flows between the separate locations can be important and go both ways. If the unity is lacking, an out-migrated section actually stands apart and finally ceases to be a part of the household.

Developmental cycle

Developmental cycle denotes the cyclical change where a household grows in size and later on disperses into several sub-units. While this cyclical pattern can be observed on a very general level over a long time perspective, the more detailed analysis of the domestic group formation tells us that the actual paths of household fission may take various forms. Here the marriage instability and the migratory patterns are clearly intervening factors.

The developmental cycle takes place in broadly two stages. First, the youths move out when they are grown up or when they get married. Second, after the death of the main property holder, the remaining household disperses into smaller units through the inheritance of wealth.

In Kilimahewa, the male youths occasionally move out of the home even when they are not married. However, the unmarried youths are seldom allocated their own land by their parents or the village authorities. The moving out is easy when one has good friends to stay with or a trading activity which provides basic income. The married youths find it easy to settle down on their own. Land prices are relatively low and young married people note that access to some land is not a problem. The young couples can easily hire or receive, as a gift, some land for cultivation of upland food crops. The young couples have also the (unpleasant) option of moving to a peripheral village which is growing up. In addition, land is borrowed for one or several years. The loan is given nominally 'free of charge' but, in practice, the youths are expected to make a gift return which is normally a sack of the harvested product.

Land allocation and house building are the social markers of the establishment of an independent unit. Here it is also worth noting that the parents' allocations to the following generations nowadays also takes other forms than land allocation. In terms of monetary value, education and monetary gifts are as important as land allocations.

Inheritance also creates multi-local households. Many elders keep the home plot and coconut and cashew trees under their own control until their death. Before that time the children may have already acquired (bought, reclaimed or received as a gift) their own plot in another location. After the death of an elder, the inheritance of land is settled by the remaining family and a village or a section leader witnesses the proceedings. If a spouse is still living the division of property can be postponed, or his or her portion is first deducted. The distribution follows a version of Islamic law where the male children get two thirds of the property while the female children get one third. Since it is most likely that the children have moved away from the plot that is allocated to them, the inheritance is likely to lead to further arrangements. For example, a distant cashew plot can be sold off. A valuable coconut plantation can be kept undivided but an agreement is made with a guard to collect coconuts regularly and to forward the proceeds to each heir in turn at consecutive harvests (which take place four times a year).

Land sales are often initiated after the inheritance process. Heirs living in towns or distant rural locations sell their land to other people who live nearby. Selling to kinsmen is a morally superior alternative but the kinsmen of the deceased are not necessarily willing or able to invest money in land. The land sale to a non-kinsman is then a practical solution. The lineages, when they exist as interest groups, need not veto land sales to keep the ancestral spirits satisfied because burial sites are not threatened by the land sales. The local burial practice of having special burial groves is such that home plots do not have a special role as a dwelling place for ancestral spirits.

The devolution of the resources to the following generation is a constant source of conflicts of interest which need to be tackled. The relations between consecutive generations are often poor in Kilimahewa. Good cooperation between a father (or a mother) and the grown-up children is far from self-evident and if good cooperation is lacking, there are far fewer opportunities to allocate labour power in an optimal way and, consequently, it becomes difficult to launch an active diversification strategy. And again, there are differences in the quality of cooperation. In Kilimahewa, there are households where a mother complains that a son visits home just when he is hungry. There are also households where the appearances of the father and son coincide and where their cooperation in business is very smooth.

Optimal household composition

I have emphasised the importance of commitment and good cooperation for a successful economic diversification. I have also listed factors which enhance the tendencies of a household to disperse. Dispersal is a natural element in the necessary change process for all households. However, a household can try to minimise the negative effects of dispersal. Thus a household cannot indefinitely suspend dispersal but it can try to generate consensus about a suitable middle ground where the composition of remaining household is balanced and the household is supportive of its economic ventures.

Household compositions are a result of natural growth rather than conscious planning. It is a very narrow perception of human nature to claim that people get married, have children or move around in order to accumulate wealth or merely to reach a balanced dependency ratio. However, it is correct to say that an exceptional household composition, combined with a poor resource base, is most likely to generate a conflict which is then settled through relocation of people.

Usually it is argued that a low dependency ratio is conducive to generating economic wealth. Yet the relationship between the dependency rate and resource base is far from straightforward. The explanation is that households with a rich resource base are able, better than poor households, to sustain an exceptional household composition. Rich households have a capacity to give, say, room to an extra nephew when the situation at his home is difficult. In poor households, it is very difficult to adjust to accommodate new household members. Thus no direct causalities between a certain dependency ratio and accumulation potential can be outlined.

The indicators of the domestic social dynamics

I have described above the key social processes which influence the household unity. On the basis of the qualitative study I have selected a number of indicators which I use to describe household dynamics. Instead of relying on a single variable (e.g. household size, weighted with age structure) I use a multiplicity of indicators where each indicator reflects a certain dimension of household dynamics. This exercise is a compromise between anthropological and economic research traditions. The quantitative indicators are still an inadequate replacement for the qualitative features that exist in reality. The trade-off is here between the comparative results (comparable also with material from other samples) and the rich idiosyncratic description of the local cases.

The graphic illustration of the household membership is shown in figure 5.1. It outlines the division of people into the resident household members and the non-resident members. Most of the non-resident members are related by close kin ties but a person does not automatically become a member on this basis. Instead, in order to be a household member, some kind of economic commitment to the household needs to be maintained, expressed through gift exchanges. As a criterion for a non-resident household member I have used the culturally perceived limit. Non-resident members are those who give or receive economic support which amounts to more than Shs. 2,000 a year. This level is just above the price of a single *kanga* cloth—a typical gift given to a woman.

Figure 5.1. Household as a minimal network

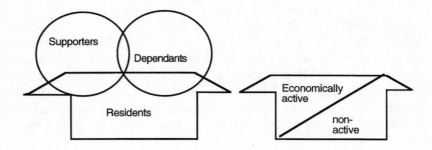

In table 5.1 I show three indicators which denote the composition of the household and serve as instruments for further economic analyses. These are the resident household size, resident dependency ratio and the number of the external supporters and dependants. The dependency ratio is calculated by dividing the number of people below 15 and over 65 years by the resident household size. All the three indicators have in common the idea that it is beneficial to have a large number of adult people who can be relied upon in case help in needed. A household is vulnerable when it either has a high dependency ratio or it does not have any external supporters.[1]

Table 5.1. Household composition by wealth group (mean values by wealth group)

Wealth group	Dependency ratio of resident household members	Number of resident household members	Number of the external		
			supporters	dependant/ supporter*	dependants
1	0.31	6.3	0	2.0	2.0
2	0.38	5.5	1.2	1.0	1.5
3	0.37	6.3	0.6	1.7	0.5

* Note: 'dependant/supporter' refers to an external member connected with two-way resource flow.

1. The indicators give only mechanical ratios for the potential vulnerability. More reliable information on the actual vulnerability can be reached through calculating the actual contributions of the various persons to the household economy over an extensive period of time. Recent observations on Tanzania indicate, for example, that child labour has increased recently bringing many children below 15 years old within the productive group again. It is also argued that in those few households where there are children above 15 at secondary schools and vocational educational institutions, the costs for the adolescents have dramatically increased the burden to their parents. Thus mechanistic age criteria are unwarranted.

The results of the indicators of household composition by wealth group are presented in table 5.1. On average the households differ very little in terms of their residential composition by wealth group. On the other hand, the relationship with the external members differs by wealth group. The rich households tend to give more support to their urban and rural dependants than what they receive in return. The poor households have a more balanced relationship with their external members, the gifts being paid in terms of labour or other gifts in return. None of the wealth groups seems to benefit substantially from urban remittances. The sample is very small but the idea of placing the domestic networking within the analysis of the household composition should be evident.

The detailed discussions on gift giving and other informal circulation show that a large number of ties are also held with people who are not related by kinship ties. This is not reflected in the column on dependants/supporters.

Table 5.2 shows some indicators that concern the relations between household members. The analysed variables are the generational change and the relations between spouses.

Table 5.2. The indicators of the household dynamics, by wealth group (absolute numbers by wealth group)

Wealth group	Generational dynamics		Cooperation between spouses		
	Growth	Fission	Good cooperation	Not good cooperation	Single headed hh.
1		3	3		
2	5	10	11	3	1
3	7	14	11	7	3

The generational change is complicated by the intervening processes of divorces and migrations. The major issue is whether a household itself has entered a phase of fission and become a potential target for resource flows to its splinter units. For this purpose, I have divided households into two groups depending on whether the spouses have married children (or, alternatively, any children over 25 years). This is, to some extent, an arbitrary (i.e. externally imposed) line. More concrete information could be reached through a qualitative assessment. What I am aiming at is a line where cessation becomes an issue. Those households which have not reached this line are facing the stage of growth while those which have passed the line are facing the phase of fission.[1] It is important

---

1. According to the classical model of Meyer Fortes there is also a third group of households—those households where the spouses have died but the inheritance is still pending. The property is held by a group of heirs over the prolonged post-mortem rituals. Cf. Seppälä (1993) for case-studies on the bending of the rules of inheritance in Kenya. In Kilimahewa it is not a local residential practice that the siblings stay side by side and share a home plot for any extended period. Instead, fission and separate compound formation take place at a relatively early stage. The exception is a distant cashew field or a coconut field which can be left undivided. This arrangement requires that there is at least one person remaining who is trustful and willing to organise the harvesting. Naturally such fields shared by siblings tend to be tended poorly.

to make the distinction and then to analyse exactly what kind of claims are made on the property in the households under fission. Although the young people cannot claim much property during the life-time of the head of household (i.e. land and property owner), they can threaten to move away and to remove their labour and thus play with the security systems built into the concept of sharing resources. This conflict creates a natural dynamism within the household composition.

Another processual indicator of household dynamics is the indicator for the cooperation between the spouses. In my operationalisation the internal cooperation is a 'soft' (qualitative) variable based on evaluation done by fellow villagers. While evaluating cooperation the villagers look specifically at the resources available to a wife. If there is mutual understanding and a supportive relationship, a woman is able to handle a number of economic assets or, at least, a man will provide resources for the benefit of a wife when she has a special need. If such trust is lacking, the husband and wife do not support each other and they can even be hostile to each other in resource use management. This kind of split may cause further splits within a household when children and other dependants take sides.

I would like to stress that the issue of good internal cooperation does not, of necessity, imply that resources are handled through 'pooling' into a 'common pot'. This practice would be difficult to implement and it is common that many resources are handled by one person only. The crucial issue is that the different parties have knowledge of what other members of a household are doing. Good cooperation means that this information is available. But information is not enough. From the perspective of diversification it is equally important that either pooling or smooth exchanges take place among household members. These methods of resource reallocation provide, at the lowest possible level, the benefits of economies of scale.

Internal cooperation is a reputational indicator which would be very difficult to replace by exact numerical indicators. For example, the direct question as to how money from cash crops is shared between spouses is likely to give unreliable answers. Another possible indirect indicator for good internal cooperation is the length of marital relationship. Marriage stability is a crucial factor which shows whether the internal conflicts have previously been solved peacefully or through divorce. The number of previous divorces and widowhoods gives a crude idea on whether stability is given a priority for its own sake. As mentioned, the average number of previous widowhoods and divorces (by any spouse) was above three for all wealth groups.

Domestic cooperation and resource circulation

The domestic economy is a locus of several kinds of economic activities. The domestic economy is an interface between monetised and unmonetised activities, on the one hand, and between reproductive and productive activities, on the other. Due to its mediating position the decisions on resource allocation are subject to different—and competing—value frames. This leads naturally to situations where the different value frames are compared with each other and the conversion of values takes place.

I have proposed that an analysis of a household should problematise the concept of the domestic division of labour. That approach gives a far too simple and static view on the resource allocation. The domestic relations do not follow a causal link where the relations of production directly determine the relations of distribution and consumption. The domestic relations of resource allocation and authority are much more complex. They are based on fights as much as rights, on debates as much as rules. Given the tendencies towards dispersal, most households are still likely to consist of several minds rather than one head and many dependants. Ann Whitehead (1981) has aptly called the debate between spouses a 'conjugal contract'. Since there are several other household members with their say, the concept can safely be enlarged to domestic contract. The important thing to notice is the fragile nature of the contract.

Another, equally seminal feature is the wide frame of reference that each small squabble draws upon. The diffuseness of the domestic relations means that any small allocative decision is part of a long term balancing exercise. When the need is large, like in the case of sickness, the resource distribution can temporarily change dramatically. The emphasis on the access to a resource, rather than the average resource allocation pattern, means the emphasis of entitlements[1] at the expense of incomes.

In Kilimahewa the pattern of access to resources shows a shift from matrilineal to patrilineal resource devolution and, consequently, a tendency towards creating strong male resource bases. Logically this tendency could mean more clearly defined resource regimes. However, this tendency is countered by the instability of marriages and the relatively easy access to land. The situation where both matrilineal and patrilineal ideologies compete with each other, entangled with different religious moralities, has led to a situation where the internal unity of households varies significantly. In this situation, good internal cooperation is an asset in itself. It lessens both short-term and long-term resource circulation.

Furthermore, good domestic cooperation has definite advantages but it should not be enhanced at the expense of external relations. If a man starts to build a household with very strictly defined limits, the exclusive proprietary attitude is bound to create cynicism and suspicions within the community. In Kilimahewa there is even hostility towards too closed and exclusive households.

---

1. Entitlement analysis generates depth on the longitudinal analysis of household resource flows. Entitlement is a rather fluid concept. Gasper (1993) shows that entitlement analysis should distinguish between vague potential claims and claims backed with strong moral or legal sanctions.

Also from the perspective of diversification strategy, the most conducive arrangement of domestic dynamics is somewhere between the extremes of individualism and sociability. A household where good domestic relations are combined with adequate and strategically placed external links is likely to be able to reallocate resources swiftly.

The effects of the diversity in agency on rural development

Under the banner of household one may find a whole rainbow of different domestic arrangements. Some of the households are merely sites for occasional encounters with a limited commitment. Others are tightly knit units of cooperation. This difference is most important if one wants to understand how a household will react in a specific situation. A dispersed household has far fewer options to commit money and labour than a united household. In economic terms we can speak of economies of scale, even if at the lowest possible level. A united household has a higher resource base from which to reallocate resources in a novel way. An atomistic individual faces far higher risks for all his/her investments.

In the theoretical chapter, Chapter 10, I shall discuss the actor-oriented theories. There I shall make statements on the situatedness of an actor.[1] Here I have tried to demonstrate that, due to the complexity of the local scene, the existing choices made within a domestic group are not predetermined by the cultural models. Instead, the household members have intimate knowledge about various household types and, due to variation, they can make their choices on marriage, residence and generational change in a reflective manner. The openness of the household front then has a causal effect on the wider rural development pattern.

A household is a site for social processes. When I give a household the status of agency, I give it under specific conditions. A household has a complex internal structure, and the cohesiveness of a household has a fundamental impact on its economic efficiency. For a household it is a central issue whether it can reinvest resources from one activity to another or whether each activity is owned by (or earmarked for) one person only. If resources can be reinvested profitably, the result is likely to have higher returns and lead to accumulation.

It is worthy of note, however, that the reallocation of the economic resources is logically distinctive from the question of whether a household has an authoritative head or a partnership structure. From the perspective of efficient diversification, all that is needed is an agreement on the final decision.

---

1. Rather than studying—as methodological individualism does—isolated individual actors, the advocated approach is one where we perceive historically loaded and spatially and temporally situated actors. Moreover, the actor is reflective on his/her external environment. This kind of approach is challenging because it creates a dialectical relationship between the actor and his/her environment.

In this chapter I have looked narrowly at the social dynamics within the household. It is often thought that a stable and clearly bounded household is the best avenue for accumulation. I have also emphasised the importance of stability and internal coherence for accumulation. Those households which are unstable may still be rational within certain limits. Good cooperation is most important in volatile economic and social settings loaded with risks and uncertainties. In the risky economic environment, it may well be that adaptability is a crucial criterion for the efficient allocation of people and resources in cases of major misfortune or crisis.

A test case for any pattern of rural development is the extent of social marginalisation that it generates. In the changing social settings, marginalisation may be sparked off from different issues. The marginalisation of some widows, thought of as witches, has been observed in some parts of Tanzania. The young girls with illegitimate children are ostracised in other communities. In Kilimahewa, people are likely to encounter several significant turns in their domestic situation during their life time. Nevertheless, it is difficult to point out a single life-cycle phase where social marginalisation will inevitably take place. Rather, the social crisis situations are seen as normal and temporary situations which can be solved through a shift in the place of living or economic activity. In this respect, the fluid domestic organisation of Kilimahewa goes hand in hand with the volatile external environment.

Chapter 6

Variety in Aims—
The Rivalry Amongst Cultural and Economic 'Capitals'

> You may have noticed that youths are having a freedom of move-
> ment. Young boys and girls are moving and wandering about. We
> have many problems with our youths.
>
> An old man

> Old men do not know anything. They think that this time is like
> the old time. They do not notice that the times are changing.
> People are busy in finding good living, income-generating activi-
> ties, the way to live, the way to get rid of problems.
>
> A young man

I have shown the multiplicity of economic practices and the complexity of
household dynamics in Kilimahewa. Among these fields it is possible to point
out some factors which seem conducive to economic accumulation. In this
chapter I will show that the very idea of economic accumulation is challenged,
but also facilitated, by the existence of other cultural orientations.

In this book I am primarily concerned with economic activities. But economic activities are not simply something which engage people when they
work as traders and peasants. Economics is also very much present in the
village council meetings, in a mosque, at a field or in a kitchen. Economics and
culture are intimately enmeshed with each other. The analysis of the interface
between economics and culture requires mental operations where those issues
which are naturally intertwined are momentarily reified and separated, so that
their character can be more systematically studied. We need to objectify the
economic transactions and cultural traits away from the texture of life in order
to be able to observe them properly. This objectification is methodologically
dangerous business because it may distort the object of analysis. In this chapter
I need to make objectifications and instrumentalisation of the cultural spheres
which, in the next phase of analysis, are brought back to their operational context. Thus I first make separations between cultural spheres only to show later
on that, in the praxis of daily life, the distinctive cultural values and practices
can be *converted* to serve purposes outside that cultural sphere. This conversion
is the linkage to the diversification theory.

Kilimahewa is perhaps an exceptionally complex village where people have
different kinds of value orientations. These orientations divide the village into
several, partly overlapping sections. The different cultural sections provide
internally coherent value frames and social hierarchies which challenge not

only each other but also economic accumulation as a central value. Thus the variety of the orientations creates a richness of competing values which has a definite effect on the functioning of the economy.

In this chapter I shall show the complex dynamics that the interface between different types of cultural and economic aims to create. First I set the scene and introduce an anthropological view on value comparisons through the concept of cultural capital. Next, in the first empirical section I present the distinctive cultural spheres of Kilimahewa. I analyse them as independent spheres of influence, but also as being selectively convertible to other cultural and economic capitals. After that I analyse the forms of economic accumulation in Kilimahewa, confronting two different strategies for economic accumulation. The first one is the traditional route of the elders based on agriculture and the charismatic leadership. The other route is that of merchandise capital used by young traders. Finally I discuss the overlap of economic and cultural capitals, and the effects that the multiplicity has on rural development patterns.

What is valuable

Economic anthropology has a capacity to ask questions which are most interesting to pose and absolutely impossible to answer and which thus lead into long debates about the theoretical foundations and methodological utility of even posing the question. One of those questions concerns what people in a given society see as valuable. Even in a distant rural village people have a mass of different alternatives as to how to allocate time and how to use money. It sounds worth posing the question of what are the criteria which direct the allocative decisions.

This question would be relatively simple to answer if all villagers were similar in their valuation pattern: if they shared similar aspirations for their future. Indeed, this is the impression one gets when reading many anthropological and economic studies. Rural villages are often presented as relatively stable locations where the continuous interaction moulds people in similar directions. Villagers are not directly seen or categorised as a homogeneous mass but this is the impression one gets when villagers are presented as members of a shared culture or as statistical objects which only occasionally are divided into different sexes or age groups.

The analysis of values and cultural orientations would be very complex if we set off from the multitude of personal views. Many villagers have collected distinctive experiences while attending urban schools, visiting distant trading places and towns and these experiences give them a special tune—a charisma or a reputation—in the village. The first preparatory step in the analysis is establishing an order in these individual life horizons. We move the analysis of values from the level of individuals to the level of institutions. We use an approach where only such values are recognised in analysis which have managed to be rooted in social institutions. The individual life horizons tend to be channelled into a limited number of alternative patterns. Each alternative is embedded in local institutions which channel behaviour into predictable alternatives. Some consistence of the value choices can thus be detected by observing the institutionalised practices.

Within Kilimahewa there is an institutional value complex relating to the main religion, Islam. But there are also the institutions of Christianity and spirit possession. In the field of politics there are value orientations for supporting the old political party and participating in communal affairs and an institutionalised practice to live without pretentious politics. These are examples of institutionalised and culturally acknowledged value orientations.

I use the concept of *cultural capital* to describe the valuable resource in an institutionally organised cultural sphere.[1] A village is a location of several social institutions and hierarchies. Each institutional setting of importance has a tendency to create a cultural totality with distinctive aims and values. Each cultural sphere has its own form of 'capital'. Capital is the scarce resource that is needed to prosper in that hierarchy. In the Muslim religious hierarchy, cultural capital is holiness which is accumulated through a good command of religious verses and appropriate behaviour. In the educational hierarchy, capital is knowledge which is acquired through attending school and the acquisition of certificates. In the wealth hierarchy, capital is defined through the command over land, people and money.

Naturally there are dozens of scarce resources and a judgement needs to be made as to what is important to place under scrutiny. Here two criteria apply. First, it needs to have an *acknowledged position* in the village which is *maintained through repetitive practices, i.e. it is institutionalised*.[2] The acknowledged position does not mean that it is accepted by all but merely that it is given recognition by all. Second, the capital needs to organise those people who aspire to it into a social order which has a degree of permanence. Usually the social order takes the form of a hierarchy. There are those who have a lot of capital and those who

---

1. The concept of cultural capital is most extensively used and analysed by Pierre Bourdieu (1984). His study shows how French people classify each other on the basis of economic wealth, education and taste. He then analyses the degrees of economic, social and cultural capital people have and shows that the class structure of France is complicated by non-economic resources. In my analysis I have a more detailed classification of different 'capitals'. Cultural capital does not have the same universal character as Bourdieu shows in his analysis. I can see capital as a resource within a sectional group.

The extension of the concept of 'capital' outside the economic sphere is controversial because it can be easily seen as a reified resource which does not require constant reproduction. However, I have used it because it fits with the analysis of resource convertibility. Thus it is not a concept of disinterested cultural analysis but a concept of economic analysis from a cultural perspective.

2. Giddens (1979) uses repetition as a criterion in his definition of an institution. Repetition leads into fairly predictable expectations and thus creates coherence in a social field where no formal organisation has been formed or where it does not have a capacity to create such coherence.

have less. Some influential people, by means of their position, are even able to give qualified opinions as to what amounts to the accumulation of capital and what is 'ignorance' or a 'subversive attitude'. In an oral society, social hierarchies need to be confirmed and reconfirmed repeatedly.

A person can, of course, have access to several kinds of capitals. Capital can be used in a consistent manner to sustain position in that sphere or it can be converted to another type of capital. This makes the process of 'accumulation' a very complex and contested notion.

Because capitals have a public character, they do not merely concern a personal identity but also the realm of public affairs. For this reason, all kinds of capitals can be used for political purposes in village politics.[1] Also, some circuits of economic accumulation in the village economy require access to cultural capital. Now we have returned to the interface between economics and culture. Economics concerns what is seen as valuable and how this value is produced and distributed, something which is well worth asking.

Cultural capitals in Kilimahewa

The village culture can be divided into different resource bases which are partly overlapping and partly separate. I call each resource bases as 'capital'. A capital has its distinctive value base but it can also, to a varying degree, be converted into other capitals. Cultural capital means a command of authority and respect which can potentially lead into economic benefits through the access to labour, entitlement to specific resources and access to a specific group of clients. As an introduction to the empirical analysis I present the variety of economic and cultural aims in Kilimahewa in figure 6.1.

I have located eight types of cultural capital in Kilimahewa. Four of these cultural capitals often go together and compose the core of the dominant (but not hegemonic) set of cultural capitals. These four cultural capitals are the Islamic religion, political authority, wisdom and traditional authority. Outside this dominant set there is the cultural capital of education. Education partly overlaps with the Christian religion. Finally, there are two cultural capitals which form structured countercultures in the village. These are related to spirit possession and youth culture. In the following I describe these cultural spheres in some detail.

The Islamic religion. The Islamic religion is a cultural capital with a high potential for convertibility. It overlaps with political capital, the age-related traditional authority and wisdom. Together these fields make a certain power block in the village.

---

1. The word 'political' needs to be interpreted here in the widest possible sense. Especially in countries like Tanzania where the hegemonic party state has practically had a monopoly for organising people, the political discourse has taken indirect forms through various cultural routes.

Figure 6.1. Cultural and economic patterns of accumulation in Kilimahewa

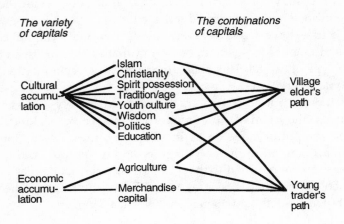

In the southern regions, the organisational structure of the Muslim community is usually more parochial and it has fewer links to the political discourse than, for example, the Muslim communities in Zanzibar. This is also the case in Kilimahewa. The national Islamic organisation called Bakwata has no formal presence in the village. The mosque is run on local resources with limited control from above. The highest local Islamic officer, sheikh, died a year ago and his post was taken over internally by the second in line, the imam, who does not have the formal qualifications to be called a sheikh. The other posts in the Mosque committee include halifa, kadhi (there are two in the village) and ordinary committee members.

The Islamic hierarchy is maintained through ceremonies and the Mosque organisation. Ordinary Muslims take part in the festivities which are community wide and carefully prepared occasions. The attendance at the mosque is limited except on Fridays when attendance rates are high. Some people prefer to hold daily prayers at home. Many people fast during the Ramadan period but even here the rules are relaxed.[1] Knowledge of the Koran is a definite measure of a person's religious devotion but most people can only chant some often repeated verses and there are few scholars with wider knowledge of the scriptures. The Koran schools have recently increased in number and currently there are four schools in the village to teach children to memorise Koran verses. The teachers are young and they do not yet stand high in the religious hierarchy.

---

1. The poor people do not fast as the ceremonial food taken at night is more expensive than normal food and the practice limits the capacity to work. Money is also a constraint in women's participation in the preparation of the festivals and the lack of money keeps poor people in the fields or at home not giving them the opportunity to visit the mosque regularly. I shall come back to the relationship of wealth and Islamic capital later.

The Islamic religion is a permissive set of principles which can be evoked in many kinds of traditional and modern contexts. Islam is directly implicated in certain institutions related to education, health care, community management and problem solving. Through these life-generating and life-maintaining institutions religion enters the daily economy as well.

Political capital. Political hierarchy has broadly three levels. The highest group is composed of the ward and village executives who are nominated from outside the village. The core group also includes the elected village chairman and the district councillor. The middle group is composed of the party-affiliated elected leaders and the bottom group consists of the ordinary citizens without political merits.

The character of the political power is relational: in order to be effective it requires the acceptance of the people governed. The Tanzanian history of village governance is full of top-down intrusions from higher authorities. The national politicians have sought to construct village communities according to their wishes. The village government can alternatively try to implement these ideas without questioning, engage in rent-seeking activities, or try to apply the policies to suit the local needs. The critical question is whether the political elite seriously seeks legitimisation for its decisions or not. The history of Kilimahewa has witnessed active leaders with popular development projects but also leaders who have ruined these efforts. During the field-work, the village was run by an unpopular chairman[1] relying on few executives. He had shown no concern for consulting villagers at large on political matters. For example, the village assembly had no meeting in 1994. No projects were being planned. The isolation of the leaders from the intermediate group and the common people had enhanced the spirit of resistance.

In this situation the position of the intermediate group of the elected village government and village section (*vitongoji*) leaders is interesting. The group consists of men and some women with credentials based on tradition and religion. They seek respect. When the official village politics is minimised, they direct the political discourse into more indirect arenas. Dispute settlement is one such field which the middle level leaders use for gaining visibility. The intermediate politicians solve disputes such as witchcraft accusations, marital disputes and thefts. However, their power depends on their intermediate position: on the one hand, their traditional basis of authority as elders, on the other, the possibility to forward the case to the ward level judicial council[2] (*baraza*) or the magistrate.

Political authority provides direct economic benefits only for a few central individuals. Inclusion in the political leadership provides access to another, more important resource. This is information on changes in policies and gov-

---

1. The chairman resigned soon after the field-work period.
2. The ward judicial councils were abolished in 1994. The reason was the lack of funds in the District Council to pay the fees of the council secretaries.

ernment interventions. The information is useful e.g. in activities like land tenure and crop trading.

Traditional authority. Traditional authority takes on a variety of forms of authority based on ethnicity, kinship, age and character. These are intertwined into a package where one element is ineffectual on its own. While traditional authority is universally recognised as a resource base, the sphere of influence for any individual is limited by the scope of his or her ethnic groups.

Kilimahewa is a multi-ethnic community where intermarriages between ethnic groups have always taken place. If a person's parents come from different ethnic groups he or she usually refers to both ethnic origins. Depending on the context a person gives special weight to either the father's or mother's side. This reflects the fact that the patrilineal wealth sphere has increasingly diluted the influence of the earlier matrilineal kin identification. The generations of migrations and the abrupt village resettlements have further fused the ethnic identity.

Ethnicity is not a major divisive issue in Kilimahewa (with the exception of the Mozambican Makonde) and the need for mutual understanding overrides the emphasis on ethnic or language-based social identities. The villagers tend to use a neutral language (Kiswahili) whenever there is a possibility for mis-understanding. One consequence of ethnic plurality is that the ethnic sub-divisions into maximal lineages or clans is even more secondary in importance. Some men, for example, do not know the clan identities of their wives.

Each ethnic group recognises one or two elderly men who are undisputed leaders of the ethnic group. They are people who have profound knowledge on past matters and who can memorise several generations of their influential ancestors. The ethnic leaders make sacrifices to their first ancestors in the village. They are also asked to make sacrifices when major calamities strike the village. The younger people hardly bother with the sacrifice business and the rituals are becoming rare occasions. Kingroup leaders are also active when a funeral collection needs to be made for a relative or for a deceased *mtani* (i.e. a person from a joking-relationship group). A leader officiates at a small meeting during the funeral to guarantee that the proceedings are well conducted. Apart from these minimal functions the wide kingroup leaders have limited direct functional relevance.

The authority of an elderly person is commonly called *busara*. In Kilimahewa, the traditional authority is heavily biased in favour of men. When traditional leaders are ranked, a crucial indicator is the number of followers. Here we find considerable differences between the leaders. Some leaders are heading large ethnic groups. It is likely that a leader was born in the area and, over the years, cemented his authority through siblings and children who are living nearby. Such an elder is given more recognition than a leader of a smaller kingroup which has more recently moved to the area.

Traditional authority is diffuse. It does not come automatically but requires a cultivated character. Another side of the coin is that the authority is convertible to political and religious capital. Traditional authority also serves as a means to access labour for one's own survival. Respected old people can be sure that they always have youngsters around who cook for them and dig the fields. It may still be difficult to enter an extensive accumulation path through the claims originating from traditional authority. The traditional authority is not backed by necessary sanctions and incentives to make it a force worth reckoning with in the world of business.

Wisdom. Busara can be separated from *upole* which denotes wisdom, good judgement, calmness and thoughtfulness. It is worthy of note that only an elderly person can have *busara* while even a child can have *upole*. *Upole* is a quality which can be recognised rather easily and which is highly valued. A person having *upole* is reliable and easy to relate to because he or she does not show shrewdness or proudness, traits sometimes associated with other types of knowledge.

Wisdom as calmness is not a privilege of the wealthy people, nor the capital of men only. There are also very poor people who are carefully listened to when they express their opinions. Thus wisdom is lateral charismatic authority with a very wide range of application. Analytically it is slightly different from other types of capital in that it is auxiliary to other types of capital (i.e. political authority, education, religious authority) and does not form its own social hierarchies. Wisdom can be shown equally in beer places and funerals. Thus *upole* only partially fulfils the formal criteria of cultural 'capital'.

Education. It is a distinctive cultural capacity to be a learned person who commands the knowledge of books. Formal education is a road to this distinctive capital but this road has few devoted travellers in Kilimahewa. The appreciation of formal education is reduced due to the limited opportunities to use it in a village context. The educated people have a tendency to leave the village whenever it is possible. Broadly speaking three groups of educated people remain in the village. The first group is the teachers who, however, are largely confined to the school and who do not have any significant leadership positions in the community. The second group of people with educational merit is the few ward level officers. Their salaries and work tasks are rather insignificant and they face largely the same livelihood problems as peasants. They may possibly engage in some rent-seeking activities to enhance their wealth. The third group with educational merits is middle-aged or elderly people with vocational training and work experience in formal sector employment who have retired to agriculture and small business ventures. Very few of them have brought machinery or other tools to the village and thus they have limited capacities to utilise their special skills in the village setting.

Education is a capital with relatively little convertibility in the village economy. Education is a resource which would require a more developed, hierarchical labour market to give distinctive value than what currently exists in the rural village of Kilimahewa.

The Christian religion. The Christians are a small minority in the village. While salvation is the aim of Christians, the fear of the Devil is an equally compelling symbol for them. Within the local Christian community there is the normal Catholic church hierarchy. Church leaders and regular church-goers form the tiny core group. In order to increase the number of followers the interpretation of the Catholic faith is rather permissive and, for example, polygamous men and their wives are accepted among the congregation (although polygamous people do not receive the sacrament).

The church is endowed with very limited economic resources. Church members tend to be people from the lower wealth groups. They do not contribute much for running the services of the church. The mission station and the parish have helped this small congregation to build good buildings but they do not financially support its daily activities.

The Christian religion has the position of representing outside values in Kilimahewa. The church leaders include some teachers and several Mozambican Makonde farmers. All these have migrated to the village from elsewhere and brought the Christian faith from their place of origin. The Mozambicans have usually migrated decades ago but some of them still do not hold Tanzanian citizenship. Thus the legal basis for their stay within Tanzania is questionable. Consequently, they form an informal underclass in the society. The active participation of Mozambican Makonde in church activities negatively influences the common attitudes towards Christians. Their participation has an adverse effect on the position of Christianity as a convertible capital. The Christian faith is a capital with little convertibility to the mainstream positions of influence in this village.[1]

Youth culture. There are some restricted pockets in the village setting where one can be given identity and respect from one's fellows but scorn or disrespect from outsiders. The social life of the youths is such a cultural sphere. The youths have their own world where any cultural trait coming from Dar es Salaam, whether it is a cloth, a song or a saying, is presented, evaluated and imitated with appreciation. The good storytellers have many listeners. Their message is strengthened by the video shows which occasionally visit the village. The video shows give a taste of the alien urban environments where prevailing moral codes are harshly smashed. The imported cultural attributes that the youths relish do not receive any understanding from elderly people. Yet it is worth remembering that the tension between the youths and the elderly people has a definite material basis.

In Kilimahewa, the youth culture has been nurtured in two secluded meeting places for young people. These meeting places are actually storage houses for coconut used by traders. They are located at the roadside in the valley some

---

1. The position of the Christians is a good example of the variations between micro-environments. Ten kilometres east or west of Kilimahewa there are areas where Christians dominate the religious scene. Thus the locational variation is immense.

distance from the village.[1] The young men who spend their time at these houses are a curious collection of wealthy traders and poor day labourers. Since those present are obviously not doing physical labour but merely waiting for work or trading opportunities, the outsiders see them as a useless group of loiterers. Some of the young men are very rough, some smoke bhang openly and act out in all ways the culture of resistance.

It is very difficult to reap respect simultaneously within the group of the youths and any other cultural sphere. Thus respect among the youths is not convertible to other forms of cultural capital. Perhaps youth culture is convertible to economic culture. What the youths can gain in this environment is crucial knowledge about the ways of trading and doing business. The youths tell vivid stories about different towns, marketplaces and villages. The youth culture is an environment for fostering young traders to the harsh life of business.

Spirit possession. I take up yet another cultural sphere which exists in ideological terms as a counterculture to the dominant ideology but which mirrors some social tensions in the whole community. This is the tradition of spirit possession. Spirit possession is looked down upon by the righteous mosque leaders and this is known by the ordinary villagers. Yet it is perfectly understandable how and why somebody can join this group. The gate is open—the members in the spirit possession guilds are a mixed group.

The support the spirit possession groups has increased recently. Earlier there were two guilds in the old Mtua village whereas there are five of them now. Each guild is led by a traditional shaman who has the power to contact spirits (*jini*). Most of shamans can contact both coastal spirits and land spirits. Each guild has a weekly session with some twenty to a hundred people participating, some of them coming from distant places. The sessions include a day-long *ngoma* and healing through spirit possession. The motive for joining the group can be a serious sickness but also a social problem like, for example, an inferior position in the community.

An interesting feature in spirit possession is its parallels with the mainstream cultural sphere, Islam. Although the guilds and spirits are not accepted by righteous Muslims, the same possession technique can be used to enable one to 'see' Mohammed. The chanting and repetitive call of Allah in the *ziara* ceremony, for example, can end with possession. And the other way round, the spirit possession session may lead a person to speak an Arabic-like language which is actually the Koranic language. The amulets that the shamans produce to protect houses and fields have scriptures in the same way as the amulets that the learned Muslims sell. The latter are protective and blessing amulets

---

1. These youths have nicknamed the area Mpepo after another river valley in Tunduru where golddiggers are making money. The coconut trade, the food trade and stealing are those activities which the youths control in their own valley and which are considered as equal to golddigging. Digging gold is an activity which, like trade, has inherently mystical logic because the rates of success are unpredictable.

inscribed with Koranic sentences. Both shamans and the learned Muslims can write with a colour on a plate and then mix the writing with rose water to make a healing drink (*kupiga mbao*). The shamans have their books for interpreting dreams and problems which are unintelligible to others but which are similar in appearance to the Arabic books that the Islamic learned people use for falagi, a method sometimes called Islamic astrology. The cross-breeding of the two traditions is thus evident. The spirit possession is actually even more complicated because it also includes the recognition of the ancestral spirits and other ethnic or clan based traits. Thus spirit possession is very familiar for a villager in its logic but simultaneously it appears as dangerous and threatening because it plays with potentially evil powers. The causes for the appearance of evil forces lie in the concrete social tensions within the community. The existence of evil powers is evident to anybody who dares to speak his or her mind. Thus the playing with spirits disturbs the ideal image of social harmony. The leading shamans are marginal people in other spheres of cultural capital. It truly requires a strong character to convert this capital into any other form of capital.

The distribution of the cultural capital

Cultural capital is an abstract term for a heterogeneous group of qualitatively different propensities. The distribution of each propensity within the sample population can be evaluated separately, in the specific context in which it is used. Cultural capital is not a single dimension, a unitary level of analysis, but remains entangled with the plurality of its expressions.

In local terms, the most simple and direct way to study cultural capital is to discuss on the sources of respectability (heshima). This is a word which can be used with positive connotations in several cultural spheres.[1] The villagers show great capacity to tolerate difference and respect cultural orientations which differ from their own.

Cultural capital is usually a propensity of an individual rather than a household. In this respect I have taken a methodological shortcut and analysed the possession of cultural capital by household heads, whether the head is a man or a woman. Usually it is still a man whose qualities are studied. This naturally simplifies the analysis at the cost of being gender biased.

In the analysis of the distribution of cultural capitals, only a qualitative evaluation can be made. I have simply asked whether a certain person has or has not a specific kind, or any kind, of cultural capital. Once there is an agreement on the criteria for the judgement, the evaluators make their judgement swiftly—a person can be likeable person, a good farmer and a reliable neighbour but when it comes to this or that type of cultural capital the evaluation can be fully

---

1. Perhaps the political sphere is an exception here. Some national leaders have insisted on being publicly addressed by the noun *mheshimiwa* (a respected person) and their arrogance has created a negative connotation to the term in that context.

negative. In this respect the category of wisdom (*upole*) is less harsh than others. A person can more easily be said to have wisdom because its character is very much in the passive potential which comes out only occasionally.

The sample household heads have been evaluated by two groups of knowledgeable villagers. The evaluation was carried out as separate discussions and the answers showed more variation than the wealth ranking, implying the subjective nature of the evaluation. If one of the groups identified a person as having a certain type of cultural capital this was noted, regardless of the evaluation of the other group. The evaluators located from none to two different kinds of capital for each person.

Table 6.1. *The distribution of cultural capital by wealth group*

Cultural capital	Wealth group 1	Wealth group 2	Wealth group 3
Number of cases	3	15	21
Number of cases with any kind of cultural capital	3	12	9
Education			
Islamic	2	4	1
Christian			
Wisdom	1	3	5
Political	1	2	1
Traditional	2	4	2
Youth			1
Possession		1	

This analysis shows that all the heads of households in wealth group one also had 'respect' among villagers. Most of wealth group two had cultural capital while wealth group three had only rarely cultural capital and, when it had, most often it was vague wisdom (*upole*) which even children can command. The small sample makes it difficult to carry the analysis further but one aspect, which is worth stressing, can be read from the table: the wealthy people take the opinion leadership positions concerning the most important cultural spheres while in numerical terms the middle wealth group still has predominance. By contrast the poor people are largely excluded from the opinion leadership positions. This fact naturally has an effect on the functioning and legitimacy of the related institutions.

The accumulation of economic capital in Kilimahewa

In Kilimahewa, economic capital is commonly understood as a sustained propensity to generate income, rather than the accumulated and stored income. Capital means potential, enabling capacity which is so well reflected by the word *uwezo* (capacity). Indeed, the village perspective on capital is an idea about dormant capacity which is not shown openly. Capital means the capacity to mobilise resources for the purpose needed, to get people working and then to have control over the harvested item, or at least over its distribution.

Naturally there are also economic resources which can be described as a command over tangible resources. Access to labour is one of the major resources in Kilimahewa. The poor people sell their labour and the rich pay only a minimal salary which covers only the daily necessities of poor. The classic antagonism between capital and labour explains a great deal of the economic dynamics, but there is never only a single factor at play. The exploitation of labour by capitalists is an important process in the village but its importance should be located in a framework which also admits other social processes as equally important. There are also other bases of authority to command labour which are numerically and practically as important as direct exploitation of labour.

Parochial elders versus young traders

The distinctive surface features which separate rich from poor are land, connections and mobility. The most simple way to be rich is to own a large coconut farm. Other cash crops (rice, sugarcane, cashew) will also do but then the effort of organising labour is much more demanding. The rich people owning many coconut trees tend to be old men. Another way to become rich is trading over long distances with large amounts of crops. This is both demanding and risky, however. It requires a strong will to be continuously on the move, creating business connections with strange people here and there while keeping one foot at home. These rich people are usually younger men. I analyse the pattern of economic change as a confrontation between the old and new pattern of accumulation.

The elders have an old established pattern of accumulation in Kilimahewa. This pattern is similar to the pattern in many other East African coastal areas. This pattern is usually described under the term 'Swahili culture', although in Kilimahewa the local term is *upepo wa Lindi*. Swahili culture is associated with mystical forces existing at the coast, with a leisurely life-style and with coconut cultivation which requires very little labour input. The coconut cultivation has traditionally been the domain of the respected old Muslim men who have also a hold on village institutions. These old men are status oriented persons and they are often visible at village events and the market place. They walk slowly in white *kanzus*—a fact which distinguishes them from those who toll with the land. Some women of advanced age can also enter this group, as exemplified by the case-study of Hadija Siri.

Coconut trees stand as a symbol for continuity and tradition in Swahili culture. A coconut tree grows for a longer period of time than a human life span, producing nuts regularly every three months with minimal care.[1]

---

1. Presenting coconut cultivation as an ancient cultural trait is very common. However, coconut cultivation was not as common before it was propagated by German colonialists

Coconut trees are also a source of economic power. The power derived from the coconut trees is exemplified by the tale about a poor man who was living and cultivating land under another man's coconut tree. The poor man complained about the destruction of the roofing of his house caused by the falling nuts. The response of the old man who owned the tree was stern. He asked: "Which was here first, you or the coconut tree?" The coconut trees are a type of property that the elders are most unwilling to relinquish. After all, they get a steady flow of income which they can use to generate complex links with their followers: webs of work tasks, kinship relations, political coalitions and other forms of mutual dependency.

The coconut trees are a means of production, a form of economic capital but they also stand for more. I have outlined distinctive kinds of cultural capital that are clustered around this economic resource. Here I only mention the trees as a symbol for political power usurped through an interwoven complex which combines together the Muslim religion and access to ancestral spirits, age and kinship ties, local administration and CCM party—all tightly brought together into a special form of kin/gift economy. The old men have controlled the major social institutions in the village through this complex for as long as they can remember. And they claim to have the longest memory!

The elders are now threatened by the commercially oriented younger men. The commercial world has recently received a new impetus through economic liberalisation measures which have facilitated trade but also placed the state institutions, the guarantors of stability and order, in a weakened position. The world of commerce links the village with new kinds of patrons who use a more straightforward and less stable kind of control over people.

Within Kilimahewa a new class of accumulators has emerged through trading activities. The case-studies of Rashidi and Hamisi are examples of such accumulators. The accumulators are mostly young people who trade over long distances. The young traders are not bound to places or trading traditions. They seek profitability and quickly abandon any item for which the profit rate falls. They trade with fish, vegetables, cashew, coconuts and consumer goods, often combining trading activities so that when one item is transported in one direction, another is taken back. These traders are always on the move. They do not own any means of transport but use buses or hire private lorries for transporting their goods.

For young traders, cashew is a major new item with a potential for large profits. Cashew was a flourishing cash crop in the mid-1970s. After that the price collapsed and the interest in taking care of the trees diminished. Its price has recently increased again creating optimism in these southern regions. At the same time the liberalisation of marketing arrangements has meant that the petty

---

in the coastal belt. It spread among African cultivators and became an important symbol of status.

traders can play a role in its marketing. This has led to an enhanced commercial orientation and supported new trading circuits (Seppälä, 1998b).

The young traders differ from the old village leaders in several respects. They have little interest in farm work and communal activities. They commonly lack the traditional signs of authority and thus they are able to escape from several related obligations which require money but, even more importantly, a lot of time. For the parochial concerns like festivals and funerals the young traders give the minimal effort and recognition which is needed so as not to receive the reputation of being arrogant or unsociable. The village elders may scorn the young accumulators, saying that they are selfish people, forgetting even their own mothers. The elders make witchcraft accusations about the rich traders. They say that the traders use medicine to attract customers and employ muted ghosts (i.e. bodies of people stolen at the moment of death) as their workers.[1]

Recently, the power of the parochial elders has been reduced because of the floods which destroyed property but also induced the relocation of the village to a new place, away from the shade of the coconut trees. The new village is situated one kilometre away from the valley where the coconut groves are found. Although the coconut trees are still an important form of property, the resettlement exercise has definitely reduced their importance. More specifically, the shift in the balance of power took place through two related aspects: first, the young and marginalised people received thier own plots in the resettlement exercise. Second, the resettlement destabilised the spatially clustered residential patterns and labour bonds. What is important to note here is the competition between the indirect cultural forms of control and the direct economic control of capital. The parochial cultural capital is no longer a necessary precondition for getting hold of labour, help or customers. The political-traditional elite has lost its means to act as a controlling gatekeeper to all economic activities in the village. As a young man says: "The old men do not know anything. They think that this time is like the old time. They do not notice that the times are changing. People are busy trying to find good living, some *miradi* (economic ventures) and a way to make a living and to get rid of problems. The old people who used to remain seated at the old village, find the living tough now."

Coexistence and conflicts: economic and cultural capitals in Kilimahewa

The coexistence of the various cultural capitals challenges the predominance of economic aims. In this way, the very criterion of what one should accumulate is opened for local discussion.

---

1. However, this does not mean that commoditisation and capitalist tendencies only receive devilish symbolic connotations as in the analysis of Taussig (1980). The ghost workers are also found in fields harvesting crops. Thus they relate to all sorts of economic accumulation. Accumulation means being distinctive and thus asocial and selfish.

In Kilimahewa, the cultural diversity has created tolerance towards different aims and cultural orientations. Cultural diversity is certainly a buffer against the feeling of deprivation which the material poverty could so easily create. For example, some very old men manage to behave in a respectable way, and to stay visible on the village scene, while actually living with very marginal economic resources, perhaps with the monetary support of a son and the practical help of a grandchild. Generally, it is quite clear who has more economic resources and who has fewer resources, but this is not the only important criterion for evaluating co-villagers. Poverty does not necessarily lead to condemnation—but poverty combined with bad manners and carelessness is certainly met with contempt.

The analysis has pointed towards some tensions between diverse cultural spheres. Due to these tensions, the community leaders cannot take for granted that their position enjoys legitimacy just because they have managed to take over the official leadership positions.

An example of dealing with the political tensions is a village meeting which was organised to discuss the efficient use of a maize mill. In this case, the problem was that the maize mill, the only surviving village project, did not produce any profit for the village purse. The meeting was the first village meeting after a long period. It took weeks to get a meeting organised and it was postponed at least once. The meeting was chaired by the divisional officer who had travelled from the town. As it happened, the village leader was absent from the meeting and it had to be postponed again. The village leader had gone to the fields in the morning and was still away in the afternoon although all the other people had returned from the fields. He had further more left a note at home that he expected to attend the meeting 'on the following day'. These measures simply exposed his lack of courage to face the villagers and their possible claims about his misuse of the resources he controlled. Although the mill is practically the only means for a leader to get 'payment' for his wide range of duties, the possible extraction of profits was not seen as acceptable.

In this conflict only about twenty villagers (all men excluding the ward secretary) showed keen interest in politics. The other villagers at the market place, many of them young traders, had to be forced to the meeting. The divisional officer officiated and opened the meeting with all the formalities, only to tell the people that the meeting had to be cancelled again. The manner of the divisional officer was very authoritarian. The tension between the official meeting procedures and the shallowness of the power of officers was almost tangible at the meeting.

Against this background it is interesting that, prior to the meeting, some youths had come forward with the idea of leasing the maize mill to a private entrepreneur. Their logic for conducting common affairs was based on a completely different logic than the one the elderly men were familiar with.

In this case, the elders with political power relied on their well established political culture where problems were solved within a political hierarchy. This power block, however, was challenged by the economic culture of the traders. The individual transactions (of the village leader) were evaluated from two competing cultural frames. When the cultural spheres came into contact, it was not clear how differing perspectives could be harmonised. It seems that cultural plurality was not only the starting point but also the end result. Nevertheless, the incident facilitated the resignation of the village leader later on.

The case of the maize mill shows that parochial elders and young traders form two central poles in the village as far as the battle over means of production is concerned.

As it happens, the young traders tend to become older over time. They invest in land which is still a very profitable source of income, and they marry a second wife to facilitate the availability of labour for both kitchen and farm. Yet another popular form of investment is building a shop which means reduced travelling although a weekly trip to a town is still needed to supplement the stock. When a young man stays longer periods in the village he can also more easily join the funerals, talk with people and rely on young relatives to do part of the tedious work. Before long, the young accumulators are drawn into the village economy through various means. Their lack of religious or political resources associated with age can in the new setting be substituted by money. A shopkeeper is more likely to be called a *mzee*, a man of age, in his late twenties than a farmer of similar age. It does not take long before a trader opens his ears for other cultural concerns and becomes a real *mzee* with all the values and manners that this implies. These people could aptly be called, using the old term, 'backsliders'. Mussa, introduced in a case-study in Chapter 3, is maturing in this particular way.

The structural effects of cultural diversity

In Kilimahewa, rural development takes place in the situation where people have very different aims and aspirations. In this situation, it is not at all self-evident that economic accumulation is the single overriding aim of the villagers. Instead, social behaviour is subject to various interpretations. Even the most neutral of our tools, like labour and money, are subject to multiple valuations. If this makes life difficult for a researcher it makes life interesting for the people living in this complex plurality.

The cultural complexity has many, even contradictory effects. I would like to emphasise the positive effect of enriching social interaction. It is admirable how well different value orientations can exist side by side in a village and how easy it is to 'borrow' a cultural trait from another social group. The disturbing effect of the variety in cultural orientations is that the different cultural orientations occasionally collide with each other. Moreover, it is not always predetermined, what code should be applied in a specific situation. When different value frames are applicable simultaneously, there are always some people who can take advantage of the situation for their own benefit.

In Kilimahewa there are some individuals who engage in rituals, work parties and meetings and who always have a monetary calculator ticking in their heads. These people can smell the discontinuities between the cultural spheres and make use of them. They can also notice the social origins of price fluctuations and attend to them in time. For them, monetary economics is a value above everything else. 'Homo Economicus' also lives in Kilimahewa.

What is the effect of the cultural diversity for the pattern of rural development? It is possible to point out cultural richness as a field of dynamism in itself. Cultural diversity helps to create a large number of social positions which provide self-respect and esteem for those involved in the related institutions. This could be termed 'modernity'. Modernity in this sense does not refer to the dominance of the western values but to the situation where a number of different value frames constantly challenge each other and create social change. Modernity expresses itself in creative cultural pluralism (Kaarsholm, 1990).

We can also deduce from the analysis that rural development takes a socially shaped path in Kilimahewa. Instead of the dominance of money, accumulation and selfishness, the values of relatedness and belonging are a vital part of the picture. The culturally oriented development is dynamic but the dynamics are horizontal, creating multi-directional development instead of unilinear and evolutionary development.

The pluralistic development has certain effects on the patterns of accumulation. From the narrow economic perspective, the pluralism first seems to make it easier to exploit people who do not fully understand the value of their land or labour. From the perspective of a capitalist it looks easy to extract resources from people who do not share the same value frame. However, this is a definite underestimation of the normal villager. It is much safer to argue that the villagers are aware of the economic values of land and labour. But instead of concentrating their efforts to directly accumulate in economic terms they divert part of their energies to tasks which enhance relatedness, security and self-respect. This conditions the capacity of the capitalist accumulators to call the shots. The accumulators are also bound to divert some of their time and resources to activities which are not directly economically beneficial.

The pluralistic village culture is not a closed culture. It is subject to different kinds of impulses. The interaction between a village and the national cultural currents is clearly visible. However, capitalist money-mindedness is only one cultural orientation among others. It has a definite pull on the young males. The other cultural currents relate to spheres like religion and politics, spirituality and football. These distract the interest of villagers in different directions. They make the village a location of changing values and aspirations.

Due to the institutional fluidity the actual conflicts between the village sections seldom break into public and open contestation. Perhaps then the conflicts are less between different village fractions and more between some local groups and external forces. I would like to point out that the diffuseness of the cultural sphere in some respects mediates the villagers' resistance to external domination and in others makes them more vulnerable. The resistance is not always direct but its effects are always noticeable. The external administrators do not have control over villagers. Neither have the political parties and other ideological leaders a hold on the villagers. Kilimahewa is not an exceptional village in the region in this respect. Gus Liebenow (1971) studied the political culture in the neighbouring Newala district in the 1960s. He outlined a long history of local resistance to colonial and post-colonial governance. The negative reputation of the southern districts is partly a result of the ungovernability of the local population. The more recent research shows that the same resistance can still be detected (Wembah-Rashid, 1998).

A hybrid position in the culture-economy nexus

Finally I return to the theoretical appropriation of cultural diversity and its connection to economic accumulation. Economists tend to perceive the cultural sphere as a hindrance for economic accumulations. According to economists, the cultural activities tend to lead the attention of the rural people into unproductive activities. Local cultural concerns deflect people's time and effort away from business ventures and enhance realms of circulation which are not based on profit calculation. In modernisation theories the rural people were classified as 'progressive' or 'traditional' according to the criterion of how single-mindedly they devoted their efforts to basic economic ventures. In some studies, a third group of 'backsliders' was noted. This referred to people who, once reaching a certain level of wealth, started to invest it in acquiring traditional status symbols. All in all, the modernisation perspective treats culture simply as a 'hindrance'. While this perspective is untenable I shall introduce a hybrid culturalist perspective which has some resemblance to the 'hindrance' argument.

In the following, I delineate two culturalist positions (a *strong* and a *weak* position) on the culture-economy nexus and a third, *hybrid* position, which I follow. The first, strong culturalist position holds that economic accumulation is just one form of accumulation of prestige among others. The second, weak culturalist position maintains that culture conditions economic accumulations. The hybrid position is then that, because some villagers are genuinely oriented primarily to other aims than economic accumulation, they can be economically marginalised by those who are concentrating their efforts, within culturally conditioned parameters, on economic accumulation. Thus the differentials in value frames enhance economic differentiation. The hybrid perspective of the economy-culture nexus requires, as preliminary methodological steps, attention to both strong and weak culturalist perspectives.

The substantivist economic anthropologists have introduced the strong culturalist view. They claim that rural people have genuinely distinctive value orientations. Thus efforts expended on cultural activities are not a 'hindrance' for accumulation but a means for a qualitatively different accumulation of, say, the remembrance of one's name after death. According to this view, the local cultural values are the only valid criteria for appraising accumulation. The question of the aim of accumulation cannot be answered without making a tour into the fundamental value judgements. I would like to keep the door open for such a debate and hold on to the observation that there are fundamental value differences even within rural communities. It is then a logical step to try to delineate different value orientations and to see how a community is divided in terms of the objects of accumulation.

According to the weak culturalist position, it is an unsatisfactory starting point to say that economic ventures and cultural values are in antithesis to each other. That view would imply that undivided attention to economic ventures would be the only feasible way for enrichment. There is a wide range of studies from Africa and elsewhere which show how, say, religious or ethnic networks function as circuits of economic cooperation. Any economic transaction is clouded by cultural codes of acceptable behaviour which require attention. Investment in cultural activities is an intrinsic element of economic accumulation.

The hybrid form of culturalist analysis concentrates on the problematique of differentiation. It acknowledges that economic activities have a cultural element, and that some people place other values higher than economic accumulation. It then continues to enquire how, under these conditions, economic accumulation takes place. One observation then is that when cultural 'investment' becomes excessive, the cultural activities hinder economic accumulation. It is also true that not all cultural investments are equally beneficial to economic accumulation. There are always some cultural investments which have a more direct connection to control over the means of production and the distribution of wealth. Thus cultural investments have different rates of return.

Chapter 7

Economic Differentiation—
A Socio-Culturally Conditioned View

> Look, nowadays one has to be careful on selecting who you can
> trust on while doing your business. Here are people who know
> how to walk, who have hands and eyes. They can say that they
> will buy cashew on your behalf. But if you dish out money to
> them, you will never see the money again.
>
> A village trader

> To multiply their options in a rapidly changing world, Africans
> have created new networks as well as multiplied their member-
> ships in existing ones. People often react to a worsening of their
> position in one social network by joining or creating others.
>
> Sara Berry: *No Condition is Permanent*

In this chapter I bring together the discussions that have been presented in
Chapters 4–6. I present a holistic analysis of the differentiation of the livelihood
strategies in Kilimahewa. The whole exercise aims to show how economic
differentiation is socio-culturally conditioned.

In order to keep this multi-dimensional discussion in bounds I have needed
to make some simplifications. The most important one is that I concentrate on a
fairly straightforward and static description. Thus I place economic differentiation as a *dependent* variable and then investigate how various factors shape it. I
mention economic mobility (i.e. a move from one wealth group to another) only
in passing. Mobility and change are central concerns in Chapter 8.

The chapter is divided into four sections.[1] The first section outlines the
differentiation of livelihood strategies, making a holistic but stereotypical model
of a livelihood strategy separately for each wealth group. The second section
looks more specifically at the leading households. I study separately the sources
of wealth for wealth group one and the social background of the village 'elite'
endowed with cultural capital. I apply some methodological experimentation to
point out variations within these two dimensions. Finally, the last section
discusses the relationship between differentiation and diversification.

---

1. The order of the research process was different. During the field-work I made a three
step analysis of differentiation. First I analysed the distribution of economic capital
between households. I have classified them into three wealth groups. Second, I studied
the distribution of cultural capital between these wealth groups. I have looked, for
example, how the access to education is distributed between the three wealth groups.
Third, I turned the analysis upside down and looked at the cultural and economic background of the village elite. This is a test to see whether the rich also govern other spheres
of life or whether a number of competitive power bases in the village can be observed.

The differentiation of the livelihood strategies

Livelihood strategy is a holistic frame for analysing differentiation. In this frame the economic, cultural and social dimensions of a household are studied side by side. In my toolbox livelihood strategy is a frame for *situated* analysis—a methodological tool which explicates the multi-layered ways a household and its members are related to the given village economy and the wider economic spheres that surround it. Thus it identifies the various factors, that shape a household economy in a specific context.

Livelihood strategy is a suitable frame to study diversification. Diversification can then be studied through the set of questions that I have made in the previous chapters concerning the involvement of a person in a new economic activity. In Chapter 4 we studied sources of income that this person and other household members can generate. In Chapter 5 we observed the importance of the structure and cohesiveness of a household. In Chapter 6 we discussed the impacts of the cultural orientation of household members. When it is admitted that a household resource allocation also has other than strictly commercial criteria we have reached the conceptual level of a livelihood strategy.

It is good to be explicit as to what can be and what cannot be validly argued through this approach. It is possible to make a detailed identification of the factors that are crucial for the analysis of a rural economy. It is possible to show which of these parameters are likely to accompany wealth and which are likely to go hand in hand with poverty. It is also possible to indicate linkages between these factors—mechanisms of diversification and resource conversion which are likely to change the socio-economic standing of a household. But it is not possible to point out which factors will inevitably indicate wealth or poverty. And it is also not possible to weight different processes of diversification and resource conversion and measure their relative importance for accumulation. The data that I have gathered is primarily based on qualitative indicators. These indicators cannot be brought together into a single numerical analysis.

Livelihood strategy can be studied with some precision for a single household. Livelihood strategy is a problematic concept if one uses it, as I do here, for aggregated groups of households, because it tends to enhance stereotypical views. When livelihood strategies of a group of households are aggregated we easily end up with a fairly static and simplistic model. In reality, the households differ enormously—and not in a coherent manner—in how their cultural, social and economic dimensions are related to each other.

The major results of the aggregated analysis of livelihood strategies in Kilimahewa are that the distribution of wealth has both economic and cultural basis.

Figure 7.1. The livelihood strategies of three wealth groups[1]

Wealth group 1	Wealth group 2	Wealth group 3
Accumulation Strategy	Reproduction Strategy	Survival Strategy
Agriculture/land entitlements		
Accumulate land	Less selling/buying land.	Selling land, opening up land
4-8 plots in various ecological areas	3-5 plots, both in valley and upland areas	1-3 plots. Moving temporarily or permanently to distant plots
Coconut/cashew in large numbers	Some coconut or cashew trees	Cashew not tended well
Adequate own food crop production; Hoarding food crops for sale.	Buying some food crops for own consumption	Buying staple food for 2–4 months a year; Engaged in collecting food from forest
Employ day labourers	Occasionally employ or work as day labourers; Organise labour parties	Work as day labourers; Organise labour parties
Income generating activities		
Trade in coconut or cashew, shopkeeping, commercial plots and buildings	Crafts, petty trade, seasonal activities, community activities, services	Extraction of natural resources, crafts, petty trade and services
Wage labour		
Remittances/gifts	Remittances/gifts; administrative tasks, teaching in the village	Remittances/gifts; piece work and day labouring in the village
Household network		
Large household size; usually polygamous; several resident and non-resident dependents	Variable household size; several supporters and dependents	Variable household size; unstable household core; only few supporters and dependents
Long-distance mobility; external trading partners	Less mobile	Movement between rural (village, field, forest) bases
Cultural capital		
Young: mobility and town connections Old: kin-based capital, Islam	Political, Islamic, kin-based capital, education, Christianity	Kin-based capital, spirit possession, Christianity.

---

1. In figure 7.1 the classification gives paramountcy to the access to economic resources. In other words the analysis of the livelihood strategy has a definite economistic bias. If the analysis gave the paramount position to, say, religious capital, the results would look different.

The livelihood strategy of the wealthy. The livelihood strategy of the wealthy tends to have several cornerstones. One of them is agriculture. As I showed in Chapter 4, the rich tend to have valuable agricultural land and cash crops like coconut, rice, groundnut and cashew. Often trading is a second cornerstone. The wealthy households have access to such forms of trading which require large amounts of liquid capital. Thirdly, the wealthy have guaranteed their security through investments in urban property, village plots and shop premises.

The wealthy households tend to be households with a long history in the area and they are likely to figure in some of the religious or communal organs where the most appreciated cultural capital resides. The wealthy have fairly stable and large male-headed households. However, some of the wealthy households are clearly of a different stock altogether. They are headed by younger traders who concentrate their efforts fully on business and agriculture and have no interest in other public affairs.

The livelihood strategy of the middle group. The middle wealth group has a rather similar package of activities and life-style to the wealthy. The difference is that the middle group has fewer resources and opportunities to take risks. Their investment pattern is likely to show a diversification to different activities, from crafts and trading to communal and personal services. The households in the middle group may command the capabilities needed for an accumulation path but they have simply not managed to make a breakthrough to the level of savings which make it possible to invest in those well-known strategies that would yield the highest profits. Occasionally, a household which previously was among the most wealthy has had a major set-back in the past which has lowered its wealth status. The problems mentioned include the bankruptcy of the shop and the destruction of property in the flood while the system of inheritance is a natural reason for social mobility downwards.

In terms of household composition and unity, the middle wealth group varies significantly. It is difficult to generalise on these issues without doing an injustice to some households which do not fit into the pattern.

The livelihood strategy of the poor. The third wealth group, the poor, is distinctive especially because of its social exclusion which exposes it to economic hazards. Among the poor households there are the small households of young couples and women-headed households. Unfavourable household composition is among the sources of vulnerability in Kilimahewa. Other possible sources of vulnerability are late immigration to the village (less contacts) and despised ethnic background (Mozambican Makonde). The poor households tend to have fewer safety networks and, as a consequence, the 'normal' problems like health problems, divorce or a crop failure have drained household resources.

Casual labouring is a simple method to make a living when one's own reserves have been exhausted. Casual labouring within agriculture may turn out to be, when used extensively, counterproductive since it competes with one's own cultivation. When its own cultivation decreases a household is forced to rely even more extensively on day labouring. This connection exists mainly for weeding work during the hunger months. As an alternative to extensive casual labouring, the poor households venture into various labour intensive income-generating activities, especially extractive activities.

Below the group of poor, there is a small group of paupers, cripples and destitutes, the *wasionauwezo* ('those without capabilities'). They are seldom economically active and thus they rely on the goodwill of the fellow family members and the alms of the mosque. Due to their dependent status they are not always perceived as independent households, even when they live on their own.

Enrichment and impoverishment. Figure 7.2 shows the strategic elements that induce mobility between the different wealth groups. It shows the main allocative strategies which are possible means of economic mobility upwards.[1] In the upward trend, trading is a very common vehicle. Occasionally, a household has moved upwards through acquiring assets like land or houses cheaply and then selling them when the market is favourable, or through cultivating a cash crop which has failed in other locations and become exceptionally valuable for local trade.

The reasons for downwards mobility are less simple to point out. The decisive factor is more often an exceptional social condition and less often an involvement in a specific economic activity. Factors like persistent health problems or an ecological disaster may bring a household all the way down from the first to the third wealth group.

The village elite

Since my statistical analysis is based on a random sample with a small number of cases, it gives very limited information about the village elite. In this section I discuss efforts which I have directed to especially cover the wealthy households. I concentrate on the issue of whether the cultural elite overlaps with the wealth group of rich people. The material used here is experimental in nature. I use different techniques to create quantitative indicators which characterise the group of the wealthy and the mighty.

---

1. The analysis of economic mobility still presents each activity as a separate component of the livelihood strategy which is an aggregate of its components. It is evident that an honest, hard-working person can move socially upwards through making extraordinary efforts in one or two fields of operation. However, I will argue later on that the way of receiving incomes is not the only key issue, but the way of circulating them onwards in equally important.

Figure 7.2. The social mobility based on individual economic and cultural resources

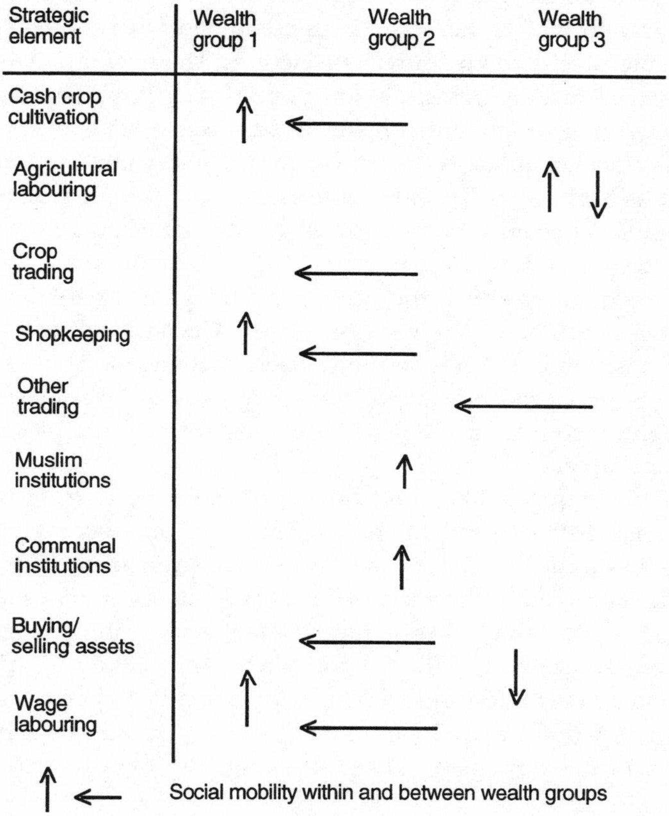

Strategic element	Wealth group 1	Wealth group 2	Wealth group 3
Cash crop cultivation	↑ ←	———	
Agricultural labouring			↑ ↓
Crop trading	←	———	
Shopkeeping	↑ ←	———	
Other trading		←	———
Muslim institutions		↑	
Communal institutions		↑	
Buying/ selling assets	←	———	↓
Wage labouring	↑ ←	———	

↑ ← Social mobility within and between wealth groups

The rich

I identified all the rich (wealth group 1) households through wealth ranking evaluations made by fellow villagers. Different people gave after some prompting relatively consistent views on those who fall within the group of rich people. Altogether 21 households were classified in the wealth group in 1994. Thirteen of them had sizeable incomes from coconut cultivation, three from cashew cultivation, seven from other cash crops, eight from trade or shopkeeping and four from salaried employment.

The local perception holds, furthermore, that there are different ways to become rich and there are also possibilities to lose this wealth. The world of economic capital (*mtaji*) has its ups and downs, like in the *mbao* game. In order to touch upon this aspect of rise and fall I did a small exercise on identifying the rich households in the past. I asked a few knowledgeable informants to list the wealthy households in the old village in the late 1970s (i.e. after the changes caused by villagisation in the 1970s had fully settled down). In the late 1970s, some fourteen households were reckoned as rich households. All of them had a sizeable coconut farm. In addition, four households were engaged in trade/shopkeeping while one received income through salaried employment. These crude figures show that, in the old village, the access to coconut trees was a major source of wealth which was sometimes combined with shopkeeping. These are also visible, well known sources of income. The evaluations show that, in the local perception, employment in town or a rural salary does not play a significant or permanent role in enrichment. In only one case, was employment mentioned as a sustainable means for wealth. It is more common to perceive employment as a phase in life spent elsewhere. The property acquired through external means becomes significant when it is invested in the local valuables, shops and coconut trees.[1]

If the lists of the rich for the end of the 1970s and 1994 are compared, we can see an increase in the variation in the sources of wealth. Coconut cultivation has still an important position but it has certainly been challenged. The ways of becoming rich are more varied nowadays than they used to be some fifteen years ago. The accumulation paths of these households are very complex as we shall see in the later chapters.

In the group of rich households, only three are headed by persons below thirty five years of age. Seven of the rich household heads are over sixty years and the rest are between thirty five and sixty years. Thus the group of the old wealthy farmers has survived to the present day. The analysis excludes a sizeable group of young people who have not quite made their way into the highest wealth group. There are several of these youths who are making big profits with the coconut and cashew trade and who have the potential to join the group of rich people. Although they have a lot of money at their disposal they are also running high risks in their business. There is a high turnover of people in trading.[2]

The overlap of the cultural and economic capitals—an analysis of the village elite

Economic capital can potentially be converted to cultural capital in many walks of life. In Kilimahewa money is used to buy a political seat, to construct a mosque and to support a football team. It is still more interesting to see how

1. I also studied the current wealth status of these fourteen households. All six households where the male head had survived where still considered rich. By contrast, among the eight households where the male head had died, only two of the main heirs were counted as rich. In one or two cases the large number of children had caused the division of wealth into small portions leading to relative decline in wealth status.

2. People leave trading because they become too old to travel, they have lost their working capital or they shift to other activities. A separate retrospective analysis of the local coconut traders from the early 1980s is revealing in this respect. Only two out of the sixteen coconut traders have continued to accumulate to the present day and both of them have actually accumulated through shopkeeping. Out of the remaining fourteen traders, three have fared moderately by continuing the coconut trade or beer club business, seven have left trading and remain as farmers with fewer resources and four have died.

cultural capital is converted to economic capital. Here the process is more indirect. People do aspire to various kinds of leadership positions but they have limited opportunities to use a position directly for personal enrichment (i.e. for command over labour and money). The conversion takes place indirectly when a position of respectability serves as a platform to receive customers, clients in patronage networks and supporters in case of dispute. The most difficult theme for analysis is the convertibility of the cultural capital to another kind of cultural capital.

Conversion between different kinds of capitals takes place continuously. Yet it is impossible to seriously play with the idea of the conversion rates where a certain amount of political capital could be converted into a certain amount of economic capital. There are no ways of counting the direct and indirect benefits accruing from cultural capital. The spell of the number magic breaks down when we get deeply into the comparison of the kinds of differences. What we can measure is the overlapping of the different cultural spheres. We can make an estimation of the overlap through counting the numbers of the people who simultaneously have influence in several spheres of life.

Next I turn to the analysis of the overlap of the different types of capital among the village elite. Village elite refers to the group of people who are at the top in terms of either economic or cultural capital. There are two methods to study membership of the elite group. The analysis can be done either in terms of some observable indicator of capital (observer analysis), or through discursive evaluation on who are seen as elite members by others (reputational analysis). I have used a method which hovers somewhere in between but which is nearer to the objectivist observer analysis. I have collected lists of people sitting on the boards of the various institutions. Most holders of leadership positions have genuine capital in that institutional field.[1] Second, I have the collected names of the big land owners, important traders and educated people. Finally I have run a wealth ranking exercise with the whole elite group.

The first column of table 7.1 shows the number of the leaders in the various village institutions. The table also shows the numbers of those who hold posts simultaneously in two institutions. The convertibility of the power is possible (but not necessary) if the same person simultaneously holds different types of institutional power. The results show that the institutional power is rather dispersed in this large village. There are some individuals who appear in many columns. The table shows that there are several cases of overlap between the village council and village section, and between the village council and CCM. The mosque committee is also well represented in various village institutions.

---

1. There are always some 'leaders' who are actually ordinary people and who are selected by their fellow villagers as lay members to represent the common man's view.

Table 7.1. The overlap of leadership positions in village institutions

	N	A Coop. union	B Village council	C Village section	D Mosque	E Church	F School	G CCM
A Cooperative union –paid member	15	x	1	1	3		1	1
B Village council –elected leader	22	1	x	9	1		3	4
C Village section –elected leader	13	1	9	x	1		2	2
D Mosque committee –elected/nominated	9	3	1	1	x		1	3
E Church committee –elected/nominated	11						2	
F School committee –elected/nominated	15	1	3	2	1	2	x	
G CCM/village leaders –elected/nominated	8	1	4	2	3			x

In comparison, the church committee has links only with the school committee.[1] The table confirms the existence of a power block as identified in the previous chapter. The assessment of leadership positions shows that the official front of the village is governed by leaders who also have credentials in Islamic and CCM posts.

The social profile of the different elites is studied in table 7.2. It shows that the village council and village sections represent fairly well both sexes and all wealth groups. Among the mosque committee there is a group of men who have generated considerable wealth mainly through coconut but also through their leadership positions. By contrast, the church leaders are generally poor people. The classification of wealth groups reveals that wealth group 1 is most over-represented in relation to its size, while wealth group 2 has the largest number of leadership positions.

On the basis of this analysis it can be concluded that the villagers are divided into cultural spheres which are partly separate and partly overlapping in terms of their membership. Regardless of their separateness the different cultural spheres are known by all the villagers. They are all fully recognised (even when despised), they can be described and people can be evaluated in terms of their rankings. It is possible to give a relatively consistent description of the rankings in the public arenas.

---

1. The table does not tell the whole truth as, for example, some members of the cooperative union are wives or brothers of influential village personalities. If these were included, the overlap between different power positions would be more considerable. Cf. Caplan (1975) for a similar type of analysis in Mafia. She aggregates the individuals into kin group in her analysis.

Table 7.2. *The social profile of the village elite*

	N	Sex		Wealth group			Special income	
		Male	Female	WG1	WG2	WG3	Teachers	Traders
A Cooperative union – paid member	15	13	2	4	11	-		1
B Village council – elected leader	22	13	9	2	12	6		2
C Village section – elected leader	13	11	2	2	7	4		2
D Mosque committee – elected/nominated	9	9	-	5	4			2
E Church committee – elected/nominated	11		5		3	7	2	
F School committee – elected nominated	15	13	2	1	9	1	5	1
G CCM/village leaders	8	8	-					

Cultural competition takes place in the public arenas. The competition for cultural esteem is conducted through subtle means and it does not require 'showing off' through a lavish and expensive personal consumption. People do not obviously express their cultural aspirations and orientations through, for example, the ways the house is constructed or decorated. What is more important are the signs of sociability through attendance at public events and showing generosity towards common causes.

Patronage relations

I have described the village as a complete social system. But is it possible that Kilimahewa has its own dynamics which are not affected by the changes on regional, national or global scenes? Or is it so that the members of the local elite are merely underdogs—clients of still bigger leaders?

If we describe a village as an autarchic unit we have missed the point. Surely an analysis of autarchy and self-sufficiency would be an ahistorical fabrication and I have not made any claim to that effect. There are ample signs of evidence which signals capitalist, administrative and religious penetration into the village. In the conventional rural studies there is seldom a lack of information on external intrusions in village life. What is more lacking is information on how some villagers appropriate and interpret these intrusions for their own benefit.

Clientage relations are an appropriate bridging concept here. I discuss briefly the clientage relations to external patrons as a source of cultural esteem or economic wealth. A clientage relation can be formed in different walks of life. It is part of the Muslim capital to have a connection with Bakwata as it is part of the Christian capital to know leaders in the Catholic hierarchy. In principle any source of cultural capital could have its own legitimisation through external patronage networks. The patrons are people clearly above the local notables but having local recognition.

In Kimakonde there is a word for clientage which is more expressive than the Swahili alternatives. *Ukalunduma* denotes the climbing on the other person's shoulders and is widely used for its metaphoric reference. In the village, the good friends of the external patrons are well known. A favourite client needs only to occasionally tell some news from the patron to maintain his position as an intermediatry between the patron and the other villagers.

Who are the patrons of villagers in Kilimahewa? First, there are three very rich urban based people who have a footing in the village. Each has created a power base and clientage although their strategies differ considerably. One person seems like a true patriarch, giving favours and contributions to those in need and during the ritual occasions to a wide public. He is very approachable, a very well liked person who is fully involved in the village affairs for both good and bad. The second person is very visible but he maintains his influence through the capitalist path, employing people, providing services for money and giving very calculated help for a specific purpose. The third person is actually just entering the group of the extremely rich and thus his influence as a patron is reduced by his limited resources and the need to turn down requests. He has a limited network of trustworthy persons who have mutually beneficial clientage tasks in the economic sphere of the village affairs. The three rich men are all occasional visitors in the village but their influence is continuous and lasting. It is worthy of note that each of them has several known clients. The clients tend to show up and exaggerate their relationship but they do not have monopoly on access to the patron. Thus the clients tend to be talkative figures, people with different experiences from various jobs and towns, and often with a meagre economic basis in their own right. Rather than gatekeepers the clients are potential mediators according to their own claims. Only one other villager has clearly entered wealth group 1 through clientage with an external patron.

It is interesting to note that these three patrons have themselves made their way up through patrons in the economic sphere. One of them had an Indian trader as a patron, another a tobacco company and the third a missionary/ businessman. None of them became rich through the CCM party or Islamic religious affiliations although in two cases these were additional merits.

There are other patrons who do not originate from the village and who have a slightly less intimate relationship with the villagers as a community. Instead, they have specific clients who have a limited function. The mission station, the town-based shopkeepers and the district administrators are such patrons. Their influence is fairly straightforward in that they give what they decide to give. They seldom provide unsolicited gifts like a ride to a hospital.

Differentiation or different values?

I have provided a special analysis of differentiation in Kilimahewa. I have continued the delicate balancing operation where the economic sphere is presented separately but is still continuously conditioned by culture.

I have shown that some cultural and economic resources tend to be intertwined with each other. Although there is a fairly good consensus within the village on the economic differentiation, there are large variations in how people value economic wealth as compared with, say, good relations or religious piety.

My village level analysis shows that concentration on accruing economic wealth should not be taken as a self-evident aim. There are large sections of the population who attach importance to different value frames. These alternative orientations, whether they are related to religion or kinship or something else, require commitment and practical involvement.

The result of the value distinctions is that the village is divided horizontally. When we concentrate exclusively on vertical accumulation, the horizontal divisions are too often brushed aside. I have tried to show that economic accumulation is one orientation among several. In Kilimahewa, orientation towards a single form of economic accumulation has been the method of a limited number of people. For most others, economic accumulation is just one issue of interest among others.

If we then say that the villagers have failed to enter a path of accumulation, we have taken the certain perspective of a developmentalist. From many other perspectives, the villagers have been successful in pursuing their livelihood strategies.

Chapter 8

Value Conversions and Accumulation—
Taking Advantage of Discontinuities in the Sphere of Circulation

> Use it when you get it, be sorry when you don't have it.
>
> Goods that are not written down in a notebook
> disappear without notice.
>
> Swahili sayings

In Kilimahewa, the villagers have varied aspirations and aims, and this variation is reflected in how they conduct exchanges. As observers we can note that,
analytically, the sphere of circulation inhabits qualitative differences, discontinuities between various exchange practices and, consequently, possibilities for
confusion—and for making use of confusion.

Some of the discontinuities in the social life seem difficult to bridge. Nevertheless, people occasionally overcome the discontinuities and *convert* an item,
an object of exchange, from one sphere to another. In such an exchange situation different *value frames* come into contact with each other and the item is converted from one social context to another. Consequently, it is given a new value.
The understanding of conversion processes requires that the essentialist interpretation of the theory of value (i.e. value based on an objective criterion like
the amount of labour[1]) is suspended and replaced with an interpretation which
starts from the premise of the multiplicity of cultural value frames.

In logical terms an exchange of, say, political support and money, can be
mutually rewarding if, after exchange, both parties have a higher level of satis-
faction. The difficulty with exchange rates is that if the exchange rates are not
anchored in an essentialist category (like the amount of labour) it is difficult to
separate an exploitative exchange from one of equal value. In logical terms, the
only situation where exploitation can be definitely measured is the situation
where exchanges make a full circle (e.g. money is exchanged in goods and then
back in more money).

---

1. Baudrillard has forcefully argued that this essentialisation of labour also means its
alienation from concrete social relations and any qualitative differences. Labour, in
Marx's theory of value, is reduced to an almost inhuman capacity for physical
endurance.

All the forms of conversion are complicated and also entail a potential for making use of value differences. The possibility leaves some openings for people with a calculating mind to reap economic benefits. There are always some who are more knowledgeable, permissive or outright eclectic in their value judgements. It is worth pointing out that the calculating mind does not necessarily mean purely commercial orientation. Instead, strategic behaviour may also require temporary investments in cultural capital. Thus the Homo Economicus is a person who knows the local culture and works through it, making use of the ambiguities that prevail in it.

I put so much emphasis on the conversion of an item from one social sphere to another because *conversion is an integral and essential part of diversification strategy*. A household which diversifies has control over the conversion process because it can conduct conversion within the household. For example, a sack of rice, originally classified for domestic consumption, can be put aside and converted to an item of merchandise or exchanged for other items just prior to Islamic festivities, when prices are exceptionally high. When these conversions are made thoughtfully, the household can optimise its resource allocation.

In the following I discuss the sphere of circulation with all its complexity. I advance from crude/general distinctions towards more complex processes. First I present the basic model of 'domains of exchange' that distinguishes three different economic logics. I apply the model to the exchanges that take place in Kilimahewa. My aim is to show how the indirect exchanges influence the price formation. In the second section I discuss theoretically and empirically the process of converting value from one sphere to another. This is the process where the 'domains of exchange' overlap. The third section separates different forms of making profit. The exploitation of the discontinuity between social spheres is seen as a common feature in the profit making strategies. Value conversions are used to conceal and naturalise unequal social relations.

I shall not do a quantitative analysis because the sphere of circulation is wider than the sphere of monetary exchanges and a concentration on countability would be harmful for the understanding of both value conversions and the less visible/unmonetised patterns of exchange.

The domains of exchange

What is the right price for a funeral prayer? Can it be estimated from the labour time that is spent on producing a prayer, with a slight profit margin added on top? Or do we get the price from the bargaining between what the customers feel is the highest price they can pay and the *kadhi* feels is the lowest he can accept? In the peripheral economy, the price setting mechanism works in complicated ways. In many transactions, monetary exchange value is unheard of. In many others, the social relationship between the parties of exchange modifies the exchange value of an item from one transaction to another. When a price is relatively stable, it can be so because of conventions which are totally removed from the considerations of the market situation.

This is not to say that 'practical reasons' or 'personal interests' were not part and parcel of every transaction—these certainly play an important role. However, many transactions also concern other things than the direct object of exchange. They concern the social bond between the parties of exchange. The sustaining of a social bond has an importance which transcends the immediate occasion of exchange. Pierre Bourdieu (1977:184) maintains that "economic power lies not in wealth but in the relationship between wealth and a field of economic relations". This is a good formulation of the basic tenet for a culturally informed economic analysis. When social relations are taken into account we end up with a complex economic system where cultural values, institution-alised practices and mere conventions shape the working of an economy.

The effect of the cultural parameters is not uniform. It slices the local econ-omy into domains where different cultural rules prevail. Each domain has an economic logic which glues together economic motives, ideological metaphors, relations between people, ways of making exchanges and the objects of exchange into a coherent whole. Local metaphors can also be constitutive for the understanding of a domain. In the local metaphors, the will of ancestors or the phenomenon of nature can be used to order the values related to economic behaviour. Thus ideas of 'growth' and 'accumulation', 'industriousness' and 'respectability', or the proper way of 'saving' and 'spending' can be derived from local metaphors (Gudeman, 1986). Thus a domain of exchange does not exist merely as an abstract construction. A domain of exchange is a crossroads where culture-specific productive activities and consumption considerations meet.

I present the basic division of the village economy into the economic domains of exchange in Kilimahewa.[1] I shall first concentrate on the distinctions between domains while, in the later sections of the chapter, I delineate the ways of crossing over divisions. There are broadly three domains of exchange. The first one is the *prestige* domain. It is the domain where cultural capital is valu-able. The second domain is the *commercial* domain. It is the domain of the busi-ness transaction and where monetary utility is valued. The third domain is the *domestic* domain. In that domain the reproductive considerations and domestic power relations have a constitutive role. The distinctions are presented in figure 8.1.

The *domestic domain* of transactions is the most important in terms of the eco-nomic value of transactions in Kilimahewa. Like in most other societies, it is suppressed under the social process of housekeeping and its economic value is undermined. Within the domain, the social relations are subject to continuous changes (due to group dynamics, spatial mobility and physical ageing) and thus the domain is characterised by a continuous 'negotiation' on rights, duties and

---

1. For an elaborated discussion on the domains of exchange see Sahlins (1972).

Figure 8.1. The domains of exchange

Item of exchange	Type of exchange	Type of unequal relationship
Prestige domain		
Protection, respect, identity, food, money.	Indirect exchange: contribution and redistribution; confiscation.	Patronage.
Commercial domain		
Commodities, food, services, money.	Direct market exchanges, network exchange, barter trade, stealing, loaning.	Exploitation, speculation.
Domestic domain		
Food, services, money, commodities.	Contributions, confiscations, gifts, loaning, stealing.	Domestic domination.

relative positions. The economic relations within the domestic domain are enhanced and money is seldom used to pay directly for labour, services or goods. Instead money can be used extensively as a gift or for domestic loans. Most of the loans that people receive take place within the domestic domain of exchange.

The *commercial domain* is characterised by values where making profit at the expense of the transaction partners is a positive value. The social and moral considerations can be brushed aside if they are detrimental to the aim of making profit. The commercial domain is most open towards external exchanges. Yet the extent of the commercial domain is relatively stable in Kilimahewa. This is so because the variety of items exchanged through the commercial domain is limited by the low purchasing power of the villagers. Within the domain, the exchange rates/prices vary according to the season and state of the market.

The *prestige domain* is related to the value considerations where parochial presence—prestige—is the highest value. As I have shown, there are different, competing ways to acquire prestige. The distinctions make the prestige domain a socially dynamic field. The dynamics are also unpredictable because the way of conducting exchanges is indirect. A common pattern of exchange is contributions (i.e. prestations) from commoners to leaders to be used for common causes, and then redistributions (which can be done with different items than those involved earlier) to those placed lower in the hierarchy. The transactions within the prestige domain are, as in the domestic domain, more than a simple concentration on accruing 'benefit' for oneself. Instead, social considerations of networking, relatedness, sharing identity and togetherness are important. Since the prestige domain has hierarchical structures, it furthermore entertains the idea of the accumulation of prestige.

The three domains of exchange usually operate in distinctive contexts which are acknowledged by the villagers. Thus, in the first analysis, the commercial domain covers transactions made in the market place while prestige goods are exchanged in ritual settings. All exchanges have their morally and culturally allotted place.

However, economic exchanges are practical activities where different intentions meet. People have a tendency to stretch the scope of the domain to serve their intentions and interests. For example, a priest can try to stretch the religious hierarchy and the related exchanges to also cover other commitments. Similarly, an old man may stretch the kinship logic into transactions with neighbours. The social logic of exchange is restricting but there are always people who would like to extend the scope of prestige transactions to the commercial domain. And the opposite is also true—those who are engaged to a considerable degree in commercial activities make similar interventions in other spheres. Thus they can use money to pay for labour parties. A commercially oriented person can also send a monetary payment to a funeral, without attending it in person. These examples show that each domain of transactions has hegemonic tendencies—tendencies to provide a 'general' model for all exchanges. In the clash of the different economic domains, the three domains tend to be blurred.

In the previous chapters I have also shown that there are a variety of ways to accumulate cultural capital, economic capital or establish a good household structure. Similarly, the three domains of exchange are internally diffuse. This is a fact which further blurs the lines between the domains.

The forms of economic exchange

Circulation is an extremely complex process where meanings are constantly negotiated and transformed. It is not a simple one-off occasion or a harmless annex to the crucial process of production, as some of the Marxist analysts argue. The sphere of circulation accommodates a number of forms of exchange. Broadly speaking the forms of exchange can be described as a continuum from direct monetary exchange to indirect non-monetary exchange.[1] In addition there are one-directional appropriations like confiscating and stealing. The continuum has at least the following variants:

- trading
- barter-trading
- selling own products
- giving contributions
- stealing

- borrowing
- confiscating
- gift exchange

---

1. The differences between different categories are fluid but qualitative in many ways. Marshal Sahlins puts it this way: "... the distinction of one type of reciprocity from another is more than formal. A feature such as the expectation of returns says something about the spirit of exchange, about its disinterestedness or its interestedness, the impersonality, the compassion. Any seemingly formal classification conveys these meanings: it is as much a moral as a mechanical scheme" (Sahlins, 1972:192).

As shown in figure 8.1, trading, barter and selling one's own produce are commercial domain actions. The other forms of exchange refer to varying extents both to the domestic and prestige domains.

I have already described the different items that are traded in Kilimahewa. The bulk of the trading is conducted in monetary terms. Most branches of trading are competitive but due to the erratic supply and erratic nature of trading, the availability of goods is far from constant. This is reflected in some prices while others are determined by conventions. Curiously, the price ratio takes into consideration the cost of the trader's labour input: a smaller amount of grain gives a lower unit price. Presumably the seller's eagerness to sell also makes it easier for a shopkeeper to lower the price.

The amount of barter trade is rather small. It is certainly smaller than in the beginning of the 1980s when many items were officially prohibited from petty trading, access to items was difficult and, consequently, dealings had to be conducted in more shady ways. There are a few occasions when professional traders engage in barter trade as a form of concealing monetary prices. Some cashew traders have noted that they have bought cashew against aluminium pots, exchanging a potful of cashew nuts for the pot itself. The case of Hassan (presented in Chapter 3) is an example of such a strategy. In general, barter-like arrangements are most typical for shopkeepers when they get involved in hoarding food crops and collecting cash crops. The traders sell cloth, food and other items against crops.

The selling of one's own produce should be separated from trading. Those selling their own produce have much more scope for determining the price than those engaged in trading (i.e. buying in order to sell). The difference is that when selling one's own products there is the possibility to value the labour input at a level which is below the normal payment because subsistence agriculture covers the bulk of living expenses. In other words, it is possible to undercut prices without causing any direct problem for working capital. The low price level of local products can be partly explained by the fact that the producers systematically undermine the value of their own labour.[1] The production of the home-made mats is an extreme case. The amount of time used for collecting fibres, making them smooth, colouring and weaving them into a mat is enormous compared with the price of the mat. Women who make the mats engage in the activity because they classify the labour effort within the bottomless pit called domestic chores.

Giving contributions is a common activity in the sphere of communal consumption. Contributions are given to leaders who are then supposed to distribute the items to the needy. The cycle of contributions is very common in Islamic activities where large amounts of food are mobilised for feeding public gatherings. Also the provisions for the poor and the upkeep of mosques are

---

1. Rural producers selling their own products can place themselves under exploitative circumstances. In other words, they cultivate their own food and thus cover their own costs for the reproduction of labour.

organised through contributions. A similar pattern is observable in the life-cycle rituals which are organised by a household but where wider kin and ethnic affiliations are mobilised.

Contributions are the basic form of indirect exchange. The person making a contribution has no guarantee that he/she will receive the same amount of a similar item in return. Actually it would be a breach in the code of conduct if a similar amount of the same item were returned directly. The idea of contributions is that the social relationship is given predominance and the economic transaction is concealed.

A gift exchange is basically a similar indirect exchange to a contribution. The difference is that gifts are given in different social contexts and they do not necessarily imply a hierarchical social relationship. In Kilimahewa, gifts of food items are continuously given to kinsmen and friends. Gifts are the material expression of the continuation of a relationship.

The scope of lending/borrowing is slightly different from gift exchanges. Typical loans are tools and money. When money is borrowed from a friend or relative, no interest is expected. Nevertheless, it is conventional to add a 'gift' at the time of repayment. The size of the gift (or interest) tends to be at the same level regardless of whether the loan was short- or long-term.

The last two forms of exchange are one-directional exchanges. Confiscation means the use of positional power to take things from subordinates. Some forms of tax collection and contributions to district funds could be termed confiscation. This is so because force is used to collect dues and the villagers have no direct benefits from them. 'Contributions' were demanded earlier for the major ceremonies of the CCM party. During the era of multi-partyism CCM has not been able to enforce collections in a similar manner.

Confiscation can also be argued to take place within domestic groups. This is a strong feminist interpretation of the role of young men (who just visit the house to eat) and older men (who can even sell food to pay for their own drinking) given by some bitter women. A more tolerant interpretation would say that domestic usurpation is compensated by other services in other situations. I shall return to this during the discussion on 'domestic domination'.

Stealing is the second form of one-directional exchange. I have already discussed the prevalence of the stealing of crops. Stealing takes also place in the village area and it is a matter of great concern. Most households try to keep at least one person at home to prevent stealing. If they cannot do that they ask the neighbours to keep an eye on the house. Stealing is morally condemned but it is also acknowledged in the village that stealing has an equalising impact on the income distribution.

The variety of the forms of exchange is thus extensive. Even monetary exchanges can take several forms. The use of money even in non-commercial indirect transactions is seldom seen as immoral.[1] Money is acceptable for most

---

1. Cf. Parry and Bloch (1989) on the discussion on the moral values attached to monetary exchanges in various kinds of social contexts. Their examples show that the relationship

of the forms of exchange. The problem is that Kilimahewa is a poor village and the circulation of money is low. Money is a scarcity commodity—during the lean months money almost disappears from the scene. What poor people have left during the lean months is food in their stores, the ability to labour in their shoulders and a large amount of imagination. These resources help to keep the transactions going even when money is scarce.

The chains of transactions

I have briefly presented the different forms of transactions. One might get the impression that the world of goods and services is neatly divided between these forms. Indeed, there are a few items which are exchanged only within a distinctive cultural sphere and which never receive a monetary value. For example, the mask of the masked dancer is an item with tremendous symbolic value which cannot be spoiled by monetary considerations.

However, the complication comes from the fact that the items tend to travel through many hands and several transactions. The sale of an item may be followed with a gift exchange, then stealing and trading, before the item is finally consumed. In other words, the sphere of circulation includes a number of secondary exchanges. In these secondary exchanges even the most definite 'commodities' become socially tamed and culturally appropriated: they receive new values. This almost always happens to the most popular female cloth, kanga, a plain cloth with colourful figures. It is most often imported from India and sold against cash for a fixed price. But it is usually given as a gift to a woman and in this transaction its monetary value is 'forgotten'.

In other words, the domain of commercial transactions is contested by the prestige domain and domestic domain. The item originating from the commercial domain is tamed during the secondary exchanges. This is exemplified in figure 8.2.

The exchanges of food items are the most common exchanges and also the most complicated. The exchanges with food can include loops where a socially tamed item is brought back to monetary exchanges. For example, a person may provide a chicken as a gift to a poor relative. The poor relative can then sell the gift onwards to get a more needed item.

The consequence of the movement of goods between the prestige domain, domestic domain and commercial domain is that the different economic domains may enter into all phases of the economic cycle. All domains are used, to some extent, in the access to labour and other means of production. All three domains shape the value given to an item in the sphere of circulation. And different economic domains shape the consumption patterns in parallel.

---

between monetary exchange and commercial values can be contested on many occasions.

Figure 8.2. A chain of the forms of exchange: The case of a bowl of rice donated to an Islamic festival

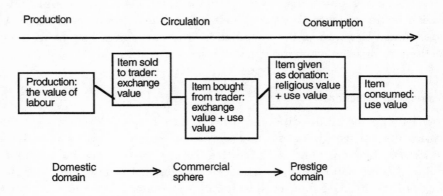

Often the production-related forward and backward linkages necessitate the linking together of transactions. Even a simple production process requires a number of exchanges. Alternatively, a household can use inter-sectoral diversification to gain access to all the raw materials. For example, the making of a hoe is a fairly simple process but still requires several exchanges before the scrap metal, charcoal and the labour of an assistant are available for a smith.[1] Building a house requires a much longer chain of transactions. In Kilimahewa, a person constructing a house for himself may, for example, cultivate groundnuts which are exchanged with maize which is then prepared as food to pay for the communal labour party at the construction site, while the expert labour is paid with money acquired through trading crops in the town. The same town visits are also used to acquire a few town based materials while most of the materials are obtained by exchange through local networks. Linkages like these look very natural.

To sum up, the circulation of the resources can take various direct and indirect forms. What is interesting here is that any single 'product cycle', however commercial it originally is, may include a chain of secondary transactions. These secondary transactions are equally central in the allocation of, and access to, resources. The secondary transactions create expectations of reciprocation and thus entitlements and dormant 'capital'. Although, for example, taking care of the well-being of the relatives and the common good of the community do not pay off directly, the investment in these social spheres through secondary

---

1. Earl P. Scott has identified similar long chains of transactions in beer brewing in Zimbabwe. "Because of the lack of cash, beer brewers must engage in two or three non-farm activities and in an equal number of stages of exchange in order to generate the cash or barter needed for the grain they require to brew seven-day or opaque beer. It is not uncommon for brewers to weave baskets, mats, trays, and the like, and to barter them for grain (or to sell them and use the cash to purchase grain) that is in turn used to make beer. This labour-intensive process of production and exchange to assemble farm labour is clearly daunting, but women struggle on due to the limited ways available to them to generate cash" (Scott, 1995:197).

transactions creates vested interest, demands for reciprocating and social networks.

So far I have discussed the sphere of exchange as if it were a simple technical matter to shift from one domain of exchange to another or from one form of exchange to another. This is not always the case. In the next section I look at those processes of circulation which break the mechanistic idea of reciprocity. I study the conversion of items where the ambiguity in the comparative value of the exchanged items is used for personal benefit.

The conversions of the values

What are conversions?

Conversion is the kind of operation where an item is transferred from one social sphere to another. After this transfer it is subjected to a new value frame. For example, an agricultural field can be converted from a measure of the lineage continuity to an economic productive resource by a mental re-categorisation. In other words, it is converted from a kinship symbol to a commodity. The trickiness of this kind of conversion is that it breaks the stable logic of fixed values. The possibility of conversion shows that values are inherently unstable: continuously negotiable and contested.

The conversion of land from kinship symbol to a potential commodity does not need to relate to any external transaction. However, it becomes an interesting issue when a conversion is done in conjunction with a transaction between people. In the context of transaction, an item is transferred from one person to another person who then fixes it in a new social context. In this process the value of the item changes. We must remember that the value of an object of exchange is not its intrinsic feature. Instead, this always depends on the relation of a person to the item. Two people can share a totally similar view on an item. Thus a transaction does not necessarily mean a conversion of its value. However, there are numerous reasons for people to place different attributes on an item.

Wealth differentials are often created through timely and clever conversions. It is important to notice that the process of converting values is a way of producing a benefit without a major labour input. Instead, the benefit results from the exploitation of the existing diversity. The value differential may be a consequence of the imperfect or segmented markets, different valuation patterns and different power positions. Whatever is the source of different social values, the value or price of the object of conversion varies accordingly.

From the perspective of the perfect market, conversion seems to be swindling. However, it is not necessary to take a highly moralising attitude against

Figure 8.3. The conversion of value

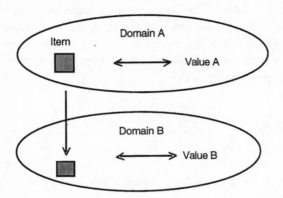

conversions. We know from the theories on value that it is difficult to establish where a profit equals the labour input (and risks and responsibilities) of the person organising production/circulation and when an exchange is exploitative. But the methodological problem of establishing boundaries should not hinder us from doing analytical, and tentatively empirical, work on the process.

Money and food as easily convertible items

There are two kinds of items which play central roles in transactions in Kilimahewa. These are food and money. These items are exchanged in all three domains of exchange. For this reason, they also have a crucial role in the processes where the borders between domains are tested, contested and either reproduced or crossed.

Food production sets the rhythm for the annual calendar of activities. The cosmological distinction between the period of arduous work and leisurely consumption is defined by food production and consumption. Food distribution also plays a role in all festivities, whether they are related to religious events, communal celebrations or life-cycle rituals. Often the food served at these public occasions is different from what is eaten daily. Food is the means to communicate togetherness and the spirit of sharing. Thus food is an item of the prestige domain of exchange. In the commercial domain, food is naturally a major item of exchange. Practically all types of food items are offered for sale. The distinction between cash crops and food for personal consumption is fluid and an item initially planned for personal consumption can be put on sale when the relative prices change. In the domestic domain of exchange, food is one of the major items of exchange. Access to food is subject to cultural taboos and conventions but these are seldom definite. The amount of food consumed by each household member is keenly observed and discussed. The continuous negotiations on the access to food makes food a key item of exchange for measuring relative power positions within the domestic group.

Thus food is exchanged in the prestige domain, commercial domain and domestic domain. The multiplicity of the occasions when food is exchanged makes food a suitable medium for conversions. Food can be subjected to several exchanges which form a chain where each exchange redefines the meaning attached to food (cf. figure 8.2).

Another item which, to the same extent, exists in different domains is money. It can be used as an expression of appreciation in the prestige domain of exchange. It is very much used in commerce. In the domestic domain of exchange, money is still rather marginal but it has proved to be a practical item in e.g. gift exchanges between household members living away from each other. The advantages of money are that it is easily transported, it has a certain degree of permanence and it is countable (although in non-commercial uses the counted amount can be secondary to the act of giving). Moreover, money tends to lose its history of previous exchange. Thus it is an excellent medium of exchange.

Together, money and food provide a backbone for the economy, occasionally bringing the separate strands together. Human encounters continuously create situations where qualitatively different items are compared. This brings cultural dynamics to the heart of economy. Economy is a practical activity for interpreting and making statements about the cultural world.

I shall return to a theoretical discussion on the conversion of values in the final chapter.

Unequal exchanges

In each domain of exchange, the unequal power relations are a source of unequal exchange. In the following section I present four ways to take advantage of unequal power relations in exchange relations. The methods of unequal exchange are capitalist exploitation and speculation in the commercial domain, patronage in the prestige domain and domestic domination in the domestic domain. Most exchanges may look neutral (i.e. reproducing the accepted hierarchy) from a cultural perspective. It is characteristic of unequal power relations that economic inequality is 'enchanted' and concealed by cultural valorisation.

Exploitation of labour in commercial domain

Capitalist exploitation is a very popular and widespread form of unequal exchange. At its basic model it takes a cycle

$$M \to L \to M'$$

where M stands for money invested to buy labour which then produces valuables worth a larger sum of money. This is certainly a process which takes place in Kilimahewa. The agricultural worker, who is paid Shs. 500 for digging a whole day, is only paid the necessary reproduction cost of his labour. He can eat for three days with that money, or provide food for his family for a day, but that is all. And he can certainly not work every day as he also need time to rest, be sick or attend to social obligations.

What are the profits for the agricultural employer in relation to the employee? Let us take the example of coconut tapping. A coconut tree is either tapped by a tapper who works as an employee, or a tree is rented to a tapper who tends to conduct the work on his own. In both cases the person doing the tapping will get approximately half of the farm-gate selling price of Shs. 13 per bottle. This deal does not look particularly bad for the tapper and actually coconut tappers are looked on more as artisans than as poor labourers. The next phase in the production cycle is that the coconut beer is transported by another carrier to the beer place for a payment of two to three shillings per bottle. The bottle will be sold at 20 shillings. The profit margin of the beer place owner is only five shillings and with that margin he needs to cover the costs of the beer place as well as pay for a barmaid. Thus we end up with a calculation:

Owner of trees	6–7 Shs.
Tapper	6–7 Shs.
Carrier	2–3 Shs.
Bar-owner/barmaid	5 Shs.
Total	20 Shs.

The 'surplus value' extracted by the owner of coconut trees through organising the tapping, but without any other labour contribution, is considerable.

In the long run, normal coconut cultivation (rather than tapping) brings higher returns and thus the rich farmers avoid resorting to tapping trees. They say that tapping coconut trees is an option for a careless farmer because it spoils the trees, making them totally unproductive after some years (and also spoils the people who drink too much alcohol). The largest surplus value from coconut trees can be acquired through selling coconuts. The following example on coconut cultivation gives some indication on the upper limit of exploitation in the village: a person cultivating coconuts needs to pay a climber one shilling per coconut (or one coconut per coconut tree); another coconut per tree is paid to the watchman who looks after the trees and cuts the grass under the trees; a coconut is then sold at some twenty shillings, giving the surplus value of eighteen shillings (if we do not count the cost of land rent) for the owner of the tree.

The coconut trader may also acquire high profits. The trader buys a coconut for twenty shillings. One more shilling is used for a labourer for carrying it to the store and another shilling for a labourer shelling it. If the trader organises transport to a distant town together with other traders, the costs of transport can be minimised. The price of transporting varies a lot depending on how this is organised. The cost of hiring a lorry can be over 20 Shs. per coconut. A few shillings are needed for loading and unloading it in another location. The selling price for a wholesale trader is between 60–70 shillings in distant locations. The following break-down shows the distribution of income:

Coconut cultivator	18 Shs.
Watchman	1 Sh.
Climber	1 Sh.
Carrier	1 Sh.
Breaking shell	1 Sh.
Loading/unloading	3 Shs
Transport	20 Shs.
Trader (including own travel expenses)	20 Shs.
Total	65 Shs.

In this equation, the owner of coconut trees gets a considerable amount of money for practically no work. He is engaged in exploitation because he receives his share as an owner of capital. A trader, for his part, works with a larger number of coconuts and receives, in a given time period, more profit than a normal farmer. It would not be fair to say that the trader is solely an exploiter—he has actually very arduous work and definite risks—but his terms of payment are certainly much better than those of his labourers. This conclusion entails the proposition that the exploitation of labour is simultaneously an expression of both capitalism (in the way it exists in the reality of imperfect markets) and screwed value conversions (marking the discontinuity between labour and commodity markets) in Kilimahewa.

Speculation in the commercial domain

Another form of conversion is speculation. It is actually also part and parcel of capitalism but it does not directly depend on the antagonism of labour and capital. Speculation may be based on price fluctuations caused by conjunctures, seasonal variations, or disruptions in the accessibility of goods. All these factors cause erratic price formation. At the same time, the conventions of pricing seem to stabilise the prices of other items. Price formation in a peripheral economy in real markets is an art in itself; describing price formation as a meeting point of aggregate supply and demand is a very unsatisfactorily explanation (cf. Raikes, 1993). In a peripheral area like rural Lindi district practically all the textbook criteria of the efficiently functioning capitalist market are lacking. There are huge discrepancies in the access to price information, capital and transport between different localities, between people in these localities, and across different seasons. There are also large variations in buying power and perceived need between localities and people according to season. Thus segmentation of both supply side and demand side actors is the only feasible starting point for the analysis. The fortunate aspect of the market deficiencies is that they enable the peripheral economy to sustain a marked division of labour and wide trading system.

The most important form of speculation is seasonal speculation. Seasonal speculation through hoarding food crops is an increasingly common practice which still arouses negative feelings but which is nowadays certainly becoming the order of the day. The crops which are subject to speculation are mainly locally produced rice and maize imported from other regions. For example, the market place price of rice can vary from Shs. 200 to Shs. 400 within a span of half a year. This seasonal fluctuation hits even harder at a poor household which needs to sell its future crop to cover the current living expenses and, in the process, gets involved in a kind of delayed barter arrangement which is likely to be most exploitative. Since rice is a luxury food the possibilities for speculation with rice are mostly geared towards satisfying urban markets. In this situation, the local speculators and traders compete with urban speculators. The urban based administrators and traders do their best to secure a good amount of rice. The deals can be made well in advance so that the harvested crop remains stored in the scattered go-downs of the original sellers. Thus the activities of the urban speculator are less spectacular. The bags of rice are later sold on the urban market where rice is consumed in competition with poorer quality imported variety.

The price fluctuation of maize is also dramatic. One reason is that a major production area (Songea in the southern highlands) is seasonally almost cut off from Lindi. The roads are impassable just before the time when the scarcity of

Table 8.1. The price of rice, maize flour and cassava in Kilimahewa market January 1994–February 1995

	Rice price	demand	Maize flour price	demand	Cassava price	demand
1994						
Jan	250	***	120	***	50	***
Feb	300	**	150	***	50	***
Mar	300	***	120	**	50	**
Apr	350	**	100	*	50	**
May	350	***	100	*	50	**
Jun	300	*	120	**	30	*
Jul	225	*	140	**	30	*
Aug	180	**	140	**	35	*
Sep	180	**	150	***	40	*
Oct	180	**	160	***	40	*
Nov	200	***	160	***	50	**
Dec	273	***	170	***	50	**
1995						
Jan	350–400	***	180	***	100	***
Feb	430	***	180	***	100	***

(The information is based on the trader's memory. The estimates of demand hinges on relative demand within one crop and they should not be compared with other crops.)

maize reaches its peak. The traders and speculators who have the means to transport maize in advance and store it properly can secure good profits. Maize is the preferred staple food in Kilimahewa and the local production is below the consumption.

The seasonal diagram of the cultivation is shown in table 8.2. It shows the various tasks done during the different months. The peak seasons for labour are the season for hoeing and planting from September onwards and the period of weeding from January onwards. The harvesting of the crops takes place over several months.

In Kilimahewa, access to the staple food is heavily cyclical. Malnutrition and a very low food intake is evident in February and March. The seasonal poverty was investigated with two questions. The first asked the number of months for

Table 8.2. Agricultural calender in Kilimahewa

	Jan	Feb	Mar	Apr	May	Jun	Jyl	Aug	Sep	Oct	Nov	Dec
Annual crops												
Rice	W	W,TP	TP, S	W, S	W, S	H	H			Pr	P	P
Simsim	W	W	H	H	H		Pr	Pr	Pr	P	P	W
Cassava	W	(H)						H	H,P	P	W	W
Millet	W	W					H	H		Pr	P	P, W
Maize	W	W	H	H	H					P	P, W	W
Pigeon peas	W	W					H	H		P		W
Sweet potato						H	H				Pr, P	
Sugarcane	Pr, H	Pr, H	Pr, H	Pr, H			P	P	P	W	W	W
Ocra	W	W	W	H	H	Pr	Pr	Pr	Pr	P	P	P
Red pepper	P	W	W	H	H	H	H	Pr	Pr	Pr	Pr	P
Groundnut	W	H	H						Pr	P	P	W
Perennial/ tree crops												
Cashew	H					F	F	W	W, H	W, H	H	
Mango	H	H								H	H	H
Pineapple	No specific season											
Banana [1]	No specific season											
Pawpaw [1]	No specific season											
Orange [1]	No specific season											
Lemon [1]	No specific season											
Coconut [2]	No specific season											
Agricultural labourers	W **	W **	H **	H **	H **	H **			Pr *	Pr **	P **	P ***
Rain	***	**	**	*	*					**	***	***

Pr = Preparing the land. P = Planting. TP = Transplanting. W = Weeding. F = Applying fungicide. S = Scaring the birds. H = Harvesting

1. First year of production. Lemon and oranges provide fruits after 5 years while bananas and paw-paws can produce much faster.
2. First harvest eight years after planting. Coconut is harvested four times a year. Weeding at convenient times.

buying the major staples. The result shows clearly that the food reserves are depleted in the poor households soon after January and the buying of food (often at high prices) is necessary.[1] The second question asked the number of the months when food is cooked only once a day. Here the response was less consistent with wealth differentiation, a fact which was explained by the different cooking practices: some women cook twice even when the amount of food is very small.

The seasonality of cultivation is the key to the timing of other economic flows in the village. After harvesting major food crops, the economic activities shoot up. Food is sold and different items are bought. During this period, the services prosper: the tea-rooms are opened again, food and drinks are sold in plenty, bicycles are repaired, new hoes are made, and the tailors receive orders. Many festivals take place during August to October when food is available and the demand for agricultural labour has lessened. Many households get a second boost in October to January when they sell cashew nuts. Since cashew is not seen as a food crop the money can be used freely without being tied to household responsibilities. During February the period of scarcity hits the village. The labour demand is equally high at the same time. The poor people need to sell their labour at the expense of maintaining their own fields. The money can be used to pay for food at inflated rates. At the same time, the rich people tap into their stored food reserves. The price fluctuation is such that the price of a sack of maize and rice normally doubles during the periods of scarcity. When these crops are sold in smaller amounts the price differentials get even higher. Another method to increase the profit margin is selling against payment in the future crop. These practices of hoarding have become common and they have a major impact on wealth distribution.

Speculation is equally caused by external policy changes. For example in cashew trading, the first five years of the 1990s have been a period of continuous changes. Each year has been unique and a person who has had access to information—or who has made a right guess—on the development of markets and prices has been able to make huge profits. Throughout the 1980s, cashew was collected by the government monopsony system where the price was set by the national marketing board. Its operations were far from efficient and the external control of pricing meant that the farmers received the residue after everything else had been deducted. (Cf. Ellis, 1980 and Jaffee, 1994 for the governmental pricing policies and Seppälä, 1998b for the overview of cashew production.) This varied naturally from one year to another, as did the modalities of payment, but the state organised buying offered few opportunities for speculation among local traders. The liberalisation of markets also increased the opportunities for speculation. The liberalisation of cashew marketing has been conducted step by step, preceded or by parallel to the demise of state marketing agencies. In Lindi region, the regional cooperative society was still supposed to

---

1. Cf. also tables 4.2 and 4. 6.

collect cashew nut in the 1990/91 season but it was too indebted to be able to finance the collection efficiently. During the following buying season, the private traders were allowed to buy cashew nuts and the official collection record of the regional cooperative diminished to a level of a quarter of the previous year's record. During the 1992/93 season, private traders were even allowed to export cashew. Yet the primary buying was officially organised through cooperatives. In practice it meant that the private traders funded the buying and the cooperatives worked as centres for weighing crops, collecting levies and paying the farmers. During 1993 the primary cooperative structure was restructured but, due to lack of financial capacities, the restructuring was of little consequence. Later on, the large-scale private traders established their own collection posts and started more direct competition. Throughout the 1990s, the petty traders had increasing opportunities to work as middlemen between farmers and the large-scale traders. The opportunities available for them varied from one district to another. The prices varied heavily throughout the buying season and the traders could double their profits by buying slightly earlier and selling later. During the latest buying seasons, the price dropped heavily at the very end of the buying season as the large-scale traders ran out of financing (or when harvesting started in India and the competitive Indian cashew entered the world market), thus leaving some speculating petty traders and farmers stranded with their stored cashew nuts (cf. Seppälä, 1998b).

Another case of speculation relates also to the imperfect markets in monopsonistic situations. In the sesame trade we find an example of the control over markets by a large Tanzanian company. The company was clearly a major agency interested in buying sesame in 1993. It announced that it had opened a buying depot in Lindi town and bought sesame at Shs. 160 a kilo. Many small traders made an effort to buy sesame and bring it to town. However, they were met with a new statement that the price announced referred to the first few tons only. The new price was only Shs. 100 per kilo. The farmers and traders were forced to sell at a loss but, consequently, the sesame production slumped the following year.

In all strategies of speculation, the right timing is essential. One can do exactly the same things as the other producers/traders. The only difference is that the successful person has managed to sell at the time when the price has been at its highest.

Patronage in the prestige domain

The conversion of values can similarly take place between cultural and economic capital. The most obvious means for such a conversion is the patronage relationship. I have already argued that often an investment in cultural capital brings primarily benefits within the realm of that capital itself but it can also be converted to monetary gains. The link between investment and benefit tends to be indirect and delayed. These factors make it impossible to calculate definite cost–benefit balances and the subsequent conversion rates between capitals.

An example of the patronage network is a chain from a wealthy local man called Hassan through local mediators, Ahamadi and Hamisi, to the villagers. Hassan is a curious figure. He has managed to accumulate a large amount of property through engaging in various kinds of economic activities which have little in common but which have fitted in well with the local conjunctures. Hassan is an industrious man with a modest educational background. He started as a lorry driver but his breakthrough was buying a coconut plantation cheaply when an Indian owner moved away after independence. Since then he has managed to accumulate another coconut plantation, a tractor, two lorries, a pick-up, a hotel and several rental properties. Hassan has a good reputation as a proper patron who helps those in need. He usually lives in town but he also has some wives in the adjoining village and during his visits he is very approach-able. Hassan listens to requests for loans (which he gives free of interest), provides transport for the sick to hospital and attends important funerals. During the Islamic festivals he slaughters animals for general consumption and thus upholds the community spirit. On the other side of the balance sheet he has had some dubious dealings concerning a major item of village property. During the early 1980s, when the villages were provided with loans for produc-tive projects, the village had acquired a tractor. The tractor was difficult to maintain and administer, however, and the village soon accumulated large arrears of payments. The bank confiscated the tractor and handed it over to Hassan who was supposed to help the village. Since the handing over the tractor has remained solely for Hassan's own use. Another major intervention has been the private cashew trade through cooperative collection posts. Hassan managed to acquire the position as sole buyer of cashew from the Kilimahewa primary cooperative society in 1992/93. He bought 90 tons of cashew at the official floor price and made a good profit. In the buying season 1993/94, the competition was much harder but he still bought a good share of the 80 tons sold through the cooperative collection post. During the season 1994/95, he was again the sole buyer as the major competitors had opened their collection posts in different localities. The price he offered at the local cooperative was lower than the price offered by the competitors but if one counts the transaction costs (travelling, waiting time, insecurity of deals in the other location etc.) a farmer could as well sell to him. Many of the small farmers sold cashew nuts directly to petty traders who sold the cashew nuts onwards either at the local cooperative society (i.e. to Hassan) or to other traders in other localities. Most interestingly, Hassan developed his own network of petty traders who bought cashew nuts directly outside the collection post. Thus he managed to dump the price in the large scale trading system, and to buy cashew nuts at a still lower price through a subsidiary petty trader system. Obviously his activities have negatively affected the profitability of growing cashew in the area.

Hassan is a patron of the community but he also has special clients. Perhaps the cooperative secretary is such a person (as was the secretary's brother who was a village chairman until thrown out after the tractor saga). I have mentioned Ahamadi and Hamisi as other clients. They use their position in the classical way, presenting themselves as gatekeepers to Hassan. Ahamadi is a poor and sick man but earlier he worked in different positions in Hassan's business and in the village organisations. He still knows Hassan personally and he can pass on good and bad words. Ahamadi is an equally poor farmer but he is most eloquent in twisting words in political speeches. He was recently elected as a district councillor, to the dissatisfaction of the 'progressive' villagers. Ahamadi is totally absorbed in parochial politics but he also makes the best out of friendship with Hassan. One example of reaping material benefits from this is when both of them acted as the weighing officers for Hassan when Hassan bought cashew.[1] It was necessary to pay a 'fee' for these 'officers' to have the cashew nuts accepted at all, and when accepted, having them graded as the first class.

This example of patronage shows that a person investing in respectability and a good name is allowed to do things which otherwise would be directly condemned. The position as a respected person with clients gives backing for making less respectable deals.

Domestic domination

The domestic arena is an arena where economic, social and cultural values are most intertwined with each other, creating a pattern where power needs to be continuously negotiated as a response to situational needs. The conversion of values is a major object for endless debates. The streams of income from commercial projects have to be divided between household members and there is no simple way to value the work accomplished in income-generating activities versus the reproductive work accomplished to keep the household members clean and fed.

In the domestic arena, the comparison of claims takes place against the background of delayed and indirect forms of exchange—a pattern which makes it difficult to measure the conversion rates. What people are often debating in their 'domestic contract' is the commitment to the common good and long-term security for reasonable entitlements, but these debates are carried out in terms of the practical issues of the day-to-day division of tasks. Thus, the hot discussions on what food is cooked and how much time each should spend at funerals may as well be indicators of the more diffuse concern of domestic politics.

It seems evident that domestic relations provide ample opportunities for accumulation by one family member at the expense of the other family

---

1. In that year most of the buying was conducted so that cooperatives were the sites of buying and the cooperative officer was involved in measuring the weight for taxation purposes but the actual sale was conducted between a producer and a trader. For this reason, a trader needed his own representatives to supervise the buying.

members. Especially some middle-aged and elderly men notoriously use the household as their private labour force, spend most of their time on village affairs or merely socialising at the beer place while visiting home mainly to eat and sleep. They contribute very little to shared consumption while they classify the contribution of the other members of the family as common property—to be managed by the male head.

The structural effects—How value conversions shape rural development patterns

The circulation of resources is a process which connects different parts of the village economy together. The qualitatively distinctive domains of exchange continuously come in contact with each other. In these encounters items are converted from one domain to another.

One effect of the continuous conversions is a lively economy which could be described in terms of modernity (i.e. cyclical change where modernity appears through new challenges to tradition, which, over time becomes a part of tradition) or even postmodernity (i.e. the coexistence of different value frames which are fragmented and subject to individual appropriations). The commercial domain of the economy provides only a part of the items that people consume. The biggest part of services and daily food is acquired through the domestic domain and some through the prestige domain.

I have spoken of the importance of the circulation for the distribution of resources. I have shown that villagers use a good part of their time and effort on the activities of circulation. Trading and speculation are seen as significant ways for enrichment. Some researchers emphasise that circulation deals only with the distribution of the resources and not with the growth of productivity. In this way it is 'unproductive'. On the other hand, one could argue that the sophisticated sphere of circulation helps to increase the division of labour among primary producers and in this way has an indirect impact on the productivity. Nevertheless, it is true that the large effort given to circulation drains resources from activities which would directly increase the total capital stock.

How do the exchange patterns influence differentiation in Kilimahewa? Is Kilimahewa a location of wild speculation and ruthless exploitation? I have shown different potential ways of conducting unequal exchanges. In practice it is very difficult to calculate which of the exchanges are actually unequal. Inequality can be counted only for the direct exchange of goods in a situation where the exchange partners share a common value frame. It is much more difficult to calculate inequality for the indirect provision of immaterial services in a situation where people do not share a common frame of reference. The countability of the inequality in exchange is guaranteed only in circular exchanges like money-labour-money.

With these reservations it can be said that the capitalist exploitation of labour has entered the village; speculation with food has become a common practice; the established patronage linkages mean a drain of resources from the village; and domestic domination goes unchecked because the patrilineality/ matrilineality controversy is unresolved and no clear domestic authority structure has emerged. These mechanisms have a historical origin and it is unlikely that the recent national level policy change from a state-dominated economy towards economic liberalisation policies has created them. Yet it is evident that economic liberalisation (conducted in piecemeal fashion through continuous policy changes), when bringing all cash crops and especially cashew within the area of private trade, has increased the scope for trade and speculation.

Chapter 9

Informal Sector and Diversification in Rural Tanzania

The most striking stylised fact about African rural households is that they have highly diversified economic activities, many of them non-agricultural.

Jan Willem Gunning: *Explaining African Economic Performance*

Given the fact that most civil servants made so much more income from their sideline activities than from their jobs, it is a wonder that they chose to remain employed at all. Most people who engaged in sideline projects saw them as an honest way to earn a living and found the notion that they might be undermining the government or Party in some way absurd.

Marja-Liisa Swantz and Aili Mari Tripp: *What Went Right in Tanzania*

In this chapter I move the analysis to the level of the national development path of Tanzania. I focus on the growth of the informal sector during the past decades. I discuss the push and pull factors which have been conducive to this process. Thus issues such as the industrial strategy during the first decades of independence, the resistance against state dominance in the years of economic crisis, and the social dynamics during the present period of structural adjustment are placed under discussion.

Although the available data is patchy, I gather comparative evidence on the tendencies towards diversification in rural Tanzania. To accomplish this I need to use statistics on income sources, main and secondary occupations, and the like. This data is unreliable and biased in many ways. Some of the side-line activities have been criminal or otherwise morally suspect and this fact has led to underreporting. In addition, the survey format has seldom been so permissive that it has allowed for the enumeration of petty economic activities. Thus the evidence on diversification is circumstantial.

The chapter is divided into four sections. The first section concerns the history of employment generation in independent Tanzania. I analyse the various push and pull factors which have led to an increasing informalisation of the economy. In the second section I concentrate on micro-enterprises, assessing the extent to which the rural micro-enterprises are either independent units or supplementary sources of income in the wider diversification strategy of a household. The third section analyses the importance of networking for the viability of small production units. The fourth and final section compares the interpretations of the political economy of rural dynamics in Tanzania. I place Hydén's 'economy of affection' side by side with neoliberal adjustment thinking and the sober 'development from below' perspective.

The history of employment and entrepreneurship

During the colonial period the efforts to raise the productive capacities of the nation were rudimentary. The development strategy fostered by the colonial government was directed towards agricultural development and even in that sector, the level of investment was low. The managerial capacities remained equally undeveloped as the educational facilities were very scarce and the racial policies of employment hindered the Africans from fully participating in entrepreneurship. Consequently, the Asians and Europeans were artificially over-represented in entrepreneurial circles.

The government of independent Tanzania was faced with constraints created by the colonial past. The envisioned solution for the engine of growth was the utilisation of state resources in capital accumulation. During the first decades of independence, Tanzania followed an industrialisation policy and agricultural policy which were based on heavy state intervention in productive activities. In order to gain control over the strategic economic factors, the government nationalised major industries, trading bodies and financial institutions. Although the act was in accordance with the development strategy it is obvious that the socialisation also aimed to reshape the racial power balance in the country.

The industrialisation strategy of the government meant the development of a substantial number of large-scale assembly and manufacturing industries and wholesale and retail marketing organs. In the early industrialisation policy, the large-scale enterprises tended to have a significant percentage of employment while medium-scale enterprises provided far less employment. The enterprises were generally formed as semi-independent parastatals and the total number of separate parastatals reached over 300 units. Since the government had full control over financial institutions and regulated the price of foreign exchange, the financing of the parastatals was dependent on governmental decisions. The output prices of the parastatals were similarly controlled. The industrialisation strategy was backed by donor funding and the system generated a major increase in productive capacity in a short period of time. However, much of it was never taken into use. The operational logic of parastatals under soft budget constraints was hardly conducive to the economic practices which would have supported the development of financially independent and profit-making institutions. When the fiscal problems of the government increased, the problem of the sustainability of the industrial strategy became obvious (World Bank, 1996:9).

During the 1980s, the industrialisation policy was changed along the lines of the structural adjustment policies. The change was slow in the parastatal sector as it has been very difficult to privatise the indebted organisations. Some positive development has taken place in the private sector and, for example, the manufacturing growth rate has increased from the figures of the early 1980s (World Bank, 1996:17). The private sector has continued to be dominated by entrepreneurs with Tanzanian Asian/foreign background. They have been able to locate local and international solutions for the financing of their operations. The entrepreneurs with Asian background have also developed extensive national networks which make it possible to make transactions within the network without the accompanying direct transfer of money. By contrast, the African entrepreneurs have been more often hampered by the lack of financial support due to the dismal functioning of financial institutions. Consequently, the micro-enterprises have had great difficulties in developing into medium and large-scale enterprises. The same observation has been made in several other African countries.

The total labour force is estimated at around 11 million in Tanzania. Less than 10 per cent has employment in the formal sector. The Labour Force Survey estimated that only 0.81 million people are employed in the formal sector as their main activity and that 60 per cent of formal employment is within the public sector (World Bank, 1996:128). In the past decades, some government establishments have grown in size. It is, however, noticeable that real salaries have fallen continuously over the past two decades until mid-1990s. Thus a majority of the public sector employees have been unable to live on their meagre salaries (Bol, 1995). For this reason they were forced to start sideline activities (Seppälä, 1999 forthcoming).

Focusing on the informal sector (i.e. micro-enterprises with five or fewer employees)[1] we can readily note that there are several push and pull factors which have generated the growth of the informal sector. First, the failure of the industrialisation strategy has meant that large private and public establishments do not provide many work opportunities. Second, and related to the first aspect, the collapse of the marketing system at the end of the 1970s meant that the customers needed to resort to informal (and forbidden) black market operators to reach consumer goods and food. Third, the decline of public sector wages directs people to the informal sector. Fourth, the decline in real producer prices of cash crops (and delays in payments) meant that the non-agricultural

---

1. The choice of concept to describe small-scale economic activities is far from self-evident. A major discussion has been conducted on the merits and dismerits of using concepts such as enterprise, micro-enterprise, non-agricultural rural employment, income-generating activity or just economic activity. In the following I shall use the size of employment as a major criterion of separation. I shall use the concept micro-enterprise to describe economic units with five or fewer employees. I shall use the concept of informal sector to describe at aggregate level the non-agricultural non-formal employment in micro-enterprises. Above the category of micro-enterprises there are medium-scale enterprises (with 20–100 employees) and small-scale enterprises (6–19 employees).

activities became a relatively more competitive source of income. Thus, in terms of employment generation, the informal sector has been an expansive sector for the past two decades.

Several studies show that the most dynamic part of rural employment generation takes place at the micro-enterprise level (Dawson, 1993; Bagachwa, 1993; Dawson et al., 1991; CIBR, 1995; Parker et al., 1995). The actual number of the people engaged in micro-enterprises depends on the definition of the lower limit, that is, the definition of when a minor economic activity can be classified as a micro-enterprise. I shall return to this issue later on.

Analysing micro-enterprises

The voluminous literature on the informal sector has convincingly shown that the understanding of the operations of micro-enterprises should be based on criteria which are different from those used in the analysis of larger enterprises.

I make a distinction between conventional enterprise analysis and permissive enterprise analysis. Conventional analysis uses the standard factor of production analysis as its starting point. A micro-enterprise is analysed in terms of its capital resources, labour resources and management skills. The inputs and outputs are estimated and a calculation is made on the efficiency of the use of production factors and the overall profitability. Conventional enterprise studies have the advantage of clarity and system accompanied by a standardised and widely accepted conceptual framework. The major problem with this approach is that the primary data tends to be poor for such a systematic analysis because the entrepreneurs seldom have a proper bookkeeping system and they tend to mix the finances of the enterprise with their personal finances. The entrepreneurs can be very elusive in their answers. For these reasons, the personal considerations and ambitions of the researcher can easily influence the results. Thus it is possible to find studies which emphasise the lack of every possible production factor as a reason for failure: some studies concentrating on technology locate the lack of tools, the educational specialists locate the lack of managerial skills while the economists locate the lack of credit. After piling up a number of 'lack' studies one starts to wonder about the utility of the production factor analysis.

The conventional micro-enterprise studies try to explain why the micro-enterprises remain as small as they are. The idea behind the studies is the striving towards a larger enterprise size as the only criterion of successful operation. A good summary of this orientation is given by Fafchams (1994). An alternative way of posing the question is to ask, how do the micro-enterprises manage to remain in operation, and even increase in numbers, given their presumed operational deficiencies. Do these micro-enterprises have strengths which remain unnoticed in the conventional production factor analysis? Any permissive enterprise analysis should try to locate such strengths.

It should be obvious for the reader that my major candidate for the strength of the micro-enterprise is its flexibility as a part of the more complex livelihood strategy. The livelihood strategy allows for the micro-enterprise to use some resources at a sub-optimal level and even to cease operations temporarily without necessarily harming the long-term existence of the micro-enterprise. All this is based on diversification. Diversification is a strategy which allows an entrepreneur to combine different elements and resources in a manner which does not serve the immediate interest of a strictly defined entrepreneurial unit but which does serve the interests of an entrepreneur.

The permissive analysis of the micro-enterprises starts from the micro-level considerations. The crux of the analysis is the performance of the social entity behind a micro-enterprise (usually a domestic group). Thus the continuity and profitability of that single enterprise does not have a definite value per se, but only in relation to the livelihood strategy of the domestic group.

The very openness of the permissive analysis of diversification as a livelihood strategy makes it problematic for comparative analysis. Given the diluted framework it is difficult to compare micro-enterprises with larger enterprises. It is certainly questionable to start from the issues of industrialisation policies and polarise the micro-enterprises and larger enterprises as the "low road" and "high road" to industrialisation. The is hardly constructive because the two modes of organising production serve different ends. Instead of polarisation it is possible to follow another path where different enterprise sizes are perceived to have distinctive advantages which lead into a complementary division of functions. According to this view, the micro-enterprises are able to carve out for themselves market niches because they can specialise in low-cost production on location and season specific markets. Their flexibility gives them advantages which are hard to measure in the standard instruments of commercial profitability. In this chapter I shall study more closely the forms of networking and flexible specialisation that are available for micro-enterprises in Tanzania.

In the following sections I aim to use the available national level data and discussion to provide an analysis which describes the operation of Tanzanian rural micro-enterprises from the perspective of diversification. Since the available studies start, with minor exceptions, from the conventional 'factor of production' perspective, it is difficult to find completely suitable data. I have collected the relevant parts of the existing surveys and I shall present them in as systematic way as possible.[1] The material used is mainly statistical and many reservations on the concepts and the reliability of data could be presented. I

---

1. The major studies with regional and national level discussions are Collier et al., 1986; Maliyamkono and Bagachwa, 1990; URT, 1991; URT, 1992; Bryceson, 1993; Havnevik, 1993; World Bank, 1993. Itala (1997) and Madihi (1997) have published recent comparative statistical data on the informal sector in Dar es Salaam. Tripp (1996 and 1997) has studied the urban informal sector in Dar es Salaam. The studies of Xavier (1997) and Trulsson (1997) also have relevant discussions which, however, concentrate on urban small- and medium-scale operators.

argue that the discussion has only superficially penetrated the characteristics of rural diversification. [1]

In the remaining parts of this chapter I aim to demonstrate the following issues related to diversification:

1) the tendency to diversify from agriculture to other income-sources has been significant throughout the past two decades.

2) the complete extent of diversification is difficult to determine because several activities are tiny part-time activities. The statistical data on diversification usually underestimates the extent of the part-time activities. The reliance on categories like 'profession' and 'enterprise' mean that tiny activities are not included.

3) The economic value of the non-agricultural rural activities has often been undervalued. More precisely, the value of the extraction of the natural resources is valued very low and the personal and communal services are omitted from several studies. The reason behind this tendency is the difficulty to give a monetary value to items which only partially enter the monetised economy.

4) Diversification is explained in some recent political economic literature as a resistance to the state. This view undermines the positive element in diversification. Diversification also implies active striving to cope with economic challenges.

Vertical diversification in rural Tanzania

The percentage of people engaged in non-agricultural activities

It is difficult to estimate the percentage of people that are engaged in rural non-agricultural activities because of the manner in which they are operated. The study of Deborah Fahy Bryceson (1990) is an interesting starting point because it explicitly discusses the division of labour as an important developmental indicator. She summarises her historical argument by stating that food insecurity has been the major concern for the rural population and whenever the food situation has deteriorated the division of labour has eroded.

---

1. Even the concept of diversification has many interpretations. When rural sociologists speak of diversification, their reference is the diversification from agriculture to non-agricultural sources of income. When agriculturalists speak of diversification they usually refer to horizontal diversification to new crops at the level of a household farming system. Vertical and horizontal diversification are suitable terms to make clear the distinction between the points of departure. I concentrate upon vertical diversification.

Diversification is a concept with yet another connotation. It is used extensively in the studies on external trade where it implies the increasing share of non-traditional exports. In countries which have only a few major tradables, it is necessary, it is argued, to diversify the export portfolio. Thus, a country which is dependent on exporting coffee and tea may diversify to exporting gold or fruits.

A more quantitative assessment was carried out by a fairly recent Informal Sector Study (URT, 1991). The Informal Sector Study estimates that 29 per cent of rural households were engaged in the informal sector in 1991. The Informal Sector Study defined informal sector activities as non-agricultural labour units with five or less employees.[1]

The Informal Sector Study was well formulated as a national survey. Yet it had the conventional problems of survey methodology: the study had to use formal questionnaires and formulate the question (on rural income formation) in such a manner that it would reveal easily comparable results. Its results can be challenged by the study of Kjell Havnevik (1993). Havnevik made a detailed study on the productive activities in the poor Rufiji district at the beginning of the economic crisis in 1979–80. Yet he estimated that 64 per cent of the economically active population were engaged in non-agricultural productive activities (Havnevik, 1993:167).[2] In my analysis I have also obtained high rates of participation in non-agricultural activities. My analysis also includes trading and services which were largely excluded from Havnevik's study.

The World Bank (1996:81) estimates that 78 per cent of Tanzanian households have more than one source of income. The poor households have slightly more often than rich households diversified income sources. Similarly, rural households are more likely to have diversified income sources than urban ones.

The difference between the Informal Sector Study (one third of households), Havnevik (two thirds of economically active people) and the World Bank (more than 78 per cent of rural households) depends crucially on what is counted as a *significant* economic activity.[3] The question is whether the tiny, temporary and marginal income sources should be classified as separate productive activities. There is no clear demarcation line on what is an economic activity and what should be left out of the analysis. Survey studies usually aim to give an overview on the 'main sources' of income. The methodology creates a hindrance to noticing minor economic activities. For example, Havnevik has located a large number of women engaged in making mats. This kind of activity is seldom noted when heads of households are questioned on the household economy. The problem is not only that the questionnaire interviews create sus-

---

1. I follow this definition. It should be noted that the definition does not refer to the lack of licensing. Thus a fully registered but very small enterprise falls within the category. This is a deviation from a conventional definition but it can be defended on the grounds that licensing does not create any decisive difference. Non-licensed micro-enterprises are also subject to market fees.

2. In 1980, Collier et al. also carried out a survey on the level of the individual and using 'occupations' as an entry point. They interviewed 1800 persons over 12 years in rural Tanzania. They counted the rates for primary and secondary occupations. Some 17 per cent of the studied people claimed to have a secondary occupation while agriculture was usually mentioned as the primary occupation (Collier et al., 1986:42–3).

3. For comparison, see Pedersen (1994b:10) for the various estimates of the prevalence of rural households with non-agricultural activities in Zimbabwe. He shows a wide variation in estimates. The difference stems from what is included in the category of non-agricultural activities.

picion among the informants. My experience is that people tend to forget such minor activities. Many minor activities are perceived as hobbies, daily necessities or social commitments. Only when directly confronted with the specific question does a person see that, say, making and selling mats is actually an economic activity.

Diversification: the combinations of micro-enterprise and other activities

Diversification is difficult to capture by means of survey studies. If we focus on the households which have mentioned that they are engaged in the informal sector, we get one set of households. Table 9.1 shows the sample of households having a micro-enterprise in the informal sector. Within these households, only 10 per cent of male and female operators concentrate solely on their enterprise. All the others also have other sources of income.

Table 9.1. The major other activity of the rural informal sector operators (%)

Other activity	Male	Female	Total
None	10.3	10.4	10.4
Wage job, govt.	2.4	2.8	2.6
Wage job, parastatal	0.6	0.3	0.6
Wage job, private	0.5	0.1	0.4
Agric+Livestock	86.3	86.4	86.0
Total	100	100	100
(n)	(794,785)	(335,631)	(1,130,416)

(URT, 1991:2/31)

The table shows that the informal sector operators overwhelmingly had agriculture as their other major source of income. Only some three per cent of operators also had government employment. This is natural given the low level of governmental employment in rural areas. The table did not allow for a combination of two informal sector activities.

The Informal Sector Study also asked whether the enterprise studied was the only micro-enterprise of an operator. The rural operators mentioned a second micro-enterprise in only three per cent of cases. Three different micro-enterprises were mentioned in only 0.4 per cent of cases. This would indicate that each person had usually only one informal sector activity. These figures are low because the threshold for the 'enterprise' category is so high. Again, minor tasks are left outside the calculation (cf. URT, 1991:1/21). It is also worthy of note that the study asked about the 'other major activity' at the level of one individual. At household level it is possible to locate more diversification.

The importance of the non-agricultural sources of income

Non-agricultural sources of income do not usually provide full-time engagement in a special activity. Instead an activity is combined with a major activity, which is usually farming and occasionally wage labour or another non-agricultural activity. This appears clearly in the analysis of the main source of income. In the Household Budget Survey 1991/92 only seven per cent of rural households mentioned 'business' as their main source of income (URT, 1992:33).

Table 9.2. The main source of income in rural households

Main source of income	% of households
Sales of food crops	47,1
Sales of livestock products	5,3
Sales of cash crops	23,3
Business income	6,9
Cash wages/salaries	11,6
Casual cash earnings	1,6
Cash remittances	0,5
Fishing	2,1
Other sources	1,7
Total	100

(URT, 1992:33) [1992=household budget survey]

It is worth pointing out that the question of the main source of income gives very limited—and easily misinterpreted—information on the economic activities.

We obtain the first estimate on the importance of the non-agricultural sources of income when we count the monetary value of the activities for the producers.

The economic crisis was hitting very hard in 1982/83 when a survey was carried out on the differentiation of rural income sources. At that time, the individual's own business brought in over 40 per cent of non-livestock cash income for the lowest and highest quintile, while the middle groups relied on a variety of income sources, including wages and remittances.

Table 9.3. Rural cash non-livestock incomes in 1982/83

| | Quintiles | | | | | |
	1	2	3	4	5	Total
Crops	48.4	48.6	54.1	31.3	27.9	32.8
Own business	41.1	19.5	17.1	20.3	63.9	47.1
Wages	9.0	20.5	10.0	29.1	4.8	11.5
Remittances	1.5	11.4	18.8	19.3	3.5	8.6

(Sarris and van den Brink, 1993:149)

In total, the category of "own business" amounted to 47 per cent of the rural cash non-livestock income. Thus even when business is seen as a secondary source of income, for a great majority of rural households it produced a substantial proportion of their cash income in the early 1980s. The figure is astonishingly high, given the difficulty in studying 'own business', which was very much out of favour (with the consequent tendency to underreport it) at that time.[1]

During the last decades, the formal sector labour force has increased. However, the real public sector wages decreased by some 80 per cent from 1970 to 1986 (Ærøe, 1991:9). After that time wage deterioration has continued. The wage deterioration has been high for government employees although, among them, some white collar workers receive substantial fringe benefits like daily allowances. The result of all this is that the importance of wages and remittances is currently much lower for the rural household than what it was during the early 1980s. The shrinking of the formal sector wages has helped the relative growth of the informal sector.

Sarris and van den Brink have calculated the relative percentage of agriculture, the informal sector and formal sector for the income generation of the rural households. They show that the poor households rely mostly on agricultural income (82 per cent). By contrast, the rich households receive the bulk of their income from 'informal sector' (81 per cent). Sarris and van den Brink have also studied the change in the relative importance since the inception of the Ujamaa policy to the time when liberalisation policies were first implemented seriously. They show that the relationship between agriculture and the 'informal sector' has been relatively constant, with the exception of the rural rich who have increased their participation in informal activities.

Table 9.4. *The percentages of informal activities and agriculture in the total household income. (Rural Tanzania 1975–1989)*

	1975–77	1978–80	1981–83	1987–89	1987–89
Rural poor					
Agriculture	81.3	81.0	81.3	82.3	82.1
Informal	16.8	17.5	18.2	17.4	17.6
Rural middle					
Agriculture	55.1	55.4	58.4	59.6	59.5
Informal	34.7	37.0	40.3	39.7	39.8
Rural rich					
Agriculture	11.4	12.2	15.1	15.5	15.2
Informal	47.6	55.6	76.9	80.4	81.4

Sarris and Van den Brink, 1993:182

The national analysis shows that the wealthier households currently receive the major part of their income from non-agricultural activities.

---

1. For example, the respondents made a questionable claim that they used a major part of their labour time outside their own farms for communal work in the study of Collier et al. (1986:49).

Micro-enterprises in Rural Tanzania

The distribution of non-agricultural activities

The Informal Sector Study used Tanzania's formal occupational classification. It then aggregated the occupations into 29 types of micro-enterprises. The types of micro-enterprises were further aggregated to six sectors. The distribution of the types of micro-enterprises is given in table 9.5.

Table 9.5. Informal sector employment by type of micro-enterprise

Sector Type of micro-enterprise	Micro- enterprises (percentage)	Informal sector employees (percentage)	Total informal sector employment ('000 persons)
Agriculture & Fishing			
Fishing	7	11	110
Mining and quarry	0	0	4
Manufacturing			
Food processing	2	1	31
Clothing making	4	1	52
Mats & Fibre	8	1	99
Wood products	7	11	117
Charcoal making	2	1	21
Clay products	4	3	47
Metal products	2	1	21
Other manufacture.	2	0	17
Construction			
House building	1	2	13
Masonry	6	7	88
Other construct.	1	1	12
Trade/restaurant/hotels			
Shop general	4	8	71
Cooked food sale	2	2	29
Fruit/vegetable. sale	2	2	33
Fish/meat sale	2	5	88
Food uncooked	3	0	40
Local beer sale	18	19	254
Charcoal sale	1	0	12
Restaurant/food stall	3	6	54
Other sale/ trading	5	4	79
Transport			
Bus and taxi	0	1	7
Other transport	3	7	59
Communal and personal services			
Shoe repair	1	0	8
Electrical repair	0	0	3
Vehicle repair	0	0	2
Traditional medicine	2	2	24
Other services	3	1	34
Absolute total numbers	1,154,136	288,861	1,419,277

(URT, 1991:1/23; 2/35)(Due to rounding off the totals are not equal with 100.)

The national analysis shows the highest participation rates in beer sales, fishing and selling fish and meat. A more recent study by Chachage Chachage (1995:69) shows that mining has recently become an important income source and that the small mines give employment to hundreds of thousands of people. This is an astonishing figure, even when it includes some other service sector employment in the mining communities. It is likely that mining has become one of the biggest non-agricultural activities in a relatively short period of time. It is also likely that it was underestimated in the Informal Sector Study because it still had a clandestine reputation in 1991.[1]

The ownership of micro-enterprises

The Informal Sector Study also asked about the ownership structures of the micro-enterprises. It used the concept 'operator' which includes all owners of micro-enterprises whether they have any employees or not. The study estimated that there are some 1.1 million operators in rural areas and that 70 per cent of operators were men. These operators employed 300,000 employees of which 66 per cent were men. It is easy to work out that an overwhelming majority of rural micro-enterprises did not have any employees. Moreover, only a small part of this employment is regular wage labour. However, the rate of employment is not insignificant. This is evident from the following table.

The category of 'other' includes family labour. This covers half of the employment in micro-enterprises. We can estimate that not more than every tenth operator has an employee who is not a household member.

Table 9.6. The labour contracts of the employees in rural micro-enterprises

Type of employment	Male	Female	Total
Paid regular— apprentice	4.0	0.2	2.7
Paid regular— other	15.2	10.8	13.8
Paid cash— part-time	33.0	5.9	23.8
Unpaid— apprentice	9.1	0.1	6.0
Other	38.7	83	53.7
Total	100	100	100
(n)	(190,812)	(98,049)	(288,861)

(Source: URT 1991, 2/35)

---

1. The Informal Sector Study was repeated in Dar es Salaam in 1995. This survey showed that the number of people engaged in the informal sector had increased by some 2.4 per cent per annum. Wholesale and retail trade had increased in relative terms and become the largest activity in the informal sector (Madihi, 1997). Unfortunately, the survey was not extended this time to rural areas.

Employees were most often mentioned in beer sales, fishing, woodwork, shops, transport (other than buses/taxes) and masonry. Employees who were not family members were mostly employed in beer sales and shops (URT, 1991:2/35–7).

The vulnerability of the non-agricultural economic activities

The rural non-agricultural activities tend to be a vulnerable source of income. The vulnerability of the micro-enterprises can be characterised with three indicators. The first is the number of the years that a micro-enterprise has existed. The second is the seasonality of the activity. The third indicator of vulnerability is the profitability of the micro-enterprise (i.e. monthly profit or the value added per unit of investment). It is worthy of note that none of the indicators directly measures vulnerability since all the three indicators also reflect other factors.

As shown in table 9.7, the average age of the rural micro-enterprises is relatively low. Especially transport, trade and the catering business have many relatively recently founded units. This can be interpreted as an indication of vulnerability but it may also be caused by the low entry requirements in these sectors, or as a consequence of the recent improvement in trading the environment.[1]

The age structure of the micro-enterprises in the mining industry is interesting. It indicates a boom of new activity in 1989–90. The number of new mining micro-enterprises (which are less than one year old) is, in comparison, very low. There is no other data which would explain (or confirm) this fluctuation in establishing mining activities.

The seasonality of the rural informal sector enterprises is very noticeable. Only communal and personal services are carried out throughout the year by more than half of all the practitioners. It is very likely that even those service providers who work the year round have a large variation in their monthly turnover.

Table 9.7. The age of rural micro-enterprises by sector
(Number of years; percentage share of the row category)

Sector	Up to 1	1 – <3	3 – <5	5 – <10	10 >	Total
Fishing	17.0	9.6	17.8	28.8	26.8	100
Mining and quarrying	2.4	38.4	4.8	37.7	16.7	100
Manufacturing	6.0	15.6	17.7	23.9	36.8	100
Construction	6.8	16.4	21.1	22.3	33.4	100
Trade/rest./hotel	17.9	25.5	22.0	18.3	16.3	100
Transport	26.1	22.3	29.1	15.2	7.3	100
Comm. and per. serv.	8.8	18.2	11.6	23.8	37.6	100
Total	13.1	20.2	20.0	21.3	25.4	100

(URT, 1991:2/5)

---

1. Cf. Seppälä, 1998d for the detailed analysis of the characteristics and competitiveness of food traders in rural Tanzania.

Table 9.8. The seasonality of the rural micro-enterprises
(The number of months operated per year; percentage share of the row category)

Sector	0–3	4–6	7–9	10–11	12	Total
Fishing	13	26	6	9	46	100
Mining and quarrying	21	23	3	23	30	100
Manufacturing	19	34	15	5	27	100
Construction	29	33	15	7	16	100
Trade/rest./hotel	19	26	15	7	32	100
Transport	23	35	13	5	24	100
Comm. and per. serv.	8	15	17	5	55	100
Total	19	29	14	6	32	100

(URT, 1991:2/10)

The monthly profit is a third indicator on the differences between enterprises. The monthly profit is counted for the months of operation only. The average value added per month (Shs. 4.200) was above the minimum wage level of Shs. 3.500.[1]

Table 9.9 shows that only mining, fishing and construction have a median profit of 5–9.900 while other sectors have below 5,000. As these three sectors are relatively seasonal, we are likely to locate relatively few of the enterprises with both a good and year-round profit record.

The fishing sector has a substantial share of enterprises with high profits. Perhaps the figures on the fishing sector indicate the complex arrangements between boat and net owners, fishermen and fish traders. It is not likely that independent fishermen would form that part of the fishing sector which receives the high profits.

The productivity of an investment gives an indication of the risks/security of the investment. Here one needs to note, however, the differences in the aver-

Table 9.9. Rural micro-enterprises by ranges of monthly profit (percentage)

Sector	Ranges of monthly profit						
	–900	1,000–2,400	2,500–4,900	5,000–9,900	10,000–19,900	20,000+	Total
Fishing	4.0	19.3	9.5	24.1	27.6	15.5	100
Mining and quarrying	12.0	24.9	7.2	44.5	8.3	3.1	100
Manufacturing	19.3	26.8	24.7	17.6	6.6	5.0	100
Construction	5.7	19.5	22.1	28.0	17.3	7.4	100
Trade/rest./hotel	14.3	22.5	24.4	20.4	9.6	8.8	100
Transport	6.1	28.0	25.2	21.7	10.6	8.4	100
Comm. and per. serv.	22.7	22.3	25.8	17.5	8.6	3.1	100
Total	14.7	23.6	23.3	20.4	10.4	7.6	100

(URT 1991:2/12)

---

1. The minimum wage has, however, decreased to a low level in Tanzania. It cannot be interpreted to mean a household subsistence level. In 1985, when the minimum wage was at a very low level, it equalled two kilograms of maize flour per day (Ærøe, 1991:10).

age size of investment and in the liquidation time of the different types of investment. Table 9.10 tells us that mining and quarrying and construction are likely to provide considerably larger value added to the unit of investment. Here it is good to remember, however, the very low level of initial investment of the rural gold diggers and the house constructors. They carry out work with minimal tools and, if other materials are needed, these are often provided by the person who works as a patron or who has commissioned the work. Given the initial low level of investment, it is easy to receive high returns on the investments.

Table 9.10. The profitability of investments in rural micro-enterprises by sector

Sector	Value added per unit of investment
Fishing	4.6
Mining and quarrying	10.5
Manufacturing	2.9
Construction	7.9
Trade/rest./hotel	2.8
Transport	0.4
Comm. and per. serv.	1.9
Total	2.4

(URT 1991, 1/19)

To sum up, the analysis of micro-enterprises shows a considerable degree of variation within the sector. There are some sectors like mining and trading which seem to be growing fast. There are others where new prospects are more limited. The understanding of micro-enterprises should start from the fact that a majority of them provide only part-time employment which needs to be supplemented by other income sources.

The political economy of diversification

In this section I discuss diversification from the perspective of political economy. The explanations for diversification are sought from rural development studies with broad and provocative approaches where two issues are worthy of separate discussion. First, in order to place the development of the rural division of labour into a political perspective, it is important to study the political relationship of the rural producers with the state. Particularly, it is fascinating to study the theory of 'the economy of affection' proposed by Göran Hydén and to compare it with the diversification theory. Second, the structural adjustment policies and the accompanying reform programmes have often been used as a frame for explaining the dynamism of micro-enterprises. I shall question this connection. In my analysis, the growth of micro-enterprises largely precedes structural adjustment. Actually, some adjustment policies (especially those aiming to reduce demand) may work against the further expansion of the informal sector in the liberalised (post-adjustment) economy.

The economy of affection

Göran Hydén (1980; see also 1983) has written a polemical interpretation of the Tanzanian economy. He has introduced into the debate the concept of 'economy of affection' which has many elements which I could endorse. His basic argument is that rural producers have their own networks and thus they can challenge the state and even the market mechanism. It is easy to agree with this view to some degree. Certainly, the market mechanism and state policies are modified by the local cultural patterns and the latter are construed on the basis of affectionate social relations. The resistance towards external interventions (especially adverse pricing and marketing policies) has been an important motivational aspect directing the livelihood strategies of rural producers.

However, there are certain issues where Hydén makes too abstract or figurative generalisations. Hydén speaks about the relative autonomy of the rural producers from wider societal processes, more specifically the autonomy of producers from the influence of the penetration of capitalist competition. In this issue his concepts are allusive. His conception of autonomous households actually entails an entitlement approach where household is understood not as an autarchic unit but within a context of locational and regional interdependence. In my view, this specification is important. The social sphere of the local producers is so wide, and their dependence on circulation so central, that there is no sense in speaking about household autonomy. However, Hydén does not advocate for household autonomy, either. Instead, he speaks of relative autonomy of a household as a part of local networks.[1] This formulation is far more compatible with empirical studies on Tanzania.[2]

We start to face problems when we try to analyse more closely how, according to Hydén, the economy of affection functions. Hydén (in Hydén and Peters, 1991:304–5) paints a picture of the African 'peasant mode of production' with following characteristics.

> First, no real exploitation of peasants by another class was occurring, although there was obviously surplus extraction going on, but that was confined within essentially lineage or clan or kinship units. Second, land tenure and the control of the means of production remained in the hands of those units—the peasants themselves—rather than in the hands of a landlord class that had alienated the land from the peasants. Third, the technology used by the peasants was very rudimen-

1. Hydén defines affection as "networks of support, communication, and interaction that exist among not only kinship units but also communities and other groups that might be described as held together on the basis of mutual sharing of positive sentiments for each other" (1991:305).

2. Nevertheless, there are also a few pockets in the Tanzanian landscape where truly capitalist agricultural labour relations are developing. See Loiske (1995) on Mbulu district.

tary and therefore there were no real functional or structural linkages—backward or forward linkages—between agricultural and non-agricultural sectors as is found in other parts of the world, where peasants have become much more integrated into either market- or state-controlled production systems... On the basis of that, I suggested that the peasants themselves were, if not fully uncaptured, then relatively autonomous and uncaptured, compared to peasants in other parts of the world.

Although this picture holds in a world-wide comparison, it provides only limited tools to understand the dynamics within rural economy. When it comes to these dynamics, Hydén lumps everything in the rural economy together and says that affection is the organising principle of production and exchange because there are no significant distinctions between people. The people are suppressed by their sameness. But what actually takes place within rural communities is an elaborate division of labour and a multiplicity of exchange networks.

In the polemical articles, Hydén presents a negative idea about the effects of the economy of affection on development. His concept of development is tied to modernisation and the economy of affection becomes in his analysis an embodiment of all evil—an antithesis of modernisation. My conception of development is totally different. I acknowledge the value of local culture and local ways for providing security and respectability; thus my conclusions on the effects of these patterns on rural development are completely different.

Hydén contextualises his argument in relative terms. He says that the market and state have not been able to penetrate rural areas because of the economy of affection. Here the economy of affection becomes the opposite to an abstract market principle which is presented devoid of any social context. This fetishist notion of 'market' is very common in liberal economic theory. When we bother to study the *realexistierende* markets we find, however, social relations always impinging on them. The social relationships within this economy tend to have a component of affection but this component is not contrary to the market principle but a local application of it. When I argue that 'cultural capital' always tends to make its inroads into the economy I argue along these lines.

In general terms I argue that what are termed 'economy of affection' or 'patron-client relationships' are not marginal phenomena, and certainly not an unchanging 'dead end' of an economy. Instead, they form a dynamic form for economic interaction. Moreover, this form is not antagonistic to the market relationship. Thus the local economy should not be analysed as a separate entity but always in relation to other economic processes. Nor should it be conceptualised as subjugated social relations determined by the wide market mechanism. Instead, the local level specialisation produces items and services which are competitive. It produces items and services at a modest price that people need and can afford to buy.

Division of labour implies that a household has a bundle of different sources of income which partly overlap and partly differ from the packages of the other households. The difference in portfolios is a precondition for exchange between the households. I simplify this to the utmost through playing with numbers. While one household may have five income sources, there are still ninety-five other economic activities in the village. The household may not need to have access to all of them but, given the similarities of consumption patterns and the 'basic needs' character of most activities, the household needs access to most of them. There are also some activities which are accessed from neighbouring villages and townships. All these relations generate exchange. This is what I have called the lively 'village economy'.

The discussion on the informal sector, on the one hand, and agricultural production, on the other, have been too compartmentalised in Tanzania. There is a vital link between agriculture and non-agricultural sources of income. Particularly, we need to emphasise the central role of the extraction of natural resources and agricultural processing. These activities provide a variety of food and consumer goods which are universally circulated into economic exchange networks. The important issue is how these activities can fully enter the analysis.

The exchange of food does not always follow the routes of commercial trade. Instead, a lot of food exchange takes place exactly according to the routes of 'affection' that Hydén delineates. Some of this production and exchange falls under the category of the 'gift economy'. The important issue here is that the produced items only tenuously leave the domestic sphere. Much of the exchange takes place within a wide group of affectionate relationships. Much of the exchange is 'delayed' exchange where a gift is reciprocated by another gift sometime in the future.

The Hydénian perspective has generated a lively debate on the contestation of power from below. This resembles the discussion that has been generated by James Scott's analysis of the 'Weapons of the Weak' (1985; cf. Tripp 1997 for Tanzania). The recent studies on rural development have emphasised the historically unexpected results of the contestation of power. The studies show that the central government control (whether during the colonial period or after it) has not been as decisive as the earlier historiography has postulated. An extremely finely tuned analysis of rural development along these lines has been written by Sara Berry (1993). In her words, rural development is a result of 'negotiation'. This does not mean concrete debates but merely that different interest groups tend to formulate stances which have an effect on the behaviour of the other groups. The political process is thus never top-down orders but an outcome of direct and indirect interest conflicts (Seppälä, 1996b). I shall return to this theme in the next chapter.

The political studies show increasing sensitivity to the motives for the diversification of livelihood strategies. Diversification to new activities is not simply either an 'exit' from the state-citizen relationship, or an entry to the market relationship. Instead, the concrete social relationships may generate superficially similar tendencies of diversification in which are embedded simultaneously (and paradoxically) a variety of motivations for making economic alliances (Tripp, 1996; 1997).

From crisis to structural adjustment—continuities in the development of micro-enterprises

The explanatory models for the growth of the informal sector, emanating from the 'economy of affection' perspective, had their heyday in the crisis years of the early 1980s. Later on the explanations which give credit to market mechanisms, fostered by structural adjustment programmes, started to gain predominance. The structural adjustment programmes have been implemented since 1986 in Tanzania. In this section I study this complete turn about in the official policy. I argue that the official policy has had less impact than expected, because the tendency towards diversification has continued from the pre-adjustment period.

As a part of the adjustment process, the entrepreneurs have been given a heavy responsibility for generating development of Tanzania. Entrepreneurs are expected to make a central contribution to the general growth of prosperity and private sector development is a widely circulated catchword to describe the ideology of development efforts in the 1990s. This orientation is in sharp contrast with the previous policies which continued from the mid-1960s to the mid-1980s. During that period, entrepreneurs were widely looked downwards upon as selfish people who were claimed to destroy societal harmony. The party officials labelled private sector entrepreneurs as racketeers, criminals and saboteurs. Private ownership was stated to contradict the socialist goals of Tanzanian society. However, the variant of socialism that Tanzania adopted was based on highly centralised power structures which turned out to be inefficient because of the bureaucracy and vested interests. It became increasingly apparent that the system could not deliver what it had promised: free basic services and a steadily increasing level of prosperity.

The change in the official policy was dramatic. However, it partly reflected a necessary acceptance of change that had already taken place behind the official policy: the economic crisis had created a growing informal sector which provided a wide variety of goods and services to the ordinary citizen. The informal sector was a buzzing scene of trade, crafts and services consisting mainly of micro-enterprises with limited capital and tools. Because of the small scale of units, the informal sector activities were difficult to uproot. The government made several attacks against the informal sector, but all in vain. The decisive episode was the 1983 Human Resources Deployment Act which was so harsh a policy, directly afflicting the ordinary people in their daily needs, that the government had to change it tactics (Tripp, 1996; 1997). After the failure of the 1983 policy, the government turned slowly towards the acceptance of the informal sector, first in practice and later on in official policy declarations. Even the central CCM party changed its nominal constituency from the workers and peasants party to a party of workers, peasants and businessmen (Shivji, 1993:222). Within a decade, the saboteurs were upgraded to developers.

Another reason for the change in the policy relates to the macroeconomic situation and the pressures exerted by the donors. The economic problems had their roots in declining agricultural production, further exacerbated by expensive social sector policies, the Ugandan war and the oil crisis. The expensive policies meant that the government had to tax rural producers heavily, thus decreasing their incentives to produce crops for the official marketing system. This enhanced the fiscal problems of the government and worsened the external trade balance. When import capacity was reduced, the heavily state-governed large-scale enterprises were unable to purchase necessary inputs and soon they were running at a very low level of productivity. Thus the official sector production decreased, making way for informal sector provisioning.

The Tanzanian economic situation was described by the word 'crisis' all the time from the mid-1970s to the late 1980s. After that period, the official figures show that the economy has strengthened. However, economists have raised doubts about whether the official figures reflect the truth. According to Sarris and van den Brink (1993:57) the so-called crisis can be interpreted as a crisis of the formal economy. Below and beside (if not above) it, the non-formal economy continued to function through its own logic.[1]

Similarly, the recent economic recovery may be rather thinly spread. It is possible that the benefits are most visible among the large-scale traders. The World Bank's poverty study ended up with figures where 36 per cent of all Tanzanians live in households classified as hard-core poor in 1991 (World Bank, 1993:3).[2] In its recent evaluation, the World Bank concludes its review of the distributive effects evasively: "Economic growth is better than in the past decades, but this will not provide dramatic improvement in living conditions" (World Bank, 1996:147).

Given this history, we need to look cautiously at the capacity of the private sector to function as the driving force of the economy. History shows that there has hardly been a 'conducive' environment for the accumulation of private sector expertise for very long. Many new institutional features supporting the private sector are still embryonic and thinly spread. And when several state governed parastatals have collapsed, the mix of enterprises is heavily weighted towards small-scale enterprises.

---

1. Sarris and van den Brink (1993:56) have estimated that the non-formal 'second economy' composed one fifth of the national economy in 1970. Since then it grew steadily and it composed a third of national economy in 1988. Maliyamkono and Bagachwa (1990) have reached the fairly similar result. It is worth noting that 'second economy' means largely unregistered and illegal practices—economic activities outside national accounts. This deviates from my use of the term informal sector.

2. Hard-core poor were defined on the basis of minimum expenditure on essentials. Households with an adult-equivalent income below Shs. 31,000 p.a. were defined as very poor.

The evidence on the growth of diversification to micro-enterprises before and after adjustment shows that a major leap had already taken place before the adjustment period. There is ample evidence that rural diversification to informal sector micro-enterprises was already high at the early stage of the crisis (Havnevik, 1993). It seems likely that the tendency towards diversification to micro-enterprises has continued among the richer households after structural adjustment. There are good grounds to argue that diversification has been an important element in the pattern of organising the rural economy throughout the years of crisis and adjustment in Tanzania. For this reason, the big changes in the national policy have had less impact than could be expected.

This conclusion needs to be read cautiously because of the varying quality of the evidence. We do not yet have any major statistics which would reveal the situation in micro-entrepreneurship after the liberalisation measures. The statistics presented largely describe the transitional period. Thus different data sources need to be used to delineate the impact of SAPs on rural entrepreneurship and diversification. The comparison of statistics on the importance of the non-agricultural economic activities as a part of rural household income are, as I have previously shown, rather problematic.

The question which follows is still whether structural adjustment is changing the economic structure so that the diversification pattern of self-employed micro-entrepreneurs will be replaced by more 'pure' capitalism and wage-labour relationships. Here the evidence seems to vary from one sector to another and the total effect is likely to be uneven. The general effect of structural adjustment has been smaller than expected.

Turbulence has continued in rural markets and in the whole economy. The turbulence is caused by the increase in the prices of imported consumer goods and social services and, at the same time, the new opportunities in some branches of production, trading and services. During this change, the private distribution mechanisms have not been able to provide unified markets and stable prices. Instead, the price fluctuations have remained high and unpredictable. As Pedersen (1994c:41) generalises, "there is little reason to believe that the segmented and unstable markets in the developing countries should turn homogeneous and stable as a result of structural adjustment policies".

The liberalisation of import and export has had direct impact on the relative competitiveness of micro-enterprises. When it comes to export, the rural small-scale producers have had very little benefit. The clearest exceptions are gold digging (in several regions of the country) and cashew nut production and trade (which takes place mainly in the southern regions). The extraction of some other natural resources (e.g. timber, precious stones and shrimps) has provided some scope for the expansion of micro-enterprises as sub-contractors. Havnevik (1993; see also Gibbon, 1997) is concerned about the short-term perspective of the exploitation of natural resources that the market liberalisation has created. According to his view, the use of resources can lead to depletion of resources without any major developmental impacts. When it comes to import, the sectors

which have previously depended on the lack of external competition are naturally influenced most dramatically. For example, rural tailoring has decreased
due to the import of the second-hand clothes.

Summary

The economic crisis of state-governed development has placed large expectations on the private sector initiatives in Tanzania. Major institutional changes
have been conducted to facilitate the expansion of the private sector. The historical record of state policies and the low level of indigenous capital accumulation
are, however, formidable obstacles to sudden changes in private sector capacities. There are rather limited prospects for rapid economic growth through the
high road of the standard capitalist enterprises apart from in a few sectors like
mining and tourism industries.

The expansion of the micro-enterprises from the 1970s onwards has created
a lively debate in Tanzania. The developments of the informal sector show that
the recent past has not been as bleak as the official statistics describe. Nevertheless, the informalisation of the economy has also created structural changes in
the economy. These can be best understood as an interaction of micro-macro
considerations. The shortages and deficiencies of the macroeconomic policies
have forced people to innovative livelihood strategies where risk aversion and
resource base diversification play a central role. The micro-level responses have
been fairly effective within the basic need oriented sectors of production. The
economic policies have later on been changed to facilitate private sector growth
through the implementation of the structural adjustment programme. However,
the major beneficiaries of the official policy change have been large traders with
import and export capacities.

Chapter 10

Diversification Theory—
Explaining the Unexpected in Rural Development

The issue of capital accumulation has been central to many studies of contemporary Africa, but has mostly been viewed as determined by large impersonal mechanisms: terms of trade, imperfections in markets, processes of capital accumulation on a world scale. Such explanations fall short of explaining the diversity of outcomes in processes of social change. There is a growing awareness that development is not unilateral and predetermined by such mechanisms. In recent studies there is a new emphasis on actors in development.

Van Donge: *Waluguru Traders in Dar es Salaam*

The theories on rural development

The theory of rural development has passed through different phases. During the last five decades different, even opposing, points of view have received a hegemonic position. The major development theories construed after the second world war looked upon modernisation of agriculture as a key solution. Later in the 1970s, modern agriculture and modern state-organised services were still given a positive value but it was increasingly perceived that the existing social formations were a hindrance to their utilisation for the common good. Instead, modernity was said to have been hijacked by a small elite and middle class which forcefully used the state apparatus and external connections to exploit the majority of the rural population. This was the position of the *dependencia* school of thought which developed later as an analysis of the articulation of the modes of production. David Booth (1992:4) has summarised well how these neo-Marxist theories made great advances on the earlier modernisation theories but, at the same time, used generalised and economistic explanatory frameworks which aspired to excessive explanatory power. The abstract level of argumentation meant that the theories failed to reflect the complexity of the real world and thus ended up with circular statements.

After these theories we have witnessed new orientations in rural development theory in the 1980s and the 1990s. The new theoretical advancement in the political and cultural studies of development policy mean that the sense of impasse which loomed over research after the demise of the dependencia theory has been avoided. The debate is as lively as ever. Two causes for this change are worth highlighting.

The first aspect causing debate is the sheer growth in the volume of studies. The analysis of rural development has grown enormously in numerical terms, leading towards the professionalisation of development studies expertise in the universities and the establishment of academic and applied research programmes. The large volume has been a breeding ground for more detailed studies on more specific topics. This specialisation is accompanied by the globalisation of the information networks which disseminate the research results.

Second, the collapse of the cold war confrontation has created a situation favourable for new political initiatives.[1] The political climate has been supportive for a heated debate on the merits and demerits of initiatives such as structural adjustment and multi-party democracy. The favourable political climate has generated research which takes stances on the crucial issues of socio-economic dynamics and the hoped for social order. The debate includes two theoretically distinctive but substantially interconnected research traditions. On the one hand, there is the neo-classical economic theory which is a highly ideological tradition using a very limited and selective repertoire of economic indicators. On the other hand, there is a vibrant tradition of political analysis with discussions on the functioning of civil society and the state. The political analysts present a variety of interpretations, including a full scale critique of the neo-classical tradition in the analysis of rural development. The two disciplinary traditions (i.e. economists and political scientists) debate on the same theme: *can external state-governed interventions provide better or worse means for generating rural development than private initiatives and enterprises?* The answers vary from pro-government stances (including the continued public sector intervention through infrastructural construction and market regulation), through middle-positions (a selective support for enhancing the 'conducive environment') to a pro-market 'hands-off' position (the running down of public institutions except the law and order component). The general tone of the discussion contrasts sharply with the excessive planning focus and interventionism of earlier decades. It seems that the critique advanced in the 1970s has been taken seriously but the package of medicine contains a radically different assortment of measures than those anticipated during those days.

The developmentalist discussion is lively and interesting. Yet the emphasis is largely on what the interventionists (state administration, market regulators, donors) should or should not do to facilitate development. Another, equally important, issue is what questions and choices the people living in rural areas find as vital, when facing the contemporary economic and social realities, and what solutions they can generate with the resources they command. This is the theme emphasised by the anthropologists.

We can locate a growing research tradition which takes the activities and aims of rural people seriously. Rural development studies have opened new

1. The international aid organisations have been forerunners in political front and, besides, active in the research front. They have policy needs for generating information which lead into reporting with highly condensed forms of expression.

paths and exposed themselves to new levels of criticism 'from below'. A strengthening tradition is the analysis of situations which do not stem from the overarching paradigm of guided modernisation. This critique has initially grown from romantic approaches to autonomous local cultures. On the other hand, the new radical research has advanced into a direction where some parts of the cultural analysis is included in the open-ended political economy framework. This research combines together the best elements of anthropological and political studies. The research incorporates ethnicity, religion and local identities as important ingredients in rural development. The new research is also sceptical about the linear model of modernisation. The researchers have shown how the developmental paths have proved to be very different in many countries from what was expected. The rural people have proved to be able to make their own conclusions on interventions, resist directives from above and thus change the societal development—and all this with a minimal organisational development of independent (non-governmental) organisations. Very often the rural people have resorted to informal economic mechanisms and taken control over a large part of the economic life, thus making the planning work in the capital look like an ivory tower exercise. The macroeconomic control mechanisms have less power than expected, because the regional and local economies take their own direction.

I have called this new politico-anthropological paradigm a paradigm of 'negotiated development' (Seppälä, 1996b). The new 'paradigm' shows development as a series of encounters where not only substantive issues are shaped but even the social identities and power relationships. When development is a result of extensive negotiations between social groups, the end result is often unexpected. The economic history of Africa has proved this true in so many ways. The determinate policies 'from above' have generated multiple responses 'from below' and the result is something which is neither modernity (i.e. westernisation) nor tradition (i.e. unchanged culture), but something completely original and new. Sara Berry has written perhaps the most realistic account in this search for the dynamics in African rural development. She states that:

> The result is neither effective state control of the countryside nor an uncaptured peasantry, but rather multiple linkages between farmers and states which affect patterns of resource allocation and agricultural performance partly by encouraging mobility and diversification of networks and income sources. ... In such contexts, access [to resources] has remained negotiable, resources mobile, and peasant agriculture surprisingly resilient in the face of economic and environmental crises. The impact of state policies and power on conditions of access to rural land and labour does not depend solely on the interest of politicians and bureaucrats, but on specific histories of debate and interaction among farmers, traders, headmen, officials, and their relatives and associates. (Berry, 1993:66)

An important question is: What kind of new methodological solution can be taken from the critical, politically and culturally guided analysis and applied to the economically oriented rural development discourse?

The outline of the diversification theory

There is one theme which repeatedly appears in this discussion but which has not received full recognition although the empirical studies have hinted at it for quite some time. This is also a theme which has been confronted by development practitioners and theorists alike. This theme has not been covered systematically partly because of its strongly non-western basis. More precisely, it is difficult to capture because it tends to undermine all the major western categories such as economy, class, enterprise, family and occupation. This is the horizontal diversification in the embedded economy. I study it through the *diversification theory*. Its core issue is the tendency of the individuals and households to diversify their activities. A central part of the diversification theory describes the tendency of the people to cross over boundaries, whether they are sectoral, geographical or cultural. Lateral mobility generates creative diversification strategies'. The lateral mobility is also a possible means for vertical social mobility. The tendency towards lateral mobility leads into an economic and social organisation which totally deviates from the models adhered to by the classical modernisation theory and its current reincarnations.

The limitation of the social scene of the diversification theory, and the strength of its explanatory power within its sphere of application, is derived from a definite epistemological position. More precisely, the theory focuses on a more specific social scene than the modernisation theory (with its national focus) and the dependencia theory (with its international focus). The diversification theory starts from the local scene and only partially involves wider level social dynamics. The ideological bias is this: whereas the modernisation and dependencia theories see external intervening agencies as the active actors and rural people mostly as passive and ignorant (cf. Hobart, 1993), the diversification theory turns this upside down.

According to the diversification theory, there are complex systems of agencies and causalities in rural settings. Although we may not explicate (in numerical terms) simple causalities between individual variables, we can, instead, parade a richness of variation. Thus, the diversification theory can use some of its ammunition to shoot down the other, simplifying, teleological and non-agentive theories and then concentrate on showing the patterns of complexity, with a firm understanding that scientific knowledge does not have, with its present tools, the adequate means to fully grasp this complexity. Rather, we should acknowledge, that much of the necessary information lies in the indigenous systems of knowledge, and it resides there in such forms (i.e. complex situated knowledge) that it cannot be directly converted to discursive knowledge of the world-wide scientific community. Therefore, what our scientific knowledge can do is to find indications of the possible patterns of co-variation, admit the limitation of abstracted generalisations, and then seek ways to go forward with a critical attitude towards causalities in social processes, and the processes of generating knowledge about them. We can say, for example, that there is a connection between crop stealing, crop trading and the economic progress of the youths, but we cannot specify their relative importance to patterns of accumulation. This process is significant, but we do not have the means to explicate how significant, and how it actually works.

Is diversification theory a resurrection of the methodological individualism, where an enterprising individual is glorified and the structural explanations, as well as institutional agencies, are simply omitted? This is not the aim, but definite dangers loom in this direction. The enterprising individual needs to be fully analysed withinthe bounds of the "duality of structure". (See the last section of the chapter.)

Is diversification theory a romantic theory of local development in self-sustaining communities? No it is not. It identifies the dynamics of power struggles, differentiation, continuous changes in social structure and economic means. But it is a singularly non-teleological theory. Diversification can be a means of accumulation or not. It may lead in economic growth or not. For the most part I have argued in the previous chapters that the dynamics are largely such that some people gain, some fall, and the total effect looks from a distance like a stagnant situation. But this is only the view from a distance.

Is the diversification theory only applicable to the most peripheral communities? Can we say that the risky agro-ecological environment, poor resource base and lack of modern infrastructure lead into this kind of complex pattern of diversification? I would like to state that this is not the case. The so called CDR economy (complex, diverse and risk prone) is prevalent in different kinds of environments. The separation of marginal areas from cash-crop areas or 'green revolution' areas is often done too hastily.

I describe the diversification theory by the following characteristics:

– Diversification theory is a systematic effort to explain the rural development through an analysis of the complexity of the local economy. It is a theory which deviates from the conventional rural development studies through its methodological orientation. The methodology is a processual and largely qualitative analysis of unaggregated elements. Methodologically, it is important to note both the ontological and epistemological critique of the current rural development theories.

– Diversification theory analyses the dynamic combination and circulation of resources within a social unit ('household' or 'enterprise') for utilitarian purposes. A preliminary step for the analysis of diversification is the full-scale survey of economic/cultural activities.

– Diversification theory is a non-essentialist theory. It is the celebration of contingencies, local specificities and unorthodox practices. It is based on the systematic analysis of the deviations from the unrealistic models of perfect markets and single-role actors.

– The tendency towards diversification has been observed in many studies on specific social groups. Some theories have explained the diversification strategies that the elites apply to exploit economic resources. Some other theories describe the diversity of the income sources tapped by the middle peasantry. Yet other theories highlight diversity as a means for the poor to avoid risks and obtain social security. Diversification theory aims to combine and systematise these observations and use them for explaining differentiation.

– The diversification theory is a critique of the *general* theories of rural development. More precisely, it challenges the modernisation theory and dependencia theory and their ways of explaining the modes of accumulation and differentiation in a rural setting. The perceived development is more towards diverse development trends where growth is not necessarily evident and where the distribution of the resources is a complicated process. The local development path can even take an opposite direction to the modernisation path.

– The diversification theory has definite limitations in its scope of application. Because of the concentration on local level studies it is difficult to include national and international actors in the analysis. Thus diversification theory needs to be supplemented with other theories.

The basic argument of the diversification theory goes as follows. Rural citizens are able to develop a nuanced division of labour and produce a large variety of goods and services. These goods and services are efficiently produced in small labour units which are so tiny that they challenge the capitalist labour relationships and the development of homogenous circuits for capitalist commodity circulation. However, rural households do not only specialise but they also combine activities together. There are different ways of combining together various activities into a livelihood strategy. The modes of accumulation can be explained through the variation in the combination of the elements: some combinations of activities are more effective than others.

It could be said that several theoretical orientations have made efforts in a similar direction. These theories have developed around concepts such as entitlement, straddling and institutional economics. What is important to note is that each concept has aimed at explaining one strand of the complexity. Diversification theory combines these arguments together.

The diversification theory acknowledges a variety of interdependencies. First, we can see that the urban and rural localities are interlinked with regional exchange networks, as well as international markets, through various mechanisms. Second, agricultural activities are dependent upon the non-agricultural activities, and vice versa. Third, the economically productive activities are conditioned by cultural and political processes. These interdependencies are rather obvious but they lead into two challenging questions. The first question is how people differ in their capacities to exploit these interdependencies. The second question is what effects these interdependencies have on the pattern of rural development.

In the following sections of this chapter I describe the diversification theory from various angles. The discussion will draw upon comparative material with reference to Sub-Saharan Africa. In the second section, I study the causes creating diversification as well as the effects diversification has upon rural development. The third section studies diversification as an entrepreneurial strategy. The focus is placed on the actor, who is construed as a situated actor with different linkages to his or her environment. Thus a capacity to carve a special niche in the economy appears as a critical element of rural entrepreneurship.

In order to simplify the presentation, I have omitted the differentiation and accumulation discourse from the second and third section and placed it separately in the fourth one. The fourth section of the chapter concerns the linkage between diversification and accumulation. I approach this issue through a critique of what I see as the current advanced positions of the discussion on rural accumulation. I discuss four elements of diversification, each requiring a crossing of the borders of the conventional economic analysis. I argue that a successful economic strategy includes continuous crossing over all these boundaries.

The final section of the chapter discusses the methodological problems of the processual analysis of the village economy. The major issue is the utilisation of the actor-oriented theories without falling into methodological individualism.

The causes and effects of diversification

In this section we look at the character of the complex, diverse and risk-prone economy, its impact on the household level diversification strategies, and the cumulative impact of household level diversification strategies on the pattern of rural development. For the sake of clarity I build the linkages in the form of causalities and study separately the 'causes', 'description' and 'effects' of diversification. I start with the factors which lead into diversification (A and B), then describe diversification (C) and then its effect on rural development patterns (D–E). The letters A–E refer to the headings in figure 10.1.

A. Structural features inducing diversification

The formal structures of the national economies are not in good shape in most African countries.[1] The prevalent situation in most of the African countries is a high rate of poverty. There are a number of processes which are likely to deepen the vulnerability of rural people, the major ones being deteriorating international terms of trade, economic and political instability, the AIDS epidemic and creeping ecological disasters. These are well known and depict a vision of a negative future for many generalists. It may still be that the deterioration of the African economies has most directly hit the wage-earning middle classes and that the poor have managed to do as well or as badly as before.

---

1. Since the early 1980s the official GDP per capita has decreased in most African countries.

Figure 10.1. The causes and effects of diversification

Complex, Diverse and Risk-prone economy

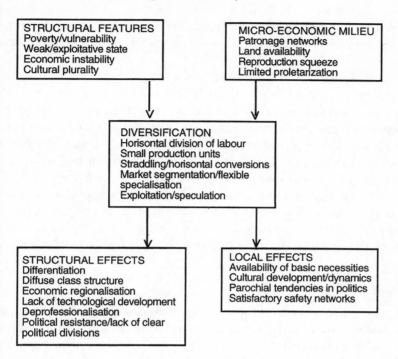

A part of the problem is the weak/exploitative state structures. Previously, the states have tried to direct economic flows from rural areas to industrialisation and infrastructural development. This has caused an antagonistic relationship between the state and the rural populations, and the consequent weakening of the legitimisation of the state. The conflict is compounded by the high-handed policies of the international financial institutions which have directed the states towards open economies and privatisation without leaving them with hardly any means of their own (i.e. not donor funded) for continuing their developmentalist agenda. What is then left of the state is the shell of a weak organisation and exploitative administrators. The natural effect of all this is economic instability.

At the same time, the political scene is open for competitive parties, interest groups and social movements. This enhances the cultural plurality which usually, although not necessarily, undermines the national economic controls. It has become more and more difficult to impose development from above. The societal development in Sub-Saharan Africa has been described as dual but the current situation could be better described by the term 'plural'. Existing plurality feeds tendencies towards diversification.

B. Micro-economic milieu

The micro-economic milieu of the rural households varies enormously and only sketchy characterisations can be made here. A major characteristic is that the smallholder type of agriculture, with heavy subsistence production, is a predominant type in Sub-Saharan Africa. This is threatened, to varying degrees, by land scarcity and rural proletarisation, on the one hand, and informalisation, on the other.

The rural areas are very much linked to the world economy. The capitalist economy makes its effect known through two major ways. First, the rural households raise and educate workers for towns who then work at a minimal wage. Second, the rural producers receive only minimal pay for the rural products as compared to the industrial products. The double effect of these two mechanisms has been named by Henry Bernstein the 'reproduction squeeze'.

The external effects are mediated by the local patronage networks. The patronage networks may have very different impacts in different cases. In some situations they facilitate the external forces in the exploitation of rural resources. In some other situations, the patronage network may be the only guarantee for a minimal internal stability and an organising principle for the rural economy.

C. Diversification

Given the structural features and the micro-economic milieu, it is convenient for rural households to diversify—engage in several different kinds of activities for the sake of increased security or profitability. Diversification means allocation of resources to several activities which may be either separate or functionally linked with one another.

Given that most rural households are engaged in food production, the other activities may be minor part-time activities. There is, however, only an incremental difference to the situation where the other activity takes a significant part of the labour time. Since most households strive towards diversification, it is only natural that they employ different strategies from one another. The effect is that there is likely to develop a wide division of labour with many special skills. It is necessary to have a distinctive skill or service to arouse interest among potential customers. The villagers are far from a homogeneous group.

An economic unit does not necessarily have to produce a unique product. It is also possible that it carves a distinctive niche through the manner in which the item or service is made available for a customer. The product may appear as special because of the specific location of selling, specific time of selling, or special side-services provided to a customer. There are plenty of small ways to gain a comparative advantage. For example, a small kiosk may survive, even if it is uncapitalised, poorly stocked and has high prices, when it is located at the margin of the village and open throughout the evening. These kinds of factors indicate complex market segmentation and flexible specialisation.

Putting together the arguments, we can first observe that there is a huge number of specialised production units, which are likely to survive. They survive through the competitive advantage of their flexible production strategy, and ruthless self-exploitation under the reproduction squeeze.

The same pattern of specialisation is, however, also conducive to circulation of resources between different activities. All means of generating extra gains (exploitation, speculation, patronage and domestic domination) can be deployed for this purpose.

It is also important to note that diversification can be profitable because of the value heterogeneity within a rural community. A transaction can also mean a conversion of a valuable from one social sphere (and value frame) to another social sphere. The value heterogeneity is a dynamic context which fuels activity at the level of circulation and feeds the tendencies towards diversification.

Diversification strategies are differentiated. Some elements of the diversification strategies are only accessible for those who command an adequate amount of liquid capital or who first have access to critical market information.

D. Structural effects

The structural effects of the tendency towards diversification are shaped by the different, even contradictory, successes of the individual histories of diversification. Some cumulative effects can be concluded, however. One obvious effect is that the class structure does not neatly follow the opposition of capital and class, occupational lines or any other single criterion. Most people are likely to have some land, some business and some patron contacts, but certain people have much more of them all.

A diffuse class structure makes it difficult to form political pressure groups whose adherents have distinctive economic profiles. This has an adverse effect on the development of organisational culture.

Another effect is that professional status is likely to have a less distinctive value in itself. A professional capacity is hardly a means for sustainable livelihood and often official posts are maintained only because of the fringe benefits and rent seeking opportunities that they provide.

The dispersal of resources to several activities means that the formation of the fixed capital is likely to be slow. Instead of investment in technology, an accumulating entrepreneur is likely to invest in social relations (which is always an insecure investment) and working capital which can be easily liquidated and moved to another branch when needed.

E. Local effects

Although the socio-economic milieu looks hostile and the diversified production units work under difficult terms, the cumulative effect of individual diversification strategies is positive at the local level. The aggregated production is likely to cover a wide spectrum of locally appreciated items, and to make them available at moderate prices. Thus the low monetary value of production is compensated by the fact that the local perception of basic needs directs the production pattern. What is produced is essential.

The organisation of the distribution and exchange of local products is complex but this complexity has its advantage—it is adjusted to cope with personal catastrophes. Thus it includes some safety networks which the market mechanisms could not provide.

The diversification pattern is likely to enhance cultural distinctions in the society, as many products and services depend on cultural distinctions.

The lively village economy is also likely to cause diffuse interest group formation which is a breeding ground for personified parochial politics. The parochial politics provide a frame of reference which is concrete and which competes effectively with national politics.

Diversification and entrepreneurship

In the previous discussion, diversification was studied in the context of rural development. Now we place the actor in perspective, and study diversification as an entrepreneurial strategy. In the entrepreneurial context, the key issue is the ways of simultaneously specialising to unique markets, combining activities to gain special advantages, and networking to stabilise the economic environment. The actor pursuing this strategy is here perceived as a situated, unique entity. Depending on the concrete research task, the actor can be defined as an individual, a household or an enterprise. Here we use a hybrid form of household, composed of several individuals involved in several enterprises. For the sake of clarity we pass over the issues of differentiation within a household (see Chapter 5) and between households (see the following section).

Market segmentation in the marginal economy

The central propensity of the marginal economy is a wide segmentation of markets leading into reduced competition and varied price scales. The markets are segmented through a wide spectrum of mechanisms. First, the segmentation can be naturally created through different types/makes of a product. For example, there can be factory made hoes available in the villages but still the villagers choose the local product which may have a shorter life-span but which has other advantages: a lower unit price and a better shape and a size which suits local conditions.[1] It is simply so that there are different tastes for products, different needs, and these factors lead into market segmentation and non-competition. Second, location is a definite aspect of the competition inducing seg-

---

1. This is an example which is well documented in Tanzania. See Müller (1980), Mothander et al. (1989).

mentation because of the poor infrastructure in rural areas. Although a product is a standard quality product, its price is completely different in an off-road village compared to an on-road village. Third, a market segment can be created through special delivery services like transport or credit services. It is much easier for the producers and traders, who know their customers intimately and who may have extra-commercial linkages with them, to offer these kinds of services. Sometimes though this knowledge may have adverse effects—the affectional relations may lead into bad debts and a collapse of business.

What is the effect of market segmentation on price formation? The previous chapters should have presented ample evidence on the segmented and unstable nature of the markets and the consequent instability in prices. One should also note the recent interest in studying market behaviour and price formation instead of the aggregate and abstract markets (Ekins and Max-Neef, 1992; Raikes, 1993). In rural Africa, the seasonal and conjectural fluctuations, extra-economic interventions, regulations and the following countermeasures, among other factors, create spatial and temporal variation in prices. Coupled with market segmentation we end up with a situation where any single figure for a price level is at best a partial truth.

The ontological propensity of the peripheral economy has been characterised by the words 'complex', 'diverse' and 'risk-prone' and the abbreviation CDR (cf. Chapter 2). It is worth noting that CDR does not refer only to the character of the environment but also to the way of operating a production unit in a turbulent environment. Complexity refers to a specific coping pattern where variable temporal arrangements can be used to utilise scarce resources in the optimal way. The business operations include complex contractual and affectionate arrangements. This leads towards the horizontal spread of activities; the creation of the secondary income sources beside food production. Finally, the complex pattern of relatedness, coupled with meagre resources and small margins (e.g. small operational capital) make risk calculation a central element of decision making and resource allocation. The 'embeddedness' of an enterprise has definite impacts on the price formation. It makes it difficult to separate the production costs for one product/service. For this reason pricing can be rather arbitrary. The combination of the different activities may also mean that the labour is fed from the individual's own farm and the reproduction of the labour power is not counted in the price equation, consequently pressing the prices down. Thus the price level can vary below and above the production costs.

Naturally one reason for the astonishingly low prices is the low circulation of money. In the scarcity of money, the prices of local products are dumped and money is, to some extent, used merely as an index of mural attachments in tightly knit exchange networks. In the low price society, the prices of imported items like canned beer are beyond any reasonable levels.

Networking

Several descriptive studies have noted the importance of networks as a practical way of organising business links in rural Africa. The networks tend to grow through a self-selection of people over a long period of time. The affective social relations of kinship, ethnicity or religion can serve as an initial source of relationship although such a criterion is neither a necessary nor an adequate basis for a mutually trustful relationship. Whatever the origin of the partnership, when a social relationship continues in a mutually beneficial way for years, it cements itself into a networking relationship.

Women show a high propensity to form networks. Women's networks usually serve multiple ends where entrepreneurship is combined with wellfarist concerns (Maula, 1997; Tripp, 1997). In women's networks there can also be a training and socialisation component well represented. Women tend to use a merry-go-round type of financial arrangement while some pooling of resources for common investment can be done (Swantz and Tripp, 1996; Maula, 1997; Swantz, 1998). Men are far less likely to form lateral networks where financial resources are shared. Instead, men tend to form loose networks which channel crucial market information. Among the men's networks it is also conventional to see more hierarchical relationships between large-scale and small-scale operators. After years of cooperation, such hierarchical relationships can include considerable loans which tie a small-scale operator to his supplier.

The backward and forward linkages in the production chain (to the providers of raw materials and markets) are natural ways of founding loose but lasting cooperation. An exemple of such a dependency relationship is the cooperation with a *mali kauli* (a middleman) who works at an urban market place in Tanzania. Rural farmers and traders may have difficulties to sell their produce at the urban market place and thus they rely on the services of the middleman. The middleman puts the owner of the produce up at a hotel and provides food, and then takes care of the goods. Since payment is due after selling (which can take many days) and the price cannot be fixed in advance, the owner of the goods needs to place considerable trust on the middleman. Such middlemen exist everywhere in Tanzania, including the southern towns.

Flexible specialisation

Flexible specialisation[1] is a term covering a number of hypotheses which together aim to give an answer to the question: how is it possible that such a large number of micro-enterprises manage to survive in a competitive economy? Flexible specialisation is actually an advanced version of network studies. Network studies have shown that the rural enterprises can survive because they

---

1. A highly relevant presentation of flexible specialisation is given in a book edited by Poul Ove Pedersen, Árni Sverrisson and Meine Pieter van Dijk (1994). It includes case-studies in the third world context.

stabilise their environment through a number of networks. The argument continues that the social networks are utilised for commercial activities in such a way that trust and commitment—the scarce resources in a less formalised economy—are increased. The problem with the older network studies was that they lacked a proper analysis of power in social relationships. Networks were seen as voluntary dyadic relationships where transactions are lateral and mutually beneficial. The relationships were described in the technical terms (backward or forward linkages, client-producer relationships) which concealed power relationships. Flexible specialisation adds two things to this model. First, it adds the hierarchical dimension of unequal power. Second, it adds the competition between agglomerates of production.

The theory of flexible specialisation is actually a theory of directed (or limited) market competition. Although similar micro-enterprises are in a competitive relationship, there are several ways for avoiding too harsh competition. One of the methods is the further specialisation into a market segment. The most interesting studies on market segmentation have recently been conducted when flexible specialisation is used as a hypothetical organisation of the entrepreneurial networks. According to this model, enterprises cannot be studied as separate units but as parts of both lateral networks of controlled competition and hierarchical networks of patron-clientship. This is graphically explained in figure 10.2. Although the theory of flexible specialisation is somewhat formal and abstract, it provides interesting tools for empirical research. Particularly, it provides tools to understand entrepreneurial behaviour in an imperfect and volatile market situation.

Figure 10.2. Flexible specialisation: relations of cooperation and competition

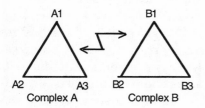

In figure 10.2, the ego is termed A2. The relationship between A2 and A3 is the relationship of controlled competition. A1 is a patron for both A2 and A3. Together the participants in the A complex constitute a productive system which competes with complex B.

The figure provides ample scope for flexible specialisation. Specialisation takes place between A2 and A3 in their relations to A1. The specialisation also takes place between complexes A and B. All in all, it shows that the terms 'cooperation' and 'competition' need to be supplemented with a mediating term like 'division of labour' or 'co-existence'. When the social relations are studied in these complex contexts, different configurations start to emerge which deviate strongly from simple market competition. Flexible specialisation appears as an all-embracing word for describing various processes like market segmentation, networking, reducing transaction costs and managing risks.

In the flexible specialisation model, an enterprise adjusts its operational size according to the market situation. The word 'flexible' refers to a management strategy whereby the range of products and the number of employees in an enterprise are adjusted according to market needs. The enterprise reacts to the external needs in a turbulent environment. The second word 'specialisation' means that the manner in which an enterprise adjusts is unique in each case. An enterprise provides commodities and services which are slightly different to those of its competitors. In this respect, the enterprise ventures into an innovative production strategy.

The flexible specialisation discussion emanates from the context of entrepreneurial link between smaller and larger enterprises. The theory of flexible specialisation has often been used in an urban context where the hierarchical relations of sub-contracting (for crafts) and the relations of urban centre and rural catchment area (for trading) are evident. In these contexts, the theory has proved to have a high explanatory capacity. When the theory is used in a rural context, the analysis needs to be adjusted to the existing organisational structures. In rural petty production and trade the importance of the hierarchical aspect of patronage is often less formalised. The patronage framework seems applicable to the larger mobile traders and shopkeepers but it has limited relevance for extractive activities, crafts and some communal/personal services. In these fields, the (direct economic) patronage relations do not create a system of controlled competition.

Another variant of the extended networking analysis is the *filière* approach.[1] This approach studies the whole production cycle from producer to consumer, looking at the concrete market situations at each level. A particular issue of interest is the set of concrete institutional links between the different stages of the production chain which generate non-competitive business practices. In some cases it is possible to observe how, say, a wholesale trader with a monopoly position can control the petty traders and their suppliers. Because of the empiricist orientation, the filiere analysis resembles some variants of the applied institutional economics. The *filière* approach is also used to analyse the price formation throughout the whole production cycle.

Peter Gibbon (1997) has recently applied the *filière* methodology to analysing the production and trading of shrimps in Tanzania. He shows how the production chain is dominated by a few large entrepreneurs with the capacity to freeze and export the produce. Thus the market liberalisation has created new patron-client relationships which have turned the petty fishermen into the sub-contractors (with share-payments) of a new industry. In southern Tanzania, the trade of cashew has developed similar hierarchical complexes which then compete

---

1. For a theoretically instructive presentation see Bernstein (1996).

with each other. In general, it seems that *filière* approach is applicable to the export of agricultural and natural resource products where the exporting agency needs to guarantee a supply of the product. But also in the domestic maize trade to Dar es Salaam, established *filières* reaching from different up-country locales through middlemen to town markets compete with each other (Bryceson, 1993; Santorum and Tibaijuka, 1992).

To sum up, the networking studies provide some ideas on how the micro-enterprises can survive through specialisation and cooperation. The new networking studies are able to deal with hierarchical power relationships in a realistic and concrete manner. The networking theory deals with a different aspect of entrepreneurship than the diversification theory and thus they are complementary to each other.

The ways of making profit

In this peripheral environment, the 'demand' and 'supply' do not meet each other as great blocks. Instead, the market works as specific markets, making it possible to take advantage of the interfaces between different systems and the conversion of values between different value frames. The ways of making profits include capitalist exploitation of labour, speculation, patronage and domestic domination. These factors were discussed in Chapter 9. Here we add only a general theoretical note.

At the most general level it can be questioned whether profit is a good indicator of economic affluence. This question needs to be raised because the risks related to a turbulent economy mean that the capacity to survive bad times, rather than profitability during an arbitrarily selected period of study, is the best test for the economic unit. The need to guarantee access to economic resources (i.e. the entitlement instead of income) requires investment in several economic clusters, networks and cultural spheres through an indirect and inse-cure ideal of reciprocity. This investment removes the cream the from initial profits but provides a hope for security. The processual economic analysis needs to consider the importance of the circulation of the resources to these safety measures and back to the unit instead of looking at profit at one specific moment. This is naturally a well known proposal but coupled with enormous research methodological problems.

The economic motivations for engaging in diversification have been debated and different explanations have been offered. A common hypothesis is that the diversification is motivated by risk-avoidance: if one activity fails there are still others which bear fruit. There are also other supply side considerations: the use of the labour time effectively throughout a year, the access to different resources, the lack of the means to enlarge involvement in agriculture, the pressing poverty etc. The curious thing is that even the wealthy households tend to be engaged in diversification strategies. In their case the calculation on engaging in side-line activities may be based on other considerations than mere risk avoidance. After all, there are ample opportunities for wealthy households to accumulate through straddling.

Productivity

The diversification theory emphasises the horizontal development at the expense of growth-oriented investments. The question is whether there are grounds to say that the prevalence of diversification works against increased productivity. Is it so that diversification is solely aiming at the conversions in the sphere of circulation—as if the economy were a mbao game in *bongo* land[1] where the resources are circulated and the foolish opponents are exploited? Or are there some significant productive investments made under the dispersed strategy of diversification?

Investment in increased productivity is hardly the main path towards accumulation in rural Africa. Certainly there are cases of investments made in investment goods, especially in good agricultural land and all kinds of urban premises. But often these investment goods, land and houses, are bought as part of culturally conditioned strategy where investment is used as a vehicle for enhancing social standing and marital alliances. Such capital cannot be easily liquidated, or used as a guarantee for business ventures. In comparison, investment in items like machinery provides less cultural capital. Thus the non-economic considerations affect the investment pattern.

The resource deployment strategy that arises from diversification is *management* rather than technology oriented. The increased productivity is reached through the efficient use of labour power, reduced transaction costs and similar matters. The diversification strategy tends to be competitive, although with limited technological capacity.

Straddling and accumulation—a reinterpretation of neo-Marxist discussion

In this section the inspiration is drawn from the neo-Marxist discussion on accumulation in rural Africa. Several neo-Marxist writers have studied situations where a person or a household has several sources of income, and the effects of such situations on societal processes. This discussion borders in many ways on our treatment of diversification. The issue requiring reinterpretation is the tendencies of actors to cross over various kinds of boundaries (between farm and off-farm income, from capitalist to non-capitalist production, across generational gaps and to distant locations) and the effect that this tendency has

---

1. In street slang, Dar es Salaam is nicknamed *bongo* land, i.e. the town where brains need to be used for survival. Thus mere capacity for physical work is not enough but a person needs street knowledge of the market, with all its opportunities and evils. This kind of 'cleverness' is also a definite advantage in the rural areas in contemporary Tanzania.

upon the stiff neo-Marxist concepts such as capitalism, class, non-capitalist production and accumulation.

Straddling between farm and off-farm incomes

There is a continuous stream of studies which show that the non-agricultural income forms a significant proportion of total income in many rural communities. The ensuing, and more interesting, questions concern how the various income sources are combined to create new patterns of accumulation and what factors determine who takes and who does not take up these strategies.

'Straddling' is a concept first developed in the specific analysis of the household level linkage between government employment and the 'middle peasantry' in Kenya (Cowen and Kinyanjui, 1977) but it is worthwhile to review this innovative discussion at length and to extend it into other contexts. Straddling implies the combination of agricultural and non-agricultural incomes in a dynamic way. Stephen Orvis describes straddling as a system of household reproduction in which "off-farm income of a various level is combined with agricultural production in an attempt to achieve current household reproduction and invest in education for enhanced future reproduction" (Orvis, 1985:12). This working definition, although specifically limited to one (Kenyan) way of straddling, clearly illustrates the basic point: the livelihood of a peasant family is dependent on farm incomes and on off-farm incomes, and both sectors are used over time to create a good combination of economic security and prosperity. It is not only important to study how incomes are generated but also how they are invested. Another point worth noting is that the unit of straddling is wider than a rural co-resident group. 'We' does not only denote the group inside the farm gate but also other related people.

Raoul Mustapha (1992) has made an analysis on Nigeria where a central concept is multiple modes of livelihood. For our purposes this concept can be seen as analogous with straddling. Mustapha refers to his own analysis in Kano where non-agricultural incomes amounted to 18, 50 and 85 per cent of the incomes of the poor, middle and rich peasants, respectively. He also makes an interesting comparison on the income-generating activities that are typical of the working class, professional classes and youths in an urban setting. Mustapha concludes that the multiple modes of livelihood contribute to economic recovery. However, his analysis does not reach the analysis of the social mobility because the initial group categories are descriptive and the analysis is static.

It seems clear that combining the analysis of straddling with the analysis of differentiation needs to be done carefully if one wants to avoid tautological arguments where straddling loses its own dynamics.

The interesting feature of straddling is that it is practised by the majority of the population and it succeeds in stirring up any simple allocation of people according to classical class categories. A concrete example is given by Per Kongstad and Mette Mönsted (1980:23) who describe households "where the husband manages his own farm producing cash crops along with a large shop and other business ventures, while his wife or wives work in their small shambas together with their children and in addition work on the farm as unpaid family labour controlling the work of labourers employed in capitalist wage-labour relations by the husband". Does this household represent a specific class (here 'middle peasantry') and, if it does, what can be concluded about the class alliances and relations of such an amorphous category?[1]

In general terms the question is whether straddling is a specific process for a specific stratum and historical conjuncture, or whether we can postulate it as a wide African pattern of accumulation. Here we proceed by stating our position before the discussion. Our answer is that straddling is very widely practised and that this part of the diversification theory merits being taken, at a minimum, as a working hypothesis or a starting point in any study on rural development in the African landscape.

There are some studies which have tentatively tried to bring diversification back into class analysis and delimit it to specific classes. Straddling is a concept initially developed by Cowen and Kinyanjui (1977) and they limited the concept to explaining the position of the class which maintains permanent employment in the state apparatus at the same time it engages in the accumulation of capital within private enterprise. They maintained, however, that the gains of the straddling middle class are limited by the state (or more precisely, international and domestic capital appropriating control and surveillance functions of the state apparatus) which sees that the straddling middle class is involved in the competitive sphere of circulation while the productive capital is left for the hegemonic class (Cowen and Kinyanjui, 1977:28). In other words, they maintain that the 'big fish' manage to enter into accumulation through the classical way of getting hold of property while this 'straddling' class is only allowed to trade with small profits. My comment is that while this separation of the two accumulation paths may be a valid distinction it can be asked whether the accumulation pattern of the hegemonic class actually fulfils exactly the same basic properties of straddling. Surely their livelihood strategy includes a variety of resources (business ventures, estate farming, salary work in the public sector, utilisation of state resources for their own benefit) and the circulation of these resources through a network where, on some occasions, one is a client of the more powerful people and, in others, a patron of the underprivileged in society.

While both the middle class and the rich have options for diversification, the third group, the rural poor, have their options which, however, may be far less profitable. Several studies show that the rural poor are equally dependent on off-farm income as the middle-groups. This conclusion has been reached both in land abundant areas in Tanzania (Chapter 9 above) and in land scarce areas in Kenya (e.g. Livingstone, 1981). The poor have options like agricultural labouring, other labouring and petty business within their reach. The pattern of

---

1. Cf. Kitching (1985) for review of this discussion.

diversification may reflect the need to use labour power effectively or the impossibility to continue farming for one reason or another. Thus, while it may be misleading to call straddling as a specific method of accumulation for the poor, it can be stated that straddling is an effective way of resource utilisation for them.

What is the geographical coverage of the reliance on straddling strategies in Africa? Gibbon, Havnevik and Hermele (1993) argue that straddling is a pattern prevalent in those smallholder areas where export crop production plays an important role. They take the highland coffee and tea areas in Kenya and the cocoa areas in Ghana as examples. In these areas agricultural production has provided surpluses which can be productively reinvested in agricultural or non-agricultural activities or in education. This cycle leads into further differentiation of incomes. Their analysis, however, does not fully explain what they mean by straddling and what makes it a pattern specific for the export crop areas. It may well be that the straddling takes place in other types of agricultural areas too but that there straddling takes a slightly different character. The other agricultural areas described by Gibbon et al. are, firstly, areas of mixed cropping of traditional food crops with auxiliary livestock and cash crops, secondly, the areas of commercial food crop production and thirdly, the areas of large-scale mechanised cereal production. In the first alternative (i.e. risk-prone diverse agricultural areas) diversification is more directed towards the extraction of the natural resources. In the areas of commercial food crop production and the areas of large-scale mechanised cereal production, we may find a low tendency towards diversification. However, these areas provide a livelihood for a very small part of the rural population in Sub-Saharan Africa.

We can now conclude that participation in straddling is neither determined by the level of income, nor the geographical circumstances. Therefore, its spread and actual forms can only be determined by empirical verification for each case. Its effects on economic differentiation can also be determined only by empirical analysis.

Reproduction squeeze and the socially conditioned local production

Are all rural producers subsumed, directly or indirectly, under the faceless force of competition? What is the independence, and active role, of 'non-capitalist' modes of production in a society where capitalism claims dominance? This is the set of questions which calls for a revisit.

Obviously a majority of rural Africans are not directly subsumed under a capital-labour relationship where wage labour represents the only means of living available to a large section of the population. The question of the penetration of capitalism can be formulated in other words where the indirect subsumption by capital is taken into consideration. At the agency level we may ask whether we are observing a division of the people into a few capitalists, some dispossessed wage-labourers, and a huge group of people who fall under neither category but who can conveniently be called 'petty commodity produc-ers', all equally subsumed under capitalism. The amorphous category of semi-independent producers has created problems for neo-Marxist analysis. I shall not open this discussion from the beginning. We start where Janet MacGaffey (1987:12–30) ends her skilful review. She presents the question whether "capital can achieve effective control of the production process without undertaking its immediate organisation and dispossessing the direct producers". She presents the answer with reference to Henry Bernstein: "The petty commodity producers are dependent on the exchange of commodities for the reproduction of the pro-ducers and the unit of production. The independence of the producers is thus circumscribed, both at the level of exchange through prices and at the level of production. Falling prices for commodities produced, relative to prices for bought commodities, result in reduced levels of consumption or intensified commodity production or both. Capital can thus put a 'squeeze' directly on production" (ibid. p. 26).

The Bernsteinian answer is curious in that it saves the hypothesis of capital-istic determination by concentrating the analysis of economy to the sphere of capitalist commodity market. The answer has a lot in common with the theory of the articulation of the modes of production in that it is very eurocentric, i.e. centred around explaining capitalism. The 'non-capitalist' mode of production is hardly analysed at all. If it is analysed it is understood as a precolonial pro-duction pattern, or its 'remnants', and occasionally as the reproduction of a domestic unit. However, this is an inadequate formulation. There are significant social processes which may take place within a limited socio-economic network and which, from the ego-centred perspective, are central patterns for organising economic life.

I have tried to show (in Chapter 4) that there is a lively stratum of produc-tion and exchange at a local level which is valuable on its own merit and not just as a functional servant of capitalism. The neo-Marxist research consistently undermines the value of production which is produced for location specific cir-culation. For example, it misses the local production of services. The neo-Marxist researchers are not the only researchers who have not noticed the service sector—the sector is also often practically non-existent in the neo-liberal studies on Sub-Saharan Africa. The services are seen, at best, as unproductive labour.[1] Yet the service sector amounts to a quarter of estimated employment.[2]

---

1. Nevertheless, there is a neo-Marxist anthropological line of discussion where services are acknowledged to be important on the politico-ideological level of an economy. It is noted that services, especially communal, ritual, religious and administrative tasks, may be an influential basis for power.

2. D. F. Bryceson argues that whereas African industrialisation has never really taken off (but is an appendix of 'derived urbanisation') the service sector (including all small-scale production for specific customers) has expanded in Africa. She refers to the UNDP calcu-lation that the percentage of the total labour force in the service sector increased from 13 to 25 per cent between 1965 and 1986–89. During the same period, industrial employ-ment remained around 8 per cent of the total labour force (Bryceson, 1993b:53). Cf.

The sweeping character of the Bernsteinian answer is disturbing in other senses too. Although a reproduction squeeze may exist on an aggregate level, the explanation does not tell why and how it squeezes some people more than others. Nor does it explain whether it would be possible to avoid the squeeze altogether in certain instances. At the agency level, we can find a lot of evidence where people have deliberately avoided commoditisation of their own labour and their produce and have limited their contact to this capitalist squeeze.

An alternative approach: capitalism as faceless competition

If one wants to study 'non-capitalist' economic relations, one needs to make room for them in the conceptual landscape. Whereas the neo-marxist analysis tries to expand the referential potentials of capitalism, I seek to limit its conceptual connotations. Instead of using it as a concept with open theoretical and empirical connotations (both resonating with functionalist class analysis) I seek here to use it in a very narrow sense.

Before entering the debate, I make some courageous propositions: First, capitalism is a non-agentive force, a structural aspect of some economic systems, which can be defined as faceless competition driving the economy towards an unknown direction. Second, this force is partly dysfunctional for capitalists (owners of the means of production) and workers (owners of the labour power). They both make social schemes to lessen the competition and give social forces control over faceless competition. The capitalists find competition on commodity markets harmful for their own interests and they scheme to limit competition. Similarly, workers try to control competition on the labour market. However, the interests of these two groups are antagonistic. They would both benefit from some competition on the other side of the fence. The capitalists would like to see competition between workers (on labour markets) while the workers would like to see competition between capitalists (on the commodity markets). The natural effect of this antagonist situation is that the capitalists and workers make social agreements among themselves and between the two groups.

This is still an abstract introduction. On the level of social actors, there are seldom pure workers and capitalists who directly face economic competition. Instead, there are people who are partly farmers, partly workers and partly capitalists; people who use the whole repertoire of the social imagination to control competition (i.e. faceless capitalism) from ruling their lives. On this concrete level, capitalism exists only as an index value in the description of the scale of competition (i.e. a function of the degree of the market information, market infrastructure, comparable commodities, homogeneity of the value frames of customers, competition enhancing agreements, separateness of the

Riddle (1986) for the analysis of the relative importance of the service sector in development theories and case-studies on the same theme.

workers and capitalists etc.). In some situations there is more capitalism, in others less.

One might argue that 'capitalism' is often empirically misplaced and theoretically misused in several analyses of rural development in Africa. This is not because capitalist processes are not taking place in Africa but because the types of social processes there so vividly deviate from any economy book models of capitalism we have in use. The actors impose social regulation on competition. The following discussion reveals how people continuously cross the boundary between the capitalist/commoditised/competitive sphere and the non-capitalist/socially controlled sphere.

In the previous chapters we have shown that there is scope for a 'non-capitalist' economy (i.e. a socially embedded economy distinctive from commoditisation and proletarisation). We have argued that there is scope for occupational specialisation, developed exchange networks and monetisation even outside capitalism.

There are several non-capitalist forms of occupational specialisation which provide people with services and goods. These are accompanied by ritual or 'economic' forms of exchange. For many people these special skills are important means to acquire a source of living. The development of the division of labour is not, by definition, a sign of capitalist development. Neither does the need to acquire consumer goods automatically mean that people have to resort to buying industrial products.

Another misleading thought is equating monetisation with commoditisation. The existence of the equivalents of money is evident from several non-capitalist societies. Where money is introduced as a medium of exchange, it does not necessarily have universal application. Neither does money, when widely used, automatically lead into the separation of price setting from social relations. Thus monetisation is a poor indicator of capitalism's triumph (cf. Parry and Bloch, 1989).

These arguments are critiques of the capitalism centred analysis. They are not empirical claims that there is not capitalist development taking place in Africa. These arguments are just theoretical and show that one should be careful not to conflate the division of labour (or, monetarisation, or differentiation etc.) with capitalism.

In summary, we have now included elements from the neo-Marxist discussion on rural African economy to a thesis which composes a part of the diversification theory. It postulates that the capitalist-labourer distinction is an ideal model with limited resemblance to African economic realities at agency level since an array of institutions intervene into the economic processes.[1] The analysis of economic life should incorporate the analysis of how people cross over borders between different capitalist and non-capitalist forms of appropriation.

---

1. The institutional economists share this observation. Cf. Bates (1989) and Ensminger (1992).

Crossing over institutional borders is an essential element of rural accumulation. Marshal Sahlins (1976) states the same in other words. He says that practical reason is always socially constituted.

In the following I study specific situations where the existence of various social rules creates possibilities for gaining economic advantage.

Temporal discontinuities and accumulation

Accumulation is a process which takes place, by definition, over a period of time. The temporal dimension of accumulation needs to be problematised; a closer look shows that the temporal dimension is a complex, multi-layered process and not a steady, neutral environment. The lineal time scale has several cyclical parallels, each with their own tempo and intensity, which create expectations for the repetition of a cycle as if it were part of nature. Given the power of the expectations of continuity, an interesting source of dynamism is the fact that each cycle may be abruptly disrupted and discontinued.

The major point on the temporal cycles is that they have a potential for discontinuity. Variation in the temporal cycles may create unexpected situations which then induce accumulation and differentiation. I study three temporal orders where the expected circulation of resources is either continued or when it is terminated. These are the agricultural/seasonal cycle, the economic policy/conjectural cycle and the life/inheritance cycle.

Seasonal cycles and discontinuities. In any agricultural society, the seasonal cycle causes a large variation in work tasks, the availability of resources and the consumption patterns. Even in a normal year, the seasonal variation hits the poor households hard which need, during the period of scarcity, to sell their labour power in order to buy food. Seasonal variation is seen as a major source for opportunistic behaviour and a major source for differentiation (Chambers et al., 1981). The situation is further complicated when the seasonal cycle is disrupted. It may happen that rains are late or the fields are flooded by too long rains. Whenever the expected cycle is disrupted, the magnitude of the seasonal factor is multiplied.

It is possible to prepare against the seasonal fluctuation by means of diversification. Kongstad and Mönsted (1980:145) have analysed the importance of seasonal cycles for a shopkeeper-farmer in Kenya. They present the following picture of the rural cyclical circulation of resources.

Here the diversification argument is connected with the annual (largely agricultural) cycle. According to the model the business venture appears to be a buffer between the family and its agricultural resources. During the period when food supplies and money circulation decrease the business resources can be utilised as a reserve. This makes the income flow steadier throughout the year.

Figure 10.3. The business cycle of a shopkeeper–farmer

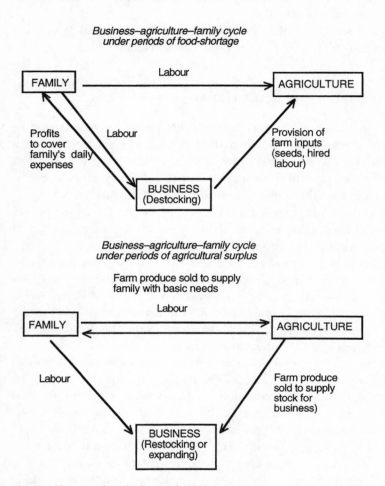

Source: Kongstad and Mönsted, 1980.

Economic policy cycles and discontinuities. The African economies seldom have clear conjectural cycles. Nevertheless, there are definite expectations of continuity for the economic policy. In countries with regular elections, the election cycle provides a setting for the accumulation of expectations. And again, unexpected disruptions can cause the collapse of the expected line of development.

Economic changes place rural producers at a definite disadvantage. Many of the items that the rural producer produces have a long gestation period (e.g. crops 3–9 months, tree crops 3–8 years) which means investment in unknown markets. In comparison, involvement in trading means investment in items which are fairly quickly liquidated. Rural producers tend also to be disadvantaged as far as price information and institutional information is concerned. They have least information to predict changes in economic policy. On the other hand, rural producers are partly cushioned from policy disruptions because they have reduced their market dependency through self-provisioning. Horizontal and vertical diversification also cushion a producer against the price fluctuation of a single commodity.

Inter-generational cycle and discontinuities. In many societies, one can identify a morally superior life-cycle model. There are also expectations and rules which govern the transfer of resources to the following generation through inheritance. The process of inheritance presents a factor for discontinuity.

Diversification provides ways to minimise the potential negative effects of inheritance. Sara Berry (1985) has magnificently analysed the accumulation processes in Western Nigeria. She has utilised a longitudinal perspective and studied the relationship between diversification and inheritance. Berry concludes that many fathers invest in the education and income-generating activities of their children. For some families this process is smooth and leads to a sustained livelihood for the children. In any case, the process of inheritance (including all types of support to the following generation) is crucial for the welfare of those who follow them. The elders need to make important decisions and it is not always evident that the elders exhibit altruism towards the followers. One of the major forms of differentiation could then be postulated between those who follow egoistic and altruist elders. Naturally, the children's own efforts count as well. In some cases children enter a competitive market and become disappointed while in some cases children receive excellent education—and then forget their backward parents.

Orvis (1989) has conducted a study which approaches the theme of inter-generational continuity from a slightly different perspective. He argues that all households in his study area in Kenya have taken a step towards inter-generational investments. According to Orvis the basic strategy of the different households has been rather similar; the issue creating differentiation is the historical period for entering the path of inter-generational investment. The households can be categorised according to the decade the male head of household started to interact with the market economy and then re-invested in household reproduction. The most successful cases are also those which entered the path during the first wave in the 1920s. The households entering the path during the following decade have also prospered relatively well. By contrast, households entering the straddling path after the second world war have had more thorny experiences. Here, the time factor is essential. Even doing the right thing is not enough if you start too late. Naturally, this kind of historical differentiation presupposes the previous altruism hypothesis (Orvis, 1989:118–177).

Ærøe (1991:263) makes a specific point in connection with the inheritance of business in building companies in Tanzania. He says that the inter-generational transfer of the enterprise *and* the management skills to the following generation is vital for accumulation. Too individualistic a pattern of management is harmful for accumulation, especially in the situation where mortality (due to AIDS) is high among entrepreneurs. The entrepreneurs may die before they have transferred their expertise to the following generation.

It is widely known that the struggles over inheritance may cause the splitting of an economic unit into parts which are unviable. One consequence of such a division tends to be abrupt sales of property by frustrated heirs. Thus inheritance is an occasion which potentially leads into transactions where outsiders—diversifying wealthy accumulators—may make large profits at the expense of the household members.

All the examples presented above point towards the same direction: When there are expectations emanating from a usual cyclical pattern. The disruption of the cycle provides opportunities for accumulation. Diversification is an efficient way to protect oneself from the harmful effects of a disruption.

Cultural capitals and accumulation

The final theme of the diversification theory is perhaps the most complicated and demanding. It concerns the critique of the economic maximisation as a shared value frame. It can be postulated universally that all people want to make their life better but there can be great variation in value judgements on what good life actually contains. Value judgements are different in various cultures and vary also according to age, sex and other factors.

The cultural framing of accumulation questions the predetermined objectification of the people. The culturalist perspective shows that different social groups aim at different ends. This plurality leads into the division of a community in sections according to the culturally constructed identities. One consequence of cultural plurality is that any single scale of differentiation is inadequate. The social differences cannot be measured with a single scale of differentiation because there are several culturally specified things which people accumulate. In other words, we can also observe social differences as lateral divisions and not only as vertical divisions.

The importance of this argument is fundamental for the diversification theory. If it were followed logically it would direct us to the cultural relativism which makes it impossible to compare people or social groups. Methodologically it is necessary to refrain from this extreme interpretation and instead take up a mediating position which has its basis in the materialistic approach.

There is one concept which mediates between lateral and vertical value judgements. This is the concept of 'cultural capital'. It can be postulated that different social realms have their own valuable symbols which can be called capital. Within the social realm this item can be accumulated and a high position reached. However, this capital can be converted into economic capital in certain situations. The convertibility of the different kinds of capital is a precondition for us to be able to speak about a united accumulation path. Bourdieu (1977) speaks about 'homologies' between different social realms (e.g. structural ordering of agriculture, ritual procedures and gender relations) which make it possible to enhance and conceal a move from one social realm to another.

There are several studies conducted in the anthropological tradition which follow this line of thought. They show how specific social realms can be mobilised for economic accumulation.[1] There are also other social realms where the accumulation of specific 'cultural capital' is actually dysfunctional for economic capital accumulation. For example, being a renowned witch is not necessarily a good qualification for making a career in business.

The argument of the diversification theory is then that it is necessary to invest in several kinds of capital in order to enter the accumulation path. Moreover, these capitals are culture specific and a subject of contestation. Accumulation may even require breaking the current cultural patterns. Sometimes the conversion process includes more of a mental operation rather than a physical one: the actor exploits the blurred conceptual boundaries and redefines a resource in a new way. In many transactions the physical exchange is accompanied by a mental change of meaning.

I have continuously stressed that diversification may lead into accumulation. This is contrary to the theories which see diversification solely as a defensive strategy of avoiding risks, spreading resources across a social group and thus a means of equalisation. How can I defend my position?

The diversification theory argues that diversification uses conversions as a method to exploit differential prices, moralities and needs that exist simultaneously in a society. Even a risk minimising household needs to diversify to cope with different social spheres. It is only a short step from passive risk minimisation, through predictive risk minimisation to active straddling. In fact, diversification can be simultaneously oriented towards accumulation and risk management.

Another often stated argument is that diversification requires extensive networking leading to social commitments which then eat all the profits. Attendance at social gatherings is part and parcel of accumulating cultural capital. Attendance may require considerable use of resources which are not directly productive. This attendance is called, in the extreme versions of lavish generosity, conspicuous consumption. Yet the difference from generosity to productive patronage may be small. Here the capacity of the actor to control the consequences of consumption is crucial. It is true that the diversification strategy may seem to operate through a large social network of contacts but it does not necessitate a large group of beneficiaries. Rather, the rules of exclusion tend to be very strict when the significant gifts and direct profits of an economic activity are distributed.

It is methodologically next to impossible to calculate the 'profits' made in capital conversions, simply because the value frames are not directly comparable. If anything can be observed it is the type of conversions and the velocity

---

1. A typical example is the study of Jane Guyer (1984) on the accumulation by chiefs in colonial Cameroon. Guyer shows how chiefs could utilise their political position to accumulate wives which, in a society where the access to labour was the critical production factor, was a precondition for the accumulation of wealth.

of conversions. Each society has its own profitable spheres and sectors. Differentiation is based partly but not totally on investment in the right sectors. Thus the type of conversions to the right capital at the right time is important. Second, the velocity of circulation of resources between sectors is an equally important criterion. The conversions need to follow one after another, instead of ending with one investment which appears to be a reliable-looking source of income. What we then see as a caricature of a good entrepreneur is a man who has always been first, who has tried many things and who moves to new opportunities whenever they open up. The speed of reaction is the important thing.

I have previously (cf. Chapter 8) discussed four ways of converting capital into a larger amount of capital. These ways are exploitation, speculation, patronage and domestic domination. They are all social relationships which include unequal power. Since unequal power exists in almost all social relationships, it is certain that most of economic relationships have one of these elements. However, one hierarchical relationship may be accompanied with a reverse obligation at another level. Social relationships are often multi-dimensional and power relations are often indirectly or directly contested. Thus we should not automatically load the four ways of converting and accumulating capital with high moral condemnation.

The actor-oriented methodology

Finally I draw together a number of methodological principles which are part and parcel of the diversification theory. It should be clear by now that the research framework is basically actor-oriented. The idea of an actor-oriented framework is shared by a multitude of theoretical approaches and thus more precision is required. The potential pitfall of any actor-oriented approach is the possibility of slipping into methodological individualism. In order to avoid that problem, the research tradition advocated here is based on the theory of practice (Bourdieu, 1977) and its sister theories such as structuration theory. These theories study actors as knowledgeable actors who are restricted by (time and space specific) cultural and economic constraints. The research along this line basically follows the model of iteration through the double entry points of the structure and the agency. The methodological road between (e.g. Marxist) structure-ontology and (empiricist) event-ontology can be called *realist* tradition (Rasmussen, 1988:6–14). This middle road is the line advocated here.

The knowledgeable actor

The methodological argument springs from the sociological discourse on the critique of the objectification of the rural population in rural development thinking. The argument stems from the Giddensian view that people are capable of knowing about many issues which affect their lives even when they cannot express themselves through discursive knowledge. The hypothesis on knowledgeable people has wide repercussions on the formulation of social dynamics between 'structures' and 'actors' in social theory.[1] The shift towards an active social scene is naturally a positive development in the rural development studies because it enhances processual thinking.

The question is still whether the knowledgeability hypothesis goes in hand with the empirical analysis of the actual flows (of dissemination and reception) of information. Instead of taking knowledgeability as just an ontological issue it should be studied whether there is a differential access to information. If there is differential access the next question is, whether it plays a significant role in rural accumulation and differentiation. It can be rightly argued that rural communities also have 'expert cultures' of their own: the knowledge is generated as a propensity of expertise and distributed under strict terms. Admittedly, most 'ancestral' knowledge of the elders is rapidly losing its audiences among the younger generations, as it is perceived as less functional. Still, there are other knowledge bases like religious knowledge and administrative knowledge which are disseminated through limited channels and which thus reproduce hierarchical structures.

The studies which actually ask about the role of knowledge in strategic action are very few. Yet it is obvious that knowledge is not always freely available in a rural community. The common practices for sharing knowledge are the frequent and extended greetings, gossip at informal gatherings and debates at a few public meetings. In rural areas, access to radio and magazines is not universal (and the information available through these channels is not always applicable to strategic choices because of its generality). The most vital items of information are commonly acquired through personal town connections, providing access to useful regional or local information. This information is not disposed of freely because its value is well understood. For example, government officers and educated people can withhold their knowledge and even withdraw behind an obscure (foreign) language. The household members can withhold information on their business ventures even from the other family members.

The discussion on knowledgeable actors has one more twist. It is convincingly argued that the researchers have difficulties to identify a stock of *local knowledge* because it is embedded in situational, culture-specific attributes. There is currently a lot of discussion on local knowledge, sub-altern history and the voices of the oppressed. The crucial question remains whether a researcher is able to present the 'local knowledge' without spoiling it during its translation to the audience of the research community.

---

1. Cf. Gould (1997) for the sociological discussion on value bases and intentionality of interests.

The 'local knowledge' approach has definite implications on the research methods. Briefly, it is argued that our understanding of the local processes is limited because, in the final instance, the methods of science cannot deal with the complexity of local knowledges. Our conception of causality, rationality and inter-relatedness is inadequate to grasp the significant processual aspects in the ways the local economies work. Local knowledges are, by definition, practical and situated knowledge which only makes sense in the specific situation, while our scientific task is a communicative and comparative project.

The dispersed actor

The actor-oriented approach is a slippery road which has been used for very diverse studies. Depending on the context, the actor has been perceived alternatively as an individual, a household or an enterprise. The actor has been perceived as a utility maximising unit within cultural and economic constraints, a passive unit which can be measured for statistical analysis, or as a rebel who never reveals his or her own secrets. In my conceptualisation the critical issue is the contextual adjustment that each actor makes. Thus an actor should not be equalled with singularity in terms of motivations and practices. An actor is always contextually bound.

The critique of the concept of identity is a helpful device for this discussion. Identity is often seen as a core characteristic of an actor, unifying various motivations and practices. A critical analysis of identity reveals that identity is often a word for the post-factum legitimisation of past deeds. Identity appears as an ideational construct which rationalises the past deeds, overlooks contradictory practices and unifies those which are remembered.

An alternative analysis of identity is a more open one. Identity describes the contextual pattern of orienting towards a set of social relationships. Since any actor grows into multiple sets of relationships, identities tend to be plural. In this formulation, relatedness appears as a crucial aspect of an agency.

An actor is the net

A central question is still how the actor *relates* to the other actors. We discuss this through the solutions that the network theories provide for the diversification theory. More precisely, we make a contrast between old and new network theories to locate applicable elements for our own actor-oriented framework.

The old network analysis has seen networking as a set of dyadic and unhierarchical social relations. The analysis of these relations premises a cooperation between two independent actors. The cooperation is mutually beneficial. The older networking studies have not asked the essential question of why cooperate with this actor rather than somebody else. The new network analysis takes up the issue of the speciality in the relationship between the two actors. The basic tenet is that the relationship between the cooperating units has a unique feature. It is based on unique history—specific historical and locational attributes.

If we perceive an actor as a productive unit, the analysis does not suggest an atomistic unit which directly confronts the faceless field of a perfect market. Instead, what we find is a pattern of cooperation where a special relationship is created through distinctive products (or distinctive products for that location), distinctive marketing methods, special transaction methods and imperfect information. The concept of flexible specialisation underlies these issues. The cooperation is possible because of the specificity of the relationship due to various reasons. Flexible specialisation is not necessarily a conscious strategy for many enterprises but a natural situation due to its specific location, specific size etc. The external relations of the actor need not be seen as either cooperation or direct competition. The third possibility is that the actors have a contractual arrangement between themselves (Rasmussen, 1988:22; Sverrisson, 1992:101–104).

The new network theory is also more precise on the distinctive types of the relationship in any network. Rasmussen (1988:20) makes the following categorisation of networks:

1. *Production* (or instrumental) networks, which contain instrumental relations,

2. *Personal* (or affective) networks, where contacts between people are rooted in sympathy,

3. *Symbolic* (or moral) networks, which are rooted in common attitudes towards a specific goal. This might be political, moral, ethnic, religious etc., but the point is that it ties people together, perhaps without their even knowing each other, who otherwise would not have any relationship.

The new network theory teaches us that the actor-oriented theory needs to move away from the abstract actor towards the situated actor. The diversification theory has only a small addition to this theme. It argues that the specific relationship can simultaneously include aspects of several kinds of networks. Thus a person can combine together elements of production oriented and personal networks, or production oriented and symbolic networks. The ambiguity in the referential aspect of the network is its strength.

The limits of the strategic analysis—structures, options and choices

It is clear that the concept of diversification strategy has the status of describing individual cases rather than explaining the societal dynamics. In this perspective the actions carried out by agencies such as the government, the international traders and even the village secretary are taken as given factors which merely set an environment for actions and reactions.

Here I raise one more methodological question pertinent to the analysis of the case material through the diversification strategy framework: Do the people really make strategic choices instead of just following tradition? Do they (we) act within the structural parameters described in an earlier chapter and actively make choices between alternatives that are embedded within them?

My answer is affirmative but it requires a certain qualification. There are structures which exist in the village community which set limits on the possible, conceivable ways of behaving. Although the analysis has been conducted through a heavy arsenal of concepts and objectifications we believe that the representations of the existing local choices can be located in this frame. A further qualification concerns the issue of whether the options are perceived as such in a conscious manner by villagers. Here we follow Giddens when he says that social rules exist when a person 'knows how to go on in a certain situation'. The person does not need be able to describe the rules in words. The set of possible alternatives does not need to be placed in the discursive consciousness ready to be told when requested.

The concept of strategic behaviour implies the intentionality in making choices. The level of intentionality is often questioned by the structurally oriented researchers. They ask whether we can expect that a person modifies the portfolio of economic activities intentionally and not just because of pressing poverty. I have argued that even poor people still have options at their disposal. Poverty may lead into quarrels, a sense of hopelessness, individualistic or defensive behaviour but all this is channelled through culturally formed options. The intentionality of diversification still exists because of the alternative choices of action.

In the end the academic analysis of livelihood strategy is then a structuration analysis: a structural analysis of the micro situation reflecting the actor-oriented perspective. As it is, the actor's own perspective can only be expressed through participatory analysis where the line between the set of questions posed by the researchers and the researched is crossed so often that it becomes diluted.[1] In the idea model of participatory research, the agenda of the research starts to resemble the agenda if not the life-world of the studied people.

The ontological premises: the character of the structure

Structural analysis has to be a necessary companion to actor-oriented analysis. When a structural analysis is conducted, a careful look is needed at the status of the 'structures'. One should be clear as to whether they represent structural contradictory forces, aggregated social groups or merely institutional players.

The Giddensian perspective is here both challenging and disturbing. It is challenging because it allows the possibility to construct structural properties with a fine-tuned, close perspective and not as societal (national) hypostatised

---

1. For an advanced presentation of this Giddensian actor-oriented perspective see Booth (1992). In the hermeneutic tradition, the knowledgeability of the studied people should ideally be combined with the 'visible researchers' who question their own grounds for deducting an interpretation. Thus the researcher is confronted with two interpretative cycles or, as it is also called, 'double hermeneutics' (Drinkwater, 1992).

forces. Thus structures appear as structural elements that structure every-day life, gender relations and temporal cycles. The Giddensian perspective is disturbing because it does not give guidance for locating the criteria of importance while doing the structural analysis (see Thompson, 1989:62–65). Thus the concept of structures is left floating, open for the researcher's personal emphasis.

The fine-tuned analysis of structures is a dynamic analysis. The end result of the diversification theory cannot be explained away through a single structure (like capital which 'squeezes' or 'exploits' the unprotected people). The structural propensities are plural, changing and have different effects. The concrete analysis of the social forces is similarly complicated. The theory leads into the deconstruction of the conventional categories of the institutional actors like the state and the aggregated actors like Muslims. The diversification theory starts from the premise that any such institutional or aggregated structure should be placed in parenthesis and subjected, in its turn, to further analysis.

It should be clear by now that the diversification theory stems from the political analysis where the actions 'from below' are valued as significant actions. This does not mean that 'small people' act in unison but rather, that the multiplicity of their strategic choices creates a level of complexity which is a central structural feature in itself. Next we study the political effects of this complexity.

The politics of resistance

Political science has contributed its voice to the discussion on reflective actors. The character of the *responses* by rural people has generated a wide debate. The earlier stance that rural people are a passive and backward mass has been overtaken by a stance that rural people can take active positions towards any change. Rural people can resist the intrusions in their lives, they can be indifferent towards intrusions, they can accommodate the intrusions or they can exit from the relationship with the intruder. The alternatives are many. The discourse then continues by asking, whether the response is effective or ineffective, unorganised or organised, and includes direct confrontations or the withdrawal from contact. These choices together compose varying patterns. It can well be that the most effective response in one situation is organised confrontation while unorganised confrontation or withdrawal are most suitable in other situations. Naturally different social groups have different strategies at their disposal (see Scott, 1985 for discussion).

During the last few years studies on rural resistance and protest have developed into an established discourse. It is increasingly perceived that the responses of the people are not predetermined by their class position. Another observation is that a person can be torn between different motivational structures. While there may be valid ideological grounds to resist powerful people, there may be other more mundane considerations which foster clientage relationships. The result of the conflicting motivations tends to be that the relationships of loyalty may take unexpected turns as the clients turn down their sympathy. In the realm of economic relationships, the vulnerability of the permanent power positions is very evident. The rich people (excluding the very rich who are beyond reach) are always suspected of having used unfair means to accumulate their property. Nevertheless, rich people can use diversification as one method of concealing the level of enrichment from envious neighbours.

At the level of structures, the diversity of the diversification strategies appears as a dynamic element which increases the flexibility in political responses. Diversity provides an umbrella under which people can seek protection against the exploiting state or market. In the insecure world, this is a definite source of security.

Conclusions

Drawing together the elements of the diversification theory leads us into a complex position. The common denominator between these elements is that diversification is potentially beneficial for accumulation. The question still is whether these tendencies towards diversification are marginal or whether they pose a serious challenge to (capitalist) development.

The indirect answer to this question can be produced through the comparison of different development theories and their analyses on the focal processes behind differentiation. Modernisation theory has, as its implicit starting-point, a premise on the division of labour which is accompanied by exchange on the competitive market. Here lateral differentiation is the primary object and the vertical differentiation of the access to resources is a necessary but rather unpredictable by-product. According to the neo-marxist theory the resources (labour and capital) are qualitatively different and thus the result of the vertical differentiation is predictable. Those having capital exploit those having labour.

The diversification theory deviates from both the modernisation theory and neo-marxist position. The diversification theory shows that the bundle of resources woven into a diversification strategy unite cultural and economic attributes. The 'contingencies' are not merely a nuisance for the theory—they constitute a basis for deducting historically specific processes.

Accumulation is attained through crossing over the barriers and taking advantage of the discontinuities. Often the barriers are merely the mental barriers of compartmentalised science. However, in several instances accumulation calls for crossing over the real barriers into true diversification. When diversification is evaluated it is important that it can be done on its own merits and not using the criteria of capitalist development. It is not fair to make a moral evaluation of the logic behind diversification if the cultural aims of that society are not perceived as important criteria. Certainly it is not fair to ask whether a pure capitalist strategy would lead into higher profits.

The diversification theory is more than a theory on a specific pattern of social organisation. Although it is inherently dynamic, it does not necessarily explain growth tendencies or the development towards a qualitatively different future. Rather, it exposes development as an affair of diffuse developments which may counter each other. In many cases, accumulation appears as a part of the null sum game where one person's gain is another one's loss. The rural African societies have their own dynamics but the direction of change, when broadly painted, does not point a qualitative leap towards a completely different organisation. The structure of rural development is already there, and it is unique.

Chapter II

Bibliography

Adams, R. H., Jr. (1994). "Non-Farm Income and Inequality in Rural Pakistan: A Decomposition Analysis." *The Journal of Development Studies* 31(1):110–133.

Bates, R. (1989). *Beyond the Miracle of the Market: The Political Economy of the Agrarian Development in Kenya*. New York, Cambridge University Press.

Bernstein, H. (1996). "The Political Economy of the Maize Filière." *The Journal of Peasant Studies* 23(2/3): 120–145.

Berry, S. (1985). *Fathers Work for Their Sons: Accumulation, Mobility, and Class Formation in an Extended Yorùbá Community*. Berkeley, Los Angeles, London, University of California Press.

Berry, S. (1993). *No Condition Is Permanent: The Social Dynamics of Agrarian Change in Sub-Saharan Africa*. Madison and London, The University of Wisconsin Press.

Bol, D. (1995). Employment and Equity Issues. *Beyond Structural Adjustment Programmes in Tanzania*. L. A. Msanbichaka and A. A. L. Kilindo. Dar es Salaam, Economic Research Bureau: 193–234.

Booth, D. (1992). "Social Development Research: An Agenda for the 1990s." *The European Journal of Development Research* 4(1): 1–39.

Bourdieu, P. (1977). *Outline of the Theory of Practice*. Cambridge, Cambridge University Press.

Bourdieu, P. (1984). *Distinction: A Social Critique of the Judgement of Taste*. Cambridge, MA, Harvard University Press.

Brown, L. C. (1985). Cashew and Cassava: Competing Cash Crops in the Farming System of the Makonde Plateau, Southern Tanzania, Reading University.

Bryceson, D. (1990). *Food Insecurity and the Social Division of Labour in Tanzania, 1919–85*, MacMillan Press.

Bryceson, D. F. (1993b). De-Agrarianization and Rural Employment Generation in Sub-Saharan Africa: Process and Prospects, African Studies Centre, Leiden.

Bryceson, D. F. (1993). Liberalizing Tanzania's Food Trade. London, UNRISD.

Caplan, A. P. (1975). *Choice and Constraint in a Swahili Community: Property, Hierarchy, and Cognatic Descent on the East African Coast*. London, Oxford University Press.

Chachage, C. S. L. (1995). The Meek Shall Inherit the Earth but not the Mining Rights: The Mining Industry and Accumulation in Tanzania. *Liberalised Development in Tanzania: Studies on Accumulation Processes and Local Institutions*. P. Gibbon. Uppsala, Nordiska Afrikainstitutet: 37–108.

Chambers, R. (1993). *Challenging the Professions: Frontiers for Rural Development*. London, Intermediate Technology Publications.

Chambers, R., A. Pacey, et al., Eds. (1989). *Farmer First: Farmer Innovation and Agricultural Research*. London, Intermediate Technology Publications.

Chambers, R., R. Longhurst, et al., Eds. (1981). *Seasonal Dimensions to Rural Poverty*. London, Prances Printer.

CIBR (1995). Dynamics of Enterprise Development in Tanzania: Final Report on the Round II Survey Data., Centre for International Business Research Helsinki School of Economics.

Collier, P., S. Radwan, et al. (1986). *Labour and Poverty in Rural Tanzania: Ujamaa and Rural Development in the United Republic of Tanzania*. Oxford, Clarendon Press.

Cowen, M. and K. Kinyanjui (1977). Some Problems of Capital and Class in Kenya, Institute for Development Studies, University of Nairobi.

Dawson, J. (1993). Impact of Structural Adjustment on the Small Enterprise Sector: A Comparison of the Ghanaian and Tanzanian Experiences. *Small Enterprises and Changing Policies*. A. H. J. Helmsing and T. Kolstee. London, Intermediate Technology Publications: 71–90.

Dawson, J., M. S. D. Bagachwa, et al. (1991). Small Enterprise Development in Tanzania: An Analysis of the Current Context and Priorities for Assistance. The Government of Tanzania and the Overseas Development Administration.

Donge, J. K. v. (1992). "Waluguru Traders in Dar es Salaam: An Analysis of the Social Construction of Economic Life." *African Affairs: The Journal of the Royal African Society* 91(363): 181–205.

Drinkwater, M. (1992). "Visible Actors and Visible Researchers: Critical Hermeneutics in an Actor-oriented Perspective." *Sociologia Ruralis* XXXII(4): 367–388.

Ekins, P. and M. Max-Neef, Eds. (1992). *Real-Life Economics; Understanding Wealth Creation*. London, Routledge.

Ellis, F. (1980). A Preliminary Analysis of the Decline in Tanzanian Cashew nut Production 1974–79: Causes, Possible Remedies and Lessons for Rural Development Policy. Economic Resource Bureau, University of Dar es Salaam.

Ensminger, J. (1992). *Making a Market: The Institutional Transformation of an African Society*. Cambridge, Cambridge University Press.

Evans, H. E. and G. Pirzada (1995). Rural Households as Producers: Income Diversification and the Allocation of Resources. *The Migration Experience in Africa*. J. Baker and T. A. Aina. Uppsala, Nordiska Afrikainstitutet: 65–86.

Feierman, S. (1990). *Peasant Intellectuals: Anthropology and History in Tanzania*. Madison, The University of Wisconsin Press.

Gasper, D. (1993). "Entitlements Analysis: Relating Concepts and Contexts." *Development and Change* 24:679–718.

Gibbon, P. (1997). "Prawns and Piranhas: The Political Economy of a Tanzanian Private Sector Marketing Chain." *The Journal of Peasant Studies* 25(1):1–86.

Gibbon, P., K. J. Havnevik, et al. (1993). *A Blighted Harvest: The World Bank and African Agriculture in the 1980s*. Trenton, Africa World Press.

Giddens, A. (1979). *Central Problems in Social Theory: Action, Structure and Contradiction in Social Analysis*. Berkeley, University of California Press.

Goldschmidt-Clermont, L. (1992). Measuring households' non-monetary production. *Real-Life Economics Understanding Wealth Creation*. P. Ekins and M. Max-Neef. London, Routledge: 265–283.

Gore, C. (1993). "Entitlement Relations and 'Unruly' Social Practices: A Comment on the Work of Amartya Sen." *The Journal of Development Studies* 29(3): 429–460.

Gould, J. (1997). *Localizing Modernity: Action, Interests and Association in Rural Zambia*. Helsinki, Finnish Anthropological Society.

Gudeman, S. (1986). *Economics as Culture: Models and Metaphors of Livelihood*. London, Routledge and Kegan Paul.

Guyer, J. I. (1984). *Family and Farm in Southern Cameroon*. Boston, Board of Trustees of Boston University.

Guyer, J. I. and P. E. Peters (1987). "Introduction." *Development and Change* 18: 197–214.

Hansen, Ø. E. (1992). "The African Peasant: Uncaptured or Participating? A Comparative Study." *Forum for Development Studies* 1: 67–86.

Hassett, D. (1985). The Development of Village Co-operative Enterprise in Mchinga II Village, Lindi Region. *Villagers, Villages, and the State in Modern Tanzania*. R. G. Abrahams. Cambridge.

Havnevik, K. J. (1993). *Tanzania, the Limits to Development from above*. Nordiska Afrikainstitutet.

Hill, P. (1986). *Development Economics on Trial: The Anthropological Case for a Prosecution*. Cambridge, Cambridge University Press.

Hobart, M. (1993). Introduction: The growth of ignorance? *An anthropological critique of development: The growth of ignorance*. M. Hobart. London and New York, Routledge: 1–30.

Hydén, G. (1980). *Beyond Ujamaa in Tanzania. Underdevelopment and an Uncaptured Peasantry*. London, Ibadan and Nairobi, Heinemann.

Hydén, G. (1983). *No Shortcuts to Progress. African Development Management in Perspective*. Berkeley and Los Angeles, University of California Press.

Hydén, G. and P. E. Peters (1991). Debate on the Economy of Affection: Is It a Useful Tool for Gender Analysis? *Structural Adjustment and African Women Farmers*. C. H. Gladwin. Gainesville, University of Florida Press: 303–35.

Ishumi, A. (1995). Maintaining Law and Order in Tanzania: Sungusungu Defence Groups. *Service Provisioning under Stress*. J. Semboja and O. Therkildsen. London, James Currey.

Itala, W. (1997). Characteristics of Informal Sector Operators. Dar es Salaam, Dissemination Workshop on the Findings of the Dar es Salaam Informal Sector Survey (DISS) of 1995 at Morogoro Hotel: 25th–28th November, 1997.

Jaffee, S. (1994). Private Trader Response to Market Liberalization in Tanzania's Cashew Nut Industry. The World Bank, Agriculture and Natural Resources Department.

Kaarsholm, P. (1990). "The Development of Culture and the Contradictions of Modernisation in the Third World: The Case of Zimbabwe." *The European Journal of Development Research* 2(1): 36-58.

King, K. (1977). *The African Artisan*. London, Heinemann.

Kiondo, A. (1991). The Nature of Economic Reforms in Tanzania. *The IMF and Tanzania*. H. Campbell and H. Stein. Harare, Southern Africa Political Economy Series.

Kitching, G. (1985). Politics, Method, and Evidence in the "Kenya Debate". *Contradictions of Accumulation in Africa; Studies in Economy and State*. H. Bernstein and B. Campbell. Beverly Hills, Sage publications.

Kongstad, P. and M. Mönsted (1980). *Family, Labour and Trade in Western Kenya*. Uppsala, Scandinavian Institute of African Studies.

Lamboll, R. (1991). A Review of Farming Systems and Farming Systems Research in the Southern Zone of Tanzania. Mtwara, Naliendele Agricultural Research Institute.

Liebenow, G. (1971). *Colonial Rule and Political Development in Tanzania: The Case of the Makonde*. Evanston, Northwestern University Press.

Livingstone, I. (1981). *Rural Development, Employment and Incomes in Kenya. Report prepared for the ILO's Jobs and Skills Programme for Africa*. Addis Ababa, ILO.

Loiske, V.-M. (1995). *The Village That Vanished: The Roots of Erosion in a Tanzanian Village*. Stockholm, Department of Human Geography, Stockholm University.

Long, N., Ed. (1989). *Encounters at the interface*. Wageningen Studies in Sociology WSS. Wageningen, Agricultural University.

Lugalla, J. L. P. (1993). Structural Adjustment Policies and Education in Tanzania. *Social Change and Economic Reform in Africa*. P. Gibbon. Uppsala, Nordiska Afrikainstitutet: 184–215.

MacGaffey, J. (1987). *Entrepreneurs and Parasites: The Struggle for Indigenous Capitalism in Zaire*. Cambridge, Cambridge University Press.

Madihi, M. C. (1997). Total Employment in the Informal Sector. Dar es Salaam, Dissemination Workshop on the Findings of the Dar es Salaam Informal Sector Survey (DISS) of 1995 at Morogoro Hotel: 25th–28th November 1997.

Maliyamkono, T. L. and M. S. D. Bagachwa (1990). *The Second Economy in Tanzania*. London, James Currey Ltd.

Maula, J. (1997). *Small-Scale Production of Food and Traditional Alcoholic Beverages in Benin and Tanzania: Implications for the Promotion of Female Entrepreneurship*. Helsinki, The Finnish Foundation for Alcohol Studies.

Mihanjo, E. P. and N. N. Luanda (1998). The South-East Economic Backwater and the Urban Floating Wamachinga. *The Making of a Periphery: Economic Development and Cultural Encounters in Southern Tanzania*. P. Seppälä and B. Koda. Uppsala, Nordic Africa Institute.

Mmuya, M. (1994). Floods and Elections in Mtwara. *Liberalization and Politics: The 1990 Election in Tanzania*. R. Mukandala and H. Othman. Dar es Salaam, Dar es Salaam University Press: 233–256.

Moock, J., et al. (1986). *Understanding Africa's Rural Households and Farming Systems*, Westview Press.

Moore, H.L. and M. Vaughan (1994). *Cutting Down Trees; Gender, Nutrition and Agricultural Change in tghe Northern Province of Zambia 1890–1990*. Portsmouth, NH, Heinemann.

Mothander, B., F. Kjaerby, et al. (1989). *Farm Implements for Small-Scale Farmers in Tanzania*. Uppsala, Nordiska Afrikainstitutet.

Mung'ong'o, C. G. (1995). *Social Processes and Ecology in the Kondoa Irangi Hills, Central Tanzania*. Stockholm, Department of Human Geography, Stockholm University.

Mustapha, A. R. (1992). Structural Adjustment and Multiple Modes of Livelihood in Nigeria. *Authorianism, Democracy and Adjustment*. P. Gibbon, Y. Ban-
gura and A. Ofstad. Uppsala, The Scandinavian Institute of African Studies:
188–216.

Müller, J. (1980). *Liquidation or Consolidation of Indigenous Technology in Tanzania*.
Aalborg, Aalborg University Press.

ODA (1979). Report of the Zonal Survey Team in Phase 2. Volume 2. The farming systems and development prospects, Mtwara/Lindi Regional Integrated
Development Programme.

Orvis, S. (1985). A Patriarchy Transformed: Reproducing Labour and the Viability of Smallholder Agriculture in Kisii. Nairobi, IDS.

Orvis, S. (1989). The Political Economy of Agriculture in Kisii, Kenya. University of Wisconsin-Madison.

Parker, R. L., R. Riopelle, et al. (1995). Small Enterprises Adjusting to Liberalization in Five African Countries. World Bank, Africa Technical Department
Series.

Parry, J. and M. Bloch, Eds. (1989). *Money and the Morality of Exchange*. Cambridge, Cambridge University Press.

Pedersen, P. O. (1994a). Cluster of enterprises within systems of production and
distribution: Collective efficiency, transaction costs and the economies of
agglomeration. Copenhagen, Centre for Development Research.

Pedersen, P. O. (1994b). De-agrarianization in Zimbabwe—a process of diversified development, Centre for Development Research.

Pedersen, P., A. Sverrisson, et al., Eds. (1994). *Flexible Specialization: The dynamics
of small-scale industries in the South*. London, Intermediate Technology Publications.

Raikes, P. (1993). Business as Usual: National and Local Food Marketing in
Kenya. Copenhagen, Centre for Development Research.

Rasmussen, J. (1988). Good-bye Theory—Hello Reality? Recent trends in social
and regional theory and its consequences for network studies in Africa.
Copenhagen, Centre for Development Research.

Richards, P. (1985). *Indigenous Agricultural Revolution: Ecology and Food Production in West Africa*. London, Hutchinson.

Richards, P. (1993). Cultivation: Knowledge or performance? *An anthropological
critique of development: The growth of ignorance*. M. Hobart. London and New
York, Routledge: 61–78.

Riddle, D. I. (1986). *Service-Led Growth: The Role of the Service Sector in World
Development*. New York, Praeger.

Roitman, J. L. (1990). "The Politics of Informal Markets in Sub-Saharan Africa."
The Journal of Modern African Studies 28(4): 671–696.

Sahlins, M. (1972). *Stone Age Economics*. New York, Aldine de Gruyter.

Sahlins, M. (1976). *Culture and Practical Reason*. Chicago, The University of
Chicago Press.

Santorum, A. and A. Tibaijuka (1992). Trading Responses to Food Market Liberalization in Tanzania. *Market Reforms and Parastatals: Restructuring in Tanzania*. M. S. D. Bagachwa, A. V. Y. Mbelle and B. Van Arkadie. Dar es
Salaam, Economics Department and Economic Research Bureau, University
of Dar es Salaam: 133–164.

Sarris, A. H. and R. v. d. Brink (1993). *Economic Policy and Household Welfare during Crisis and Adjustment in Tanzania*. New York and London, New York University Press.

Scott, E. P. (1995). "Home-Based Industries: An Alternative Strategy for Household Security in Rural Zimbabwe." *The Journal of Developing Areas* 29: 183–212.

Scott, J. C. (1985). *Weapons of the Weak: Everyday Forms of Peasant Resistance*. New Haven and London, Yale University Press.

Sen, A. (1981). *Poverty and Famine. An Essay on Entitlement and Deprivation*. Oxford, Oxford University Press.

Seppälä, P. (1993). *The Changing Generations: The Devolution of Land among the Babukusu in Kenya*. Jyväskylä, Gummerus.

Seppälä, P. (1996a). "The Politics of Economic Diversification: Reconceptualising the Rural Informal Sector in South-East Tanzania." *Development and Change* 27(3): 557–78.

Seppälä, P. (1996b). "Negotiated Development—A New Paradigm for Social Dynamics in Rural Africa." *Nordic Journal of African Studies* 5(2): 71-83.

Seppälä, P. (1998a). Introduction. *The Making of a Periphery: Economic Development and Cultural Encounters in Southern Tanzania*. P. Seppälä and B. Koda. Uppsala, Nordic Africa Institute: 7–38.

Seppälä, P. (1998b). The Recovery of Cashew Production in Southern Tanzania. *The Making of a Periphery: Economic Development and Cultural Encounters in Southern Tanzania*. P. Seppälä and B. Koda. Uppsala, Nordic Africa Institute: 117–136.

Seppälä, P. (1998c). The Informal Sector in Lindi District. *The Making of a Periphery: Economic Development and Cultural Encounters in Southern Tanzania*. P. Seppälä and B. Koda. Uppsala, Nordic Africa Institute: 233–262.

Seppälä, P. (1998d). Tanzania—Decisive Liberalization Path. *Liberalised and Neglected? Food Marketing Policies in Eastern Africa*. P. Seppälä. Helsinki, UNU/WIDER: 76–123.

Seppälä, P. (forthcoming 1999). Professionalisation of the Labour Force in Tanzania. *Occupational Change, Identity and Morality in Africa*. D. F. Bryceson.

Shipton, P. and M. Goheen (1989). *Bitter Money: Cultural Economy and Some African Meanings of Forbidden Commodities*. Washington D. C., American Anthropological Association.

Shivji, I. G. (1993). *Intellectuals at the Hill: Essays and Talks 1969–1993*. Dar es Salaam, University Press.

Shuma, M. (1994). The Case of the Matrilineal Mwera of Lindi. *Chelewa, Chelewa: The Dilemma of Teenage Girls*. Z. Tumbo-Masabo and R. Liljeström. Uppsala, Nordiska Afrikainstitutet: 120–132.

Skjønsberg, E. (1989). *Change in an African Village: Kefa Speaks*. West Hartford, Kumarian Press.

Sverrisson, A. (1992). Innovation as a Collective Enterprise: A Case Study of Carpenters in Nakuru, Kenya. Research Policy Institute, University of Lund.

Swantz, M.-L. (1998). Notes on Research on Women and Their Strategies for a Sustained Livelihood in Southern Tanzania. *The Making of a Periphery: Economic Development and Cultural Encounters in Southern Tanzania*. P. Seppälä and B. Koda. Uppsala, Nordic Africa Institute: 157–194.

Swantz, M.-L. and A. M. Tripp, Eds. (1996). *What Went Right in Tanzania: People's Response to Directed Development*. Dar es Salaam, Dar es Salaam University Press.

Taussig, M. (1980). *The Devil and Commodity Fetishism in South America*. Chapel Hill, University of North Carolina Press.

Thompson, J. B. (1989). The Theory of Structuration. *Social Theory of Modern Societies: Anthony Giddens and His Critics*. D. Held and J. B. Thompson. Cambridge, Cambridge University Press: 55–76.

Tripp, A. M. (1996). Contesting the Right to Subsist: The Urban Informal Economy in Tanzania. *What Went Right in Tanzania: People's Response to Directed Development*. M. L. Swantz and A. M. Tripp. Dar es Salaam, Dar es Salaam University Press: 43–68.

Tripp, A. M. (1997). *Changing the Rules: The Politics of Liberalization and the Urban Informal Economy in Tanzania*. Berkeley, University of California Press.

Trulsson, P. (1997). *Strategies of Entrepreneurship: Understanding Industrial Entrepreneurship and Structural Change in Northwest Tanzania*. Linköping, Linköping University.

URT (1985). The Economic Environment of Farmers in Lindi and Mtwara Regions: An Assessment of Constraints and Potentials. Mtwara/Lindi Regional Integrated Development Programme (Peter Oates).

URT (1991). Tanzania: The Informal Sector Study. The United Republic of Tanzania, Planning Commission and the Ministry of Labour and Youth Development.

URT (1992). Household Budget Survey 1991/92: Volume 1: Preliminary report: Tanzania mainland. Bureau of Statistics, President's Office, the Planning Commission.

Wembah-Rashid, J. A. R. (1975). *The Ethno-History of the Matrilineal Peoples of Southeast Tanzania*. Vienna, E. Stiglmayr.

Wembah-Rashid, J. A. R. (1998). Is Culture in South-Eastern Tanzania Development-Unfriendly? *The Making of a Periphery: Economic Development and Cultural Encounters in Southern Tanzania*. P. Seppälä and B. Koda. Uppsala, Nordic Africa Institute.

Whitehead, A. (1981). 'I'm Hungry, Mum': The Politics of Domestic Budgeting. *Of Marriage and the Market: Women's Subordination in International Perspective*. K. Young, C. Wolkowitz and R. McCullagh. London, CSE Books: 88–111.

World Bank (1993). Tanzania: A Poverty Profile.

World Bank (1996). Tanzania: The Challenge of Reforms: Growth, Incomes and Welfare. Volume I: Main report.

Xavier, B. (1997). Industrial Change under Structural Adjustment: Tanzania 1993–1996. Helsinki, The World Bank/Helsinki School of Economics.

Ærøe, A. (1991). *Rethinking Industrialization: From a National to a Local Perspective*. Köpenhamn, Handelshögskolan i Köbenhavn.

Annex I

Field-work methods

Field-work has been carried out in three separate phases during a period of three years. The first phase generated a regional overview and three village studies (Seppälä, 1995). This was utilised for the generation of the conceptual framework which was consistently applied in the second phase. That phase concentrated on case studies and ended with a small supplementary survey (Seppälä, 1996). The third phase was a testing of the framework and the qualitative deepening of the case-studies. The primary assistants employed during the first phase were graduates from the University of Dar es Salaam and during the second phase the local teachers and other *wasomi* from the village.

While discussing with people I focused separately on three levels of analysis: the village level institutions, household level economy and, thirdly, on different income sources and patterns of transactions.

Village hierarchies and institutions. Village economy includes collective institutions like village government, village projects, the marketing cooperative, market place, saving societies, the communal labour institutions, religious bodies etc. These were studied through group interviews and participant observation.

Household economy. The householding patterns were elaborated through a simple interview based on the PRA method emphasising visual sharing. Similarly agricultural resources were studied through a separate activity where the fields were inspected, cropping pattern mapped and the crop incomes analysed in an agricultural calendar framework.

New methods had to be developed to analyse household diversification and the conversion/reallocation of resources from one activity to another. A useful new PRA method was a household budget analysis, conducted using cards with pictures exemplifying different income sources and uses. The cards were placed on the ground for an interactive analysis. Beans were used as equivalents of money. The interviewed person related the household budget over time by giving a narrative while simultaneously moving beans from on top of one card to another. Through this method even illiterate people could provide comprehensive information on their use of money and other economic resource flows.

Finally, the income-generating activities of the households were studied more formally using a questionnaire which gave systematic results on the basis of the concepts generated during the preliminary phase. All the conducted surveys were formulated after PRA exercises and interviews to provide a basis for the quantitative data. I carried out an analysis of a random sample of population (39 households) selected on a fair distribution across the geographic area of the village. The households were classified through a separate wealth ranking exercise on the basis of the wealth criteria generated in group discussions. Three evaluators ranked the households individually and these evaluations were compared to find out in which wealth group each household would fall. In the end, only 3 households fell in the group of rich households, 15 in the middle group and 21 in the lower group. This division (8, 38 and 54 percent, respectively) reflects the general evaluation of the relative differentiation in the village.

In the main text I return several times to the sample stratified into these three groups. I compare the wealth groups in terms of their social indicators, agricultural production and the other income sources. Since the number of households within wealth group 1 (i.e. rich households) is only three households the results cannot say much on their character. However, a random sample of households would have been very large to include an adequate number of rich households. In order to circumvent this, I have made other studies which concentrate specifically on the rich people.

Income sources. The field-work started by the empirical listing of the income-generating activities. These were analysed in PRA exercises called matrix classification. Income-generating activities were classified according to criteria such as gender and age of the operators and the number of persons involved with it. In the next step, an expert on each activity was interviewed and some basic information was written down. The typical characteristics of a person engaged in an income-generating activity were listed. The following aspects were mapped for each activity:

– production chain from production to consumption
– seasonality
– profile of the operators
– labour arrangements
– other economic aspects of production
– importance for individual operator
– social implications and reputation.

This kind of material is easily directed towards empirical collection of the skill specific information. This was not the aim of the study. However, the empirical skill profiles were a necessary stepping stone while advancing towards the analysis of the diversification strategies.

Exchange patterns. Many of the exchange patterns follow affectual relationships like kinship or neighbourhood. That is why efforts were made to localise the kinship pattern and its economic implications. The study does not concentrate on these issues, however. The kinship patterns are not made into a separate sphere but taken more as practices within the overall configuration of the social relations. Other social networks studied were those based on religion, politics, friendship and economic cooperation. I also studied the scope of stealing, giving gifts and barter trade. In order to localise limited spheres of exchange, ritual objects, religious exchanges and political networks were mapped whenever possible. This kind of information gave an idea about the most evident restrictions that cause divisions in the sphere of circulation.

Annex II

The ensemble of diversity: Kilimahewa village[1]

I am sorrowful for Godly calamity
All of us are sorrowful
Our village: our village Mkong'ondo
We all weep because of floods
I am sorrowful to this calamity
We are sorrowful to God for bringing the floods to us
He has brought us this calamity
Our village, our village Mkong'ondo
All of us left the old village
We all ran
We came to settle at Kilimahewa because of floods
God sent us the floods
People weep for their lost property
People weep for their shops
Our youth from Nyengedi organised looting
On the pretext of floods

While running from the floods
We all came to settle at Kilimahewa
We are thankful to our government
First thing we got was maize flour
Second item was clothes
Third item was household utensils
Without them we would have perished in hunger
If this calamity came during night time
All of us would have died from floods
We thank God it came during morning time
All of us were aware
We ran to Kilimahewa
We then thanked our God
He made us aware of the floods; we thank him
We all then became happy

---

1. An analysis of the southern regions of Mtwara and Lindi is presented in the book edited by Pekka Seppälä and Bertha Koda (1998).

At Kilimahewa he paid us back
The first thing we got was maize
The second thing we got was millet
The third thing we got was fingermillet
The fourth thing we got was cassava
All of us are now safe

Because of the God-brought disaster
Shop-keepers are weeping
Coconut farmers are weeping
We are sorrowful to God for the disaster

A song composed by a village musician

In this Annex I present some characteristics of the village studied. The major part of the book is based on a case-study of a village called Kilimahewa.

Kilimahewa is situated at a meeting point of different ecological environments. It is situated on the coastal uplands but it also accommodates a section which is slightly lower and which has valuable alluvial land in the valley. This valley area borders Lukuledi river which is one of the major rivers in south-east Tanzania. Immediately north of the village the escarpment and forests of Rondo plateau start. A few kilometres south of the village there are cashew dominated areas and the Makonde plateau. Thus within walking distance a large variety of agro-ecological zones are available for various kinds of crops.

The residential village is planned in an orderly manner and rather dense. Residential plots of one acre have various food crops but the sandy soils are not very productive. Normally a household also has a cashew plot in uplands and a coconut and food plot in the lowlands. The distances to various fields run in kilometres. The village is large with some 4,500 inhabitants. Ethnically they are a mixture of Makua, Makonde, Mwera, Yao and Ndonde. Most are Muslims by religion but some are Christians and some deny adherence to either major religion.

Next I present the history of Kilimahewa which entails several upheavals. The upheavals have left their marks on the population. Each upheaval has also created social divisions which exist in equally many layers so that, as a result, Kilimahewa can be best described through its sophisticated social structure. Due to the social structure, it is difficult to establish a hegemonic position in the village.

The actual location of the village has changed several times during this century. The continuous resettlements have marked different epochs in the life of the village. Lindi region has a remarkable history of long distance trade and some of that trade passed alongside the river Lukuledi. The older name of the village is Mtua and several anecdotes associate this name with a resting place. In one version the resting place is connected with the slave trade while missionaries are mentioned in another. Still a different explanation given refers just to putting down a water pot, in Kiswahili *kutua*. The old village is also called Mkong'ondo, according to the old name of the valley where it is situated.

Later on, the village has accommodated a few Indian shopkeepers. Although their shops have been small, their mere existence shows a continued tradition of external trade contacts. It is intriguing that neither the caravan traders nor the Indian shopkeepers have left any physical landmarks in the landscape. Their impact continues, if at all, in the large interest in trading.

The elders give informed but conflicting views on the ethnic origin and settlement history of the village. As it happens, each leading elder of an ethnic group tends to give more weight to his own group in the local history. It is likely that the Mtua area was first inhabited by Makonde with Namkutuka as their leader. He was followed by Wamakua, Wayao and Wandonde.

Originally Mtua village used to lie in the fertile river valley. Mtua was dramatically reshaped during operation Vijijini in 1974 when Mtua village's land use was reorganised and the people from surrounding hamlets and smaller villages were incorporated into it. The villagisation enhanced the differentiation between households. The rich households of Mtua lost some agricultural land but they still gained the biggest advantage from the resettlement. The immigrating households were located under the coconut plantation of the existing village and, having less resources in the area, became often the labourers of the coconut tree owners. The villagisation also enhanced men's domination over their wives and sisters because land was largely allocated to 'households' and thus the men.

A flood catastrophe forced a second resettlement when the Lukuledi river flooded in 1990. The flood caused huge damage practically smashing down the village in the river valley. Several people died and the main part of movable property was either destroyed by floods or stolen in the following chaos. The government came in to rescue the displaced people. First it gave relief help and soon resettled the villagers in a safer location one kilometre west above the valley. The new area had been previously used for cashew and other upland crops. The new village was named Kilimahewa. The government deserves praise for its prompt action. At the same it can be noticed that the help also ended abruptly a half a year after it had started and just after national elections (cf. Mmuya, 1994). The resettlement was compulsory and the land losers (who had owned farm land in new village area) were not compensated. The new settlement was built quickly as the forested area was visited by lions which scared people. The disadvantage of the resettlement was that it increased the distance to the fertile valley where most agricultural work is done. An old man, while complaining about the negative effects of the resettlements, summarises views held by many: "Look at me, I have no resources (*uwezo*). I have moved three times. When I start to cultivate I have to move away. A cashew field is as far as the village of N. How could I cultivate that field?"

During the last five years the villagers have cleared their new home plots, built new houses and cultivated old and new fields. Currently the village looks as if the floods were in the distant past. However, the consequences of the abrupt change linger in the village in many ways. All the people do not unanimously agree that life has changed for the worse. A poor man gives a statement which pointedly diverts from the opinion of the old man: " I find that the conditions are now better than they were in the old village. Now we have got the experience of self-reliance and everybody is working hard. At the old village some people were like capitalists and landlords. You could find a man just resting on his chair and making somebody else do the work, asking him to collect coconuts and carry them somewhere. Now I carry out my own work and nobody will command me... In the new village everybody has a place or plot to work".

These examples, while brief, show that the resettlements have shaken the established social order in the village. The changes have never been complete and the old dispositions have stayed as a layer in the people's memories. Different people tend to stress different historical epochs which have been more favourable to them. All this complicates the contemporary social setting.

In tables 1 and 2 there are population censuses from the time before and after the floods. As the figures show, the village has grown rather than decreased in size. The governmental help was an attraction which pulled some people from surrounding areas to the village. Also the land allocation pattern of giving land to all youths of age was an incentive to move back to the home village and to establish a family. Nevertheless, the exhaustion of the soil in the new home plots has already started a new process of outmigration to other areas with more easy access to land.

As the population census shows, women outnumber men in every age group except the oldest one. The census was conducted before the women were exempted from poll tax and thus the exemption cannot be the reason for the bias in the sex ratio. A more likely reason is the men's continuous outmigration to look for urban employment. Men from these areas are known as traders in Dar es Salaam. They are even given a shared name (i.e. a kind of constructed ethnic group) of Wamachinga (cf. Mihanjo and Luanda, 1998).

Table 1. Village population structure in old Mtua village

Age groups	Males	Females	Total	Sex ratio
0–4	214	242	456	88.4
5–14	439	467	906	94.0
15–24	345	392	737	88.0
25–34	236	258	494	91.5
35–44	193	231	424	83.5
45–54	146	172	318	84.9
55–64	90	124	226	72.6
64 +	130	96	226	135.4
Total	1793	1982	3775	90.5

Source: Population census 1988

Table ·2. *Population in new Kilimahewa*

Population group	Males	Females	Total	Sex ratio
Small children	193	204	397	94.6
School children	744	947	1691	78.6
Working aged	1100	1220	2320	90.2
Disabled	23	17	40	135.3
Aged (60+)	27	12	39	225.0
Total	2087	2400	4487	87.0

Source: Village archive 1994

One should read the figures of the censuses, especially the figures of the village archive, with some caution. A major problem with all census data is that they are based on a one-shot exercise while the village population changes quite dramatically depending on the agricultural seasons. Many people move to live in the small huts beside the fields to protect fields from birds and later on to harvest the crop. Some of these settlements are becoming permanent. Thus many villagers actually live in several places. Consequently, the census studies provide different information depending on the season when the study is conducted.

Village administration and civic institutions

The state exists in the village through its administration which for decades has tried to penetrate rural social relations, entering as a third party between farmer and trader, husband and wife, elder and junior. State penetration is a heuristic term which well describes the aim of the state to legitimate itself through a multiplicity of interventions. In many villages the state penetration has lost both its legitimisation and its concrete means to show off. In Kilimahewa, the flood gave the state an exceptional situation to extend its arm and show its usefulness. The flood aid was directed to construct buildings that serve all villagers. Kilimahewa has a newly built office building, a ward centre accommodating a ward executive officer, community development officer, agricultural officer and educational officer. The list of officers sounds impressive but the truth is that the resources and salaries of the officers are negligible and they are seldom seen in the office. The office block also accommodates a village chairman and a village executive officer as well as a CCM office. Another building constructed by flood aid is a cooperative godown. The cooperative was originally purported for village use. In 1993 the cooperative organisation was restructured and the neighbouring six villages were amalgamated to the new larger unit with Kilimahewa as its centre. Nevertheless, the fundamental change in the cooperative front had already occurred earlier when the regional cooperative union went practically bankrupt and it could no longer finance its own crop collection.[1] Thus the new local cooperative society is merely a shadow of its earlier predecessor.

Also other institutions were built with the help of flood aid. The government helped with school construction. It also provided a milling machine which is currently the only village project bringing income to the village administration. A health clinic has so far no premises of its own but it uses a corner of the ground floor of the village cooperative. The Catholic mission has funded the building of a church. A businessman originating from the village has funded the Mosque construction. The district council has supported the building of a roofed market place. In comparison with many villages, Kilimahewa has good premises for public functions.

Paradoxically, now that the village has good buildings it has very little activities taking place inside them. In comparison, the old Mtua had several village projects in its heyday. There was a milling machine, a shop, cattle, a tractor and a *bega-kwa-bega* farm. These projects came to an end because of mismanagement. The dissatisfaction with village leaders in the running of common projects finally prompted a coup in the village administration in 1992. At the same time it must be noted that it is far more difficult to run a village project in the 1990s than it was during the previous decades. The central government support for village projects (e.g. loans, by-laws, distribution mechanisms) has decreased continuously over the past two decades and currently a village government has practically no government recognition and support.

The political institutions have similarly lost a part of their earlier stamina. Politically Kilimahewa is clearly a CCM stronghold. Officially women and youth have their party wings within CCM but in practice these wings are passive and their projects have died out. The opposition parties are known in the village and their advantages and disadvantages are debated openly. There are individual supporters for NCCR-Mageuzi but so far none of them has stood for a public seat.

The uniting rituals

What brings people together in the village? What are the forums where they share information, where moral landmarks are nailed down and where compelling value frames are formulated? The answer is that there is no single occasion where all the villagers are present but there are several cultural institutions which are so popular that all the people need to take stance on them. These institutions are focal points which unite people in debates even when they dis-

---

1. During the 1992/93 season the primary cooperative society was able to buy 90 tons of cashew by the order of a Lindi based businessman. During 1993/94 it received orders for 80 tons of cashew. Half of the cashew was ordered by the cooperative union (with central bank backing) and the other half by three traders. The cooperative does not collect other crops or provide any inputs. It has only a handful of paid members in the village.

agree in their opinions. In the following I present the central civic institutions which are vital for the village life.

The Muslim festivities have high participation rates as almost all the villagers are Muslims. The main points in the ritual calendar are Ramadan (fasting period ending with Iddi-El-Fidli), Ziara (or visits) and Maulid (celebrating the Prophet's birthday). One person can participate in several Ziara and Maulid festivities in various locations. The rituals do not have specific dates in the secular calendar but follow the Islamic moon calendar.

July starts a general festival period in the village. That is the time when a *ngoma* dance is organised almost every night in one corner of the village. Ngoma can be organised for relaxation but sometimes it is part of a circumcision ceremony, a wedding or other ceremonies. Many of these ceremonies are conducted during the festival period when food is in plenty and the weather is comfortable.

Another traditional institution with economic importance is *mkumi,* a labour party. Lately it has lost popularity due to increased wage labouring. The practical arrangements of mkumi have always differed between villages in southern regions; in this village mkumi has usually been organised on food crop fields and the payment has been food or beer. It is the poor people who take part and organise mkumi. The social basis for the labour party is the neighbourhood. In old Mtua the settlement pattern had developed kin-based clusters and it was common to organise mkumi in those groups.

Other important institutions forming communal spirit are related to life-cycle ceremonies. Circumcision ceremonies attract people—especially when a masked dancer appears in the coming out ceremony. Male circumcision is done at the tender age of six to ten years and the economic importance for the youth is limited to new clothes. A similar rite of passage to social personhood is also done for girls but without circumcision. Compared with circumcision, marriage ceremonies are rather modest. A Kadhi is supposed to officiate the marriage ritual and a boy to pay a bridewealth which can be paid in instalments so that only a part is paid before the marriage is consummated. Divorces are naturally even less publicised occasions but in terms of economic importance they are equally significant. A funeral is always a major occasion in the village and participation at a funeral is a common social happening. Funerals are said to be increasing for one reason or another. Participation is high and rather organised. An ethnic group with a joking-relationship to the deceased is involved in practical arrangements like the provision of food and firewood.

The institutions that properly unite people in a village are largely the informal cultural institutions which have been described above. By contrast, the formal organisations have a less significant uniting function. For decades, the party and governmental officers have discouraged the practice of forming formal non-governmental organisations. The officers have done their best to monopolise the organisational culture. There are very few organisational forms which have managed to oppose this hegemony. One exception is the few rotational saving groups of women. Rotational saving groups have been organised informally (i.e. without government contact) but with strict rules. Rotational saving groups have been most common among women engaged in activities like trading which provide some income the year round. In the flood of 1990, most groups died but, later on, at least seven new women's groups were formed to participate in a special loan scheme launched jointly by the Rural Cooperative Development Bank and district council.

The youths have had no non-party organisation until last year when a football club Kongo was formed. In a short time the club has grown to 300 paying members. The active members have taken up agricultural labour tasks to fund their club. The club even fenced a football field to be able to sell tickets to its matches. This strategy worked only for one month. After that rains and the vandalism of the poor spectators ruined the fence.

The representativeness of the village

Kilimahewa is one village among thousands in rural Tanzania—yet it is a unique micro-environment which has a regional reputation and which exhibits qualities distinctive from all the surrounding villages. These differences are a basis for functional exchange relations between the neighbouring villages. Inside the village, the social stratification has historically taken a shape which differs from other villages in the area.

I consider the representativeness of the village in terms of one variable: the diversity of the economic activities (i.e. the degree of the division of labour). The question is whether there is more or less diversity in Kilimahewa than in other villages in Tanzania. The following factors speak for less than average diversity:

- The village confronted catastrophic floods in 1990. The people had to start again from scratch. Survival was a paramount issue—anything else was luxury.
- The village has a tradition of coconut cultivation. This factor unites it with the coastal culture which is commonly associated with leisurely life-orientation and backwardness.
- The ethnic diversity of the village increases social individuation which may be detrimental to economic security and thus increases the risk for engaging in special projects. Ethnic diversity feeds insecurity, thefts and witchcraft.

The following factors speak for larger than average economic diversification:

- The village size is well above that of the average villages in the region.
- A major road connects the village to several district capitals—a factor which boosts trading activities. There is a clear distinction compared to villages without any passable road connection.
- The village borders the cashew dominated areas and it is infected by the considerable upsurge of cashew income during the last three years. How-

ever this change concerns Kilimahewa much less than the 'cashew dependent' villages in the neighbouring district.

In order to have comparative evidence I have made an analysis of the diversity
of the (non-agricultural, non-wage labour) income-generating activities in four
villages: Kilimahewa, Rutamba, Nazimmoja and Utende villages in Lindi district (cf. Seppälä 1998c). The first two villages are rather similar in terms of size
and have a ward centre status. The third one is a divisional centre and practically a township. The fourth one is a small village. The variation of these four
villages, in terms of the diversity of income-generating activities, was smaller
than one could expect. All the villages accommodated between 50 and 60 types
of income-generating activities. There were some activities like specialised
shops, openly operating moneylenders and mechanics which only exist in Nazimmoja. However, also small and remote villages tend to have their own specialities—either due to cultural reasons or as a consequence access to a certain
natural resource. Examples are making canoes and carvings. The conclusion is
that the concentration of people into a large village may increase the numbers of
people in profitable activities but the effect on diversity is not very dramatic.

In general terms it is untenable to compare this village and ask whether it is
a representative case for Tanzania or even for South-East Tanzania. The concept
of the typical village is quite unfounded in many respects. Take the agro-ecological variation: according to the large agro-ecological zoning survey exercise,
there are some 10 agro-ecological zones ranging from coastal lowlands to fertile
uplands, from unpopulated forests to overpopulated cash-cropping areas in
South-East Tanzania. An agricultural economist emphasises micro-ecological
variation: "variability even within zones is such that it is recommended that
each village included ... should be individually classified according to its agricultural characteristics and policies adjusted to fit local variation." (URT,
1985:23). If we leave agriculture and look at the cultural variation, we can find
an equally perplexing amount of variation. In south-east Tanzania there are a
dozen ethnic groups, both Muslim and Christian communities and both commercially and subsistence oriented communities. Variation is a major characteristic of the rural areas.